Rainer Werner Fassbinder and the German Theatre

Using extensive and untapped archival material as well as a series of
in-depth interviews with Fassbinder's main theatre associates, this book
offers commentary on and insights into Fassbinder's plays, his
dramaturgies and staging practice. David Barnett helps to unlock the
much-discussed theatricality of Fassbinder's films by showing its many
concrete sources. The first study of Fassbinder's work in the theatre, as
a playwright and director, this book gives a full contextualization of his
work within the upheavals of its times. Readers are introduced to the
cultural history of the West German theatre in the late 1960s and early
1970s. Radicalism in society meets experiment on stage as Fassbinder
emerges from the cellar theatre scene of Munich, co-founds the
antiteater, and is then integrated into the most subsidized theatre in
Europe, before being offered his own theatre to run for one fateful
season.

DAVID BARNETT is Lecturer in Drama Studies at University College
Dublin. He is the author of *Literature Versus Theatre*, a study of the
later plays of Heiner Müller in performance (1998). He has also
published widely on contemporary German drama, metatheatre and
postdramatic theatre.

CAMBRIDGE STUDIES IN MODERN THEATRE

Series editor
David Bradby, *Royal Holloway, University of London*

Advisory board
Martin Banham, *University of Leeds*
Jacky Bratton, *Royal Holloway, University of London*
Tracy Davis, *Northwestern University*
Sir Richard Eyre
Michael Robinson, *University of East Anglia*
Sheila Stowell, *University of Birmingham*

Volumes for Cambridge Studies in Modern Theatre explore the political, social and cultural functions of theatre while also paying careful attention to detailed performance analysis. The focus of the series is on political approaches to the modern theatre with attention also being paid to theatres of earlier periods and their influence on contemporary drama. Topics in the series are chosen to investigate this relationship and include both playwrights (their aims and intentions set against the effects of their work) and process (with emphasis on rehearsal and production methods, the political structure within theatre companies and their choice of audiences or performance venues). Further topics will include devised theatre, agitprop, community theatre, para-theatre and performance art. In all cases the series will be alive to the special cultural and political factors operating in the theatres examined.

Books published

Rainer Werner Fassbinder and the German Theatre

David Barnett

University College Dublin

CAMBRIDGE
UNIVERSITY PRESS

CAMBRIDGE
UNIVERSITY PRESS

University Printing House, Cambridge CB2 8BS, United Kingdom

Cambridge University Press is part of the University of Cambridge.

It furthers the University's mission by disseminating knowledge in the pursuit of education, learning and research at the highest international levels of excellence.

www.cambridge.org
Information on this title: www.cambridge.org/9780521855143

© David Barnett 2005

First published 2005

A catalogue record for this publication is available from the British Library

ISBN 978-0-521-85514-3 Hardback
ISBN 978-0-521-10724-2 Paperback

For Georgina

Contents

Illustrations

List of illustrations

Acknowledgements

This book would not have been possible without the help and generosity of a great deal of people. In terms of Brecht's 'erst kommt das Fressen, dann kommt die Moral' (roughly: 'eat first, ask questions later'), I am most grateful to the Humboldt Foundation, who funded me as a Research Fellow for a year's stay in Germany. I also thank the School of Music and Humanities at the University of Huddersfield for granting me a year's sabbatical and the money to pay for teaching cover.

Juliane Lorenz and Annemarie Abel at the Rainer Werner Fassbinder Foundation have also been exceptionally helpful in opening up and guiding me through the holdings of their archive on many occasions. I would also like to thank all those who gave up their time to allow me to interview them: Harry Baer, Karlheinz Braun, Rudolf Waldemar Brem, Margit Carstensen, Irm Hermann, Hans Hirschmüller, Kurt Hübner, Yaak Karsunke, Gunter Krää, Renate Leiffer, Juliane Lorenz, Joachim von Mengershausen, Peer Raben, Günther Rühle, Jörg Schmitt, Hanna Schygulla, Heide Simon, Volker Spengler, Eberhard Wagner and Gerhard Zwerenz.

There is also a host of Fassbinder's associates, archivists and others who have provided me with materials which have greatly deepened my understanding of Fassbinder's work in the theatre (and I repeat some of the names already mentioned with pleasure): Wilfried Beege (photographer), Karlheinz Braun (publisher), Rudolf Waldemar Brem, Corinna Brocher (Rowohlt), Denis Calandra (University of South Florida), Margit Carstensen, Frank Fellermeier (assistant to Peer Raben), Steffi Friedrichs (Theater Bremen), Stefan Hemler (LMU, Munich), Irm Hermann, Hans Hirschmüller, Yaak Karsunke (critic),

Acknowledgements

Frau Katzidef (Bundeswehr-Archiv), Brigitte Klein (Theatersammlung Frankfurt), Renate Leiffer (independent assistant director), Juliane Lorenz, Dr Neumann (Stadtarchiv Bochum), Peer Raben, Günther Rühle, Ulrike Schiedermair (Deutsche Akademie der Darstellenden Künste), Bruno Schneider (independent film-maker), Dr Schneider (Stadtarchiv Frankfurt/Main), Heide Simon, Gerrit Thies (Kinematek, Berlin) and Eberhard Wagner.

I should also like to thank all those at CUP who have supported this project. Dr David Bradby has encouraged me ever since I submitted my first proposal, and Dr Vicki Cooper, Alena Dvorakova and Becky Jones have overseen the production process with great care. A final note of gratitude goes to Dr Geoff Westgate, who took the time to read the whole manuscript and offer a vast array of keen insights that had clearly passed me by while writing.

Introduction

Fassbinder: life, film and theatre

Rainer Werner Fassbinder may well have died on 10 June 1982 at the age of thirty-seven, yet the spectre of his biography has eclipsed the forty-two films he left behind, and the rest of the work has remained an underrated footnote to the excesses of his life. The publication, in the same year as his death, of three books by two close associates and an author with whom Fassbinder had worked in various capacities helped to establish a series of Fassbinder legends which have never really forsaken him or his reputation.[1] The biographical interpretation of his work followed and has more or less been a staple of Fassbinder criticism, with a couple of notable exceptions. Psychologizing accounts which include his work more as an excuse for revelations and speculations have been written by Ronald Hayman, Robert Katz and Peter Berling. The new monograph on the artist that was released to mark the twentieth anniversary of his death contains the line that Fassbinder's life was 'identical to his film work'.[2] The biographical interpretation of his work was not helped in the slightest by a television film, *Ein Mann wie EVA* (*A Man like*

---

[1] Kurt Raab and Karsten Peters, *Die Sehnsucht des Rainer Werner Fassbinder* (Munich: Bertelsmann, 1982); Harry Baer with Maurus Packer, *Schlafen kann ich, wenn ich tot bin. Das atemlose Leben des Rainer Werner Fassbinder* (Cologne: Kiepenheuer und Witsch, 1982); and Gerhard Zwerenz, *Der langsame Tod des Rainer Werner Fassbinder. Ein Bericht* (Munich: Schneekluth, 1982).

[2] Michael Töteberg, *Rainer Werner Fassbinder* (Reinbek: Rowohlt, 2002), p. 112. Even this book, which addresses Fassbinder's work seriously, dabbles with tittle-tattle and biographical exegesis.

EVA), directed by Radu Gabrea in 1983, which highlighted all the worst clichés about Fassbinder's life. The idea of casting a woman (Eva Mattes, an actress Fassbinder worked with on several occasions) in heavy make-up as 'Fassbinder' was shrewd and could have produced an interesting sideways glance at him. But EVA (an allusion to Fassbinder's abbreviated initials, RWF) is spiteful, unstable, wilful, emotionally exploitative, hypocritical, squalid, tyrannical and vindictive. Herbert Spaich, a biographer who does not get bogged down in pat psychological interpretations, called the film 'the height of bad taste'.[3] A recent film by Rosa von Praunheim, *Für mich gab's nur noch Fassbinder. Die glücklichen Opfer des Rainer Werner Fassbinder* (*For Me There Was Only Ever Fassbinder. The Grinning Victims of Rainer Werner Fassbinder*), made in 2000, is just another sensationalist account which pays almost no attention to artistic output in the slightest.

To an extent, Fassbinder was partially responsible for the prominence of his life in interpretations of his film work. As Thomas Elsaesser points out, the 'rumour-machine' was a way of attracting attention, ultimately to the films, and thus creating an audience and a dialogue.[4] That the film work has been so neglected in favour of scurrilous depictions of a life is nothing short of a scandal.

Fassbinder is one of the great multi-media artists of his generation. His sensitivity towards medium and his ability to understand crucial distinctions between artistic genres led to a sizeable body of work that far outstrips the already astonishing tally of forty-two films. He was at home in the cinema, on television and in the theatre, yet the last has been much neglected.

---

[3] Herbert Spaich, *Rainer Werner Fassbinder. Leben und Werk* (Weinheim: Beltz, 1992), p. 115. In this book, all translations from the German have been done by the author unless otherwise acknowledged.

[4] Thomas Elsaesser, *Fassbinder's Germany. History Identity Subject* (Amsterdam: Amsterdam University Press, 1996), p. 10. Elsaesser's book is one of the few major works that refuses outright to engage with Fassbinder's biography as a way into his creative output. The book, focusing predominantly on the film work, is one of the sharpest analyses available.

Fassbinder was a playwright, a theatre director and a stage actor. He wrote sixteen published dramas (of which five were radical adaptations of classic texts), two radio plays, and there are various texts, adaptations and fragments which either remain in the archives or have been lost over time. After training at acting school and work as an extra, Fassbinder entered the theatre at the age of twenty-one in 1967, when he stepped in for an injured actor at the small, independent *action-theater*. Its forced closure in 1968 allowed Fassbinder and his team to set up the *antiteater*, which grew to national prominence within a year. Fassbinder was 'discovered' by one of the most important figures in West German theatre, Kurt Hübner, in 1969 and was invited to become an in-house dramatist and then director at Hübner's Bremer Theater. In the following years directing commissions arrived from some of the most prestigious theatres in the Federal Republic. In 1974, seven years after his first tiny role and still in his twenties, Fassbinder was given his own part-publicly funded theatre in Frankfurt. Yet these impressive credentials are overlooked and erased in the critical literature. Mauro Ponzi, who wrote a short, comparative biography of Fassbinder and Pasolini, barely considers the drama work at all, even though both film-makers spent a great deal of time working in the theatre.[5] Christian Braad Thomsen, one of the great popularizers of Fassbinder's film work outside Germany, believes that we cannot properly understand the drama because it was written for specific actors with specific styles in mind. However, this argument is at best questionable, since it rather renders the investigation of almost any drama, from the ancients via Shakespeare to Beckett, pointless. Thomsen concludes: 'for Fassbinder, theatre was undoubtedly a "film school"'.[6] Wallace Steadman Watson asserts that 'one can make only limited claims for the importance of Fassbinder's work in the theatre', which he views, like Thomsen, as ephemeral and too closely shackled

---

[5] Cf. Mauro Ponzi, *Pier Paulo Pasolini. Rainer Werner Fassbinder* (Hamburg: Europäische Verlagsanstalt, 1996).

[6] Christian Braad Thomsen, *Fassbinder. The Life and Work of a Provocative Genius*, tr. Martin Chalmers (London: Faber and Faber, 1997), pp. 47 and 59.

to its times.[7] However, such opinions, espoused by authors who are not theatre specialists themselves, are openly contradicted by the major upswing of practical interest in Fassbinder's theatre work in the 1990s and early years of the twenty-first century (cf. the table of productions in the epilogue to this book). The plays are being produced and performed regularly and often, both in the German-speaking countries and further afield. Their appeal clearly transcends their immediate contexts and has found resonance in contemporary society.

Fassbinder himself did little to dispel the impression that he was never really interested in the theatre. Filming almost always took precedence over theatre commitments, and after the acclaimed production of Claire Luce Boothe's *The Women* as *Frauen in New York* at the Schauspielhaus Hamburg in 1976, he was never to work in a theatre again. Yet these facts belie a more active engagement. Fassbinder was never afraid of revealing his debt to his experiences in the theatre, even though they were usually couched in terms that viewed them as secondary to his film achievements. In 1971/2 he said the theatre had taught him 'how to work with actors and how to tell a story'.[8] By 1974 he explained how dearly he valued the depths of relationships developed over a rehearsal period in a theatre: when he worked on the film *Martha* with Karlheinz Böhm, everything went swimmingly. But after seven weeks of work on *Hedda Gabler* at the Theater der freien Volksbühne in Berlin, the emergence of complexity and 'chasms' in his relationship with the actor was 'absolutely central'.[9] Even in an interview in which he said he was never really that interested in theatre and would never direct another play again, Fassbinder added a few pages later that he *would* consider returning there to direct a play more like a film, 'concretely, directly, together with people who were

---

[7] Wallace Steadman Watson, *Understanding Rainer Werner Fassbinder. Film as Private and Public Art* (Columbia: University of South Carolina Press, 1996), p. 57.

[8] Rainer Werner Fassbinder, *Die Anarchie der Phantasie. Gespräche und Interviews*, ed. Michael Töteberg (Frankfurt/Main: Suhrkamp, 1986), p. 38.

[9] Ibid., p. 52.

interested and affected by it'.[10] Fassbinder went on to stage *Frauen in New York* a few months after the interview and hatched various plans to return to the theatre in the last seven years of his life. These plans ultimately came to nothing.

Where theatre *is* mentioned in the longer studies, it is almost exclusively presented with factual inaccuracy or other material error. Although such mistakes are usually minor – a wrong date, a failure to understand the boundary between Fassbinder's work at Munich's *action-theater* and the *antiteater* – they betray the fact that almost no concerted work has been done on the history of his theatrical activities. Even Joanna Firaza, who has written and published a doctoral dissertation on Fassbinder's dramas, is reliant on other people's accounts and, although she offers many interesting and important insights into the texts and their contexts, she displays a palpable lack of knowledge of the original productions themselves.[11]

The second problem in the existing literature on Fassbinder's theatre concerns theatrical aesthetics and their deployment by critics. For the most part, Fassbinder is portrayed as an Artaudian, a sensual, irrationalist director, fascinated by the unsayable in performance. Fassbinder's interest in Artaud is well documented: Artaud provides the epigraph to the much-misunderstood film *Satansbraten* (*Satan's Brew*) in 1976, is recited by Fassbinder as a voice-over in his only documentary, *Theater in Trance* (1981), and the film *Despair* (1977) is dedicated to him, Van Gogh and Unica Zürn. Such a view was pioneered by Michael Töteberg in an article in which he argues that the *action-theater* was 'the Munich branch of the Living Theatre'.[12] Although he suggests that Fassbinder's aesthetic is somewhere between Artaud and Brecht, his belief that the *action-theater* owed much of its energy to the ecstatic revolutionaries from America owes much to one

---

[10] Ibid., pp. 76 and 80.

[11] Cf. Joanna Firaza, *Die Ästhetik des Dramenwerks von Rainer Werner Fassbinder. Die Struktur der Doppeltheit* (Frankfurt/Main *et al.*: Peter Lang, 2002), pp. 11, 20–5 or 112, for example.

[12] Michael Töteberg, 'Das Theater der Grausamkeit als Lehrstück. Zwischen Brecht und Artaud: Die experimentellen Theatertexte Fassbinders', *Text und Kritik*, 103 (1989), pp. 20–34, here p. 22.

production, *Antigone*, in which Fassbinder stepped in for an injured actor midway through the run. Non-specialists have championed the Artaudian Fassbinder and dismissed a Brechtian influence. Jane Shattuc attempts to historicize the assertion by claiming Brecht was part of the 'established left' and therefore not such an oppositional figure, although this was not really the case in the late 1960s.[13] There had been a 'Brecht boycott' in the Federal Republic which had followed the building of the Berlin Wall in 1961. Elsewhere, critics are keen to follow Fassbinder himself on Brecht. In an interview of 1971, Fassbinder associated Brecht with coldness and abstraction, whereas he preferred the Hungarian Ödön von Horváth, who was more concerned with relationships between everyday people.[14] In 1975 Fassbinder elaborated on this position, when asked about Brecht's influence. He believed he had been influenced

> as much as anybody in Germany has been influenced by Brecht, but not especially . . . What's important to me and everyone else is the idea of alienation[15] in Brecht, and my films have the character of the Brecht didactic pieces. But they are not so dry as the *Lehrstück* ['the learning play']. That's the thing that disturbs me about Brecht's *Lehrstücke*, the dryness; they have no sensuality.[16]

---

[13] Jane Shattuc, *Television, Tabloids and Tears. Fassbinder and Popular Culture* (Minneapolis: University of Minneapolis Press, 1995), p. 87.

[14] Christian Braad Thomsen, 'Conversations with Rainer Werner Fassbinder', in Laurence Kardish (ed.), in collaboration with Juliane Lorenz, *Rainer Werner Fassbinder* (New York: Museum of Modern Art, 1997), pp. 85–9, here p. 88.

[15] 'Alienation', the mistranslated *Verfremdung* of Brecht, is better rendered as 'defamiliarization', making the familiar strange and thus stimulating curiosity. This study will prefer the latter rendering.

[16] Quoted in Klaus Bohnen, '"Raum-Höllen" der bürgerlichen Welt. "Gefühlsrealismus" in der Theater- und Filmproduktion Rainer Werner Fassbinders', in Gerhard Kluge (ed.), *Studien zur Dramatik in der Bundesrepublik Deutschland* (Amsterdam: Rodopi, 1983), pp. 141–62, here p. 156. The interview originally appeared in English in the magazine *Film Comment*, November/December 1975, p. 14.

The 'dry' or 'cold' Brecht discussed here is used as a brickbat by critics against Brecht the theorist when addressing his part in Fassbinder's development. I shall be returning to Brecht and his role in Fassbinder's theatre practice in chapter 2, and will be exploring a different, more sensual interpretation of Brecht.

Fassbinder and the West German theatre

We see, then, that in the various histories of Fassbinder and his work, the dramatist and theatre director receive fairly short shrift. And even when commentators do consider the drama, the analysis lacks the edge of primary research. What is left unwritten is the remarkable climb of a minor actor from a small role in a little-known theatre's production of a Greek classic to a figure of great stature within the West German theatre system. At the peak of his directing career, Fassbinder was offered contracts at some of the most important theatres in Germany by some of the most innovative *Intendanten*[17] and was finally entrusted with his own experimental theatre before he was thirty. Equally exceptional is the fact that in this brief seven-year period, Fassbinder had also made over twenty-one feature-length films for cinema and television. Although this book is exclusively dedicated to Fassbinder's work in the theatre, it should be clear to those familiar with the films that Fassbinder's aesthetics owe a great deal to a sense of artifice, or theatricality. This quality arose from his extensive experience of the theatre, which engaged his creative focus for a full and intensive year and a half before he made his first feature. Fassbinder was acutely sensitive to the differing demands of a medium, something he exhibits at the age of twenty-one: 'In the world of television, I am most interested in the possibilities afforded by the TV film, whose fundament is not theatre plays but solely texts written for the possibilities

---

[17] The term is untranslatable but broadly means 'artistic directors'. However, these are the people who run and shape the theatres in German-speaking countries and consequently have powers that transcend the more demarcated job title of 'artistic director'.

of the television.'[18] Klaus Ulrich Militz argues that new media are 'not born into an empty world', and that the new medium pressurizes the old, so that the old must learn from the new.[19] Fassbinder did not mistake the theatre for a cinema or a television set, but engaged with all three to generate new forms of theatre and performance.

In addition to Fassbinder's work as a director, I shall be examining the plays themselves, the conditions of their production and their contribution to a post-Brechtian theatre. Fassbinder's dramas have been treated in scholarship, but only with a limited focus on a small number of works, and then with little, if any, discussion of Fassbinder's approach to theatrical production or direction. Shorter, article-length criticism is mainly textual rather than dramaturgical. Only Firaza has dedicated a whole book to Fassbinder's drama, but even she has not quite delivered the promise of her study's title, namely an aesthetics.

A closer examination of the oeuvre reveals something far more interesting than the literary quality of the texts or their relationships to various genres. Firaza notes that heterogeneity is the only unifying factor in Fassbinder's drama.[20] The playwright paces impatiently from style to style, playing with the possibilities of one before moving onto another in his next play. He takes up the *Volksstück* (a genre discussed in chapter 1), the melodrama, the experimental play, the burlesque, satire and the radical adaptation. Yet even the concept of genre is problematic. As Benjamin Henrichs points out, Fassbinder's works are all 'bastards of form'.[21] The theatre imports ideas from the cinema, and provincial perspectives from his native Bavaria are seen through the lens of America. Each play demonstrates a new approach,

---

[18] Rainer Werner Fassbinder, 'Wie stelle ich mir meine zukünftige Berufstätigkeit vor?', in *Filme befreien den Kopf*, ed. Michael Töteberg (Frankfurt/Main: Suhrkamp, 1984), p. 123.

[19] Klaus Ulrich Militz, *Media Interplay in Rainer Werner Fassbinder's Work for Theatre, Cinema and Television* (unpublished PhD thesis: University of Edinburgh, 2000), p. ii.

[20] Firaza, *Die Ästhetik des Dramenwerks*, p. 13.

[21] Benjamin Henrichs, 'Fassbinder, Rainer Werner. Oder: immer viel Trauer dabei', *Theater heute*, Sonderheft 1972, pp. 69–70, here p. 70.

an alternative perspective, a fresh consideration. However, at the very heart of Fassbinder's drama is a fascination with language as a social phenomenon. The ability, but more often, inability to communicate, the violence exerted through language, and the dependencies language creates are investigated through a kaleidoscope of forms.

Fassbinder's work in the theatre is not solely of interest within the man's development as an artist. His career in the theatre allows us to explore the West German theatre system itself. Fassbinder's career takes us through all the major crises and debates that surround the most subsidized theatre in Europe. The *Kellertheater* scene that flourished in post-war Germany was a direct challenge to the conservative, stagnant, yet well-funded theatres that were still the norm in Germany at the time. In a Germany that was both facing up to its catastrophic past and looking to forms of art that challenged bourgeois concepts of literature and theatre, smaller private theatres were starting to offer aesthetic competition. That Fassbinder's association with the *antiteater* gained it a national profile, distinguished the company in that it was able to offer an alternative not only to its own more immediate rivals in Munich, but to the state-supported theatres as well. The success of the *antiteater* generated an interest in Fassbinder and his approaches to production that was to channel him into the system itself: Kurt Hübner, one of the most innovative *Intendanten* in Germany, engaged Fassbinder as a playwright and later as a director at the publicly funded theatre in Bremen. This came at a time when more adventurous *Intendanten* were seeking a new kind of theatre, one which called into question the orthodoxies of the older generation and their conservative conceptions of theatre. The *Regietheater* ('directors' theatre') that was taking off in the late 1960s became a haven for Fassbinder and his radical ideas on staging. Once established as a theatre director in his own right, Fassbinder was left to deal with one further issue that had dominated West German theatre politics ever since the student revolts of 1968: *Mitbestimmung* ('collective decision-making'). Fassbinder's period as the head of the Theater am Turm in Frankfurt was in many ways his theatrical Waterloo. The challenge of running a theatre under the principles of collectivity was untenable, and his initial enthusiasm and subsequent disenchantment mark the end of an era in the theatre history of the Federal Republic. Fassbinder thus presents himself as an important figure in all the major debates surrounding the post-war theatre's problematic metamorphosis from the polite pastime of the middle classes into a more inclusive, more experimental and more exciting institution.

This book is thus a contribution to a much-neglected area of Fassbinder's working biography, a critical examination of both Fassbinder's drama and its production, and an exploration of West German cultural politics at a time of great crisis and upheaval, around and in the wake of the turbulent year of 1968. I have consulted the broad source material in a bid to gain a clearer idea of the productions and their rehearsal and performance styles. Extensive interviews were also undertaken with almost all the central figures from Fassbinder's early days in the theatre in Munich and the later period, including actors, ensemble members and theatre critics who followed his progress. I have also visited the archives of the major theatres and cities in which Fassbinder worked after his auspicious beginnings in Munich. The evidence from all the sources is contradictory, and the reader should understand that each description of a production is provisional. I have, however, tried to give as helpful, critical and authoritative a set of sketches as possible in order to establish the methods and the principles of Fassbinder's work in the theatre.

In the first chapter I shall be discussing the *action-theater*, the collective Fassbinder joined as a stand-in before establishing himself as one of its central members. The theatre will be considered within the context of both a highly subsidized theatre system and the network of *Kellertheater* in the Munich of the late 1960s. The second chapter moves on to deal with the *antiteater* and its distinctive performance style. The central importance of the 1968 student movement and its effects on cultural paradigms will be compared to and contrasted with the *antiteater*'s practices. Chapter 3 charts Fassbinder's uneasy integration into the system, and his various commissions to direct at the cream of the German theatres. Here the ideas of the *Regietheater* will be explored and Fassbinder's place as a director will be assessed. The fourth chapter will then consider Fassbinder's spell as the head of the Theater am Turm (TAT) together with the attendant difficulties of a limited budget and the principle of *Mitbestimmung*, that last hang-over of the days of revolt in 1968. The fifth chapter then looks at Fassbinder's aborted plans after his final theatre production in Hamburg, evaluates Fassbinder's resonance on the German stage after his death in 1982 and investigates West Germany's greatest post-war theatre scandal when the Schauspiel Frankfurt tried to perform *Der Müll, die Stadt und der Tod* (*Rubbish, the City and Death*) in 1985. An epilogue reviews Fassbinder's achievements in the theatre and speculates on the reasons for his continued popularity.

1   The roots of the *antiteater*

Public theatres in the Federal Republic of Germany and the crisis of the *Staatstheater*

The German theatre system is the envy of the Western world. Its virtues are twofold: it is exceptionally well funded and it is decentralized. The public money that flows into it, provided by national and regional taxation, has one central function – it makes drama and theatre virtually independent of the market. In 1953, 93 million DM were distributed throughout West Germany, a figure which had risen to 391 million DM in 1967, and passed the billion mark in 1975.[1] With such huge underwriting from the state, theatres can experiment free from the economic realities of actually having to pay their way. Directors can be more daring and dramatists are able to make ever more challenging demands on actors, set-builders and directors in their plays. Large subsidy (reckoned to cover approximately 80 per cent of a theatre's costs in the 1970s)[2] also affects the role of the actor and the audience. Unlike in Britain, actors in Germany are exposed to a more diverse range of dramaturgies and acting styles and theoretically have fewer preconceptions as to how to approach a speech or a role. The audience, too, is exposed to a broader interpretation of what theatre might be, and, after the onslaught of more experimental direction in the 1960s, has become discerning towards the sophisticated fare on offer and indeed weary of

---

[1] Source: Deutscher Bühnenverein (ed.), *Vergleichende Theaterstatistik 49/50 bis 84/5* (Cologne: Deutscher Bühnenverein, 1987), p. 46.

[2] Cf. Günther Rühle, *Theater in unserer Zeit* (Frankfurt/Main: Suhrkamp, 1976), p. 289.

'traditional' interpretations of playtexts. Such positive effects naturally have to be qualified by certain disadvantages. One might find (primarily directorial) self-indulgence or complacency at certain venues, and less cosmopolitan and more conservative institutions hang on to more conventional notions of theatre than their more progressive counterparts. Another corollary and limitation of such public investment is the role and power of local politicians. Theatre may be more divorced from the market in Germany, but it is tied more tightly to the main parties and their representatives. However, a party's political hue is not necessarily a yardstick by which to gauge how it may act. While one can understand why the conservative CDU (Christian Democratic Union) opposed the appointment of a former student and colleague of Brecht's as *Intendant* in Düsseldorf, the more left-wing SPD (Social Democratic Party of Germany) ejected the radical innovator Kurt Hübner from Bremen. The influence of local politicians on the theatre in Germany will feature at certain key moments in this study.

Decentralization is also a crucial factor in German theatre. Whereas Britain and the USA have undisputed theatre capitals, London and New York, Germany benefits from the geopolitical landscape that preceded unification in 1871. Up until then, Germany was a dense patchwork of larger and very much smaller states, many of which had their own theatre. After the abolition of the monarchy and the founding of the Weimar Republic in 1918, the many theatres were nationalized. Following the Second World War, about a third of the theatres lay in ruins or were unusable. Theatres were included in West Germany's extensive programme of reconstruction. New theatres were erected, older ones rebuilt or refurbished. A new theatre in Münster in 1954 started the ball rolling, even though the rebuilding of the theatre in Bochum was completed the year before. New theatres sprang up in Düsseldorf, Stuttgart, Frankfurt, Cologne, Berlin and a host of other cities. Twelve new theatres were inaugurated in 1966 alone. The completion of the *Staatstheater* and *Stadttheater* (literally 'state theatre' and 'city theatre') in Karlsruhe effectively marked the end of the building boom in 1975. Although the number of theatre seats in the country had more than doubled between 1949 and 1985, the number of stages owned by the theatres had risen almost threefold from 104 to 286.[3]

Decentralization, like state funding, has important effects. The West German theatre scene has significant centres up and down the country. This owes as much to Germany's pre-unification history as it does to post-war regionalization policy, a strategy aimed at breaking up the power of central government. Berlin, Hamburg, Munich, Frankfurt and other cities have developed into centres of theatrical excellence. The system is so dispersed that even less important cities, such as Bochum or Bremen, can take advantage of a ground-breaking team in order to establish themselves as cultural forces. The lack of a centre also encourages 'cultural competition' because there is no one theatre or location that might dominate. Theatres vie for the services of certain directors or the appointment of certain *Intendanten*. Creative individuals are not forced to serve one particular master, thus enriching the cultural life of the nation rather than merely a region. The historical quirk of Germany's late nationhood has vastly increased the possibilities for a diverse and stimulating theatre.

In theory, then, the German theatre is one of the most attractive in the West. Its financial independence and its variety distinguish it from the more conservative and limiting structures of other European and American apparatuses. However, theatre in West Germany in the 1950s and 1960s was not in good shape.

The malaise, which became a full-blown crisis, began with the restoration of theatrical affairs in the years following the collapse of the Third Reich. The tone was set by Gustaf Gründgens, an *Intendant* who continued to work in Germany throughout the Nazi period.[4] As Vice President of Der Deutsche Bühnenverein, he set out a conservative agenda in a speech to his fellow *Intendanten* in 1948 when he exhorted them to stage 'productions which were true to the text'

---

[3] Source: Deutscher Bühnenverein (ed.), *Vergleichende Theaterstatistik*, p. 30.

[4] Gründgens' career in the theatre is the subject of Klaus Mann's novel *Mephisto*, which was filmed by István Szabó in 1981. Neither Mann nor Szabo suggests Gründgens was a Nazi, but both criticize his careerism and opportunism as he purveys culture within a barbaric regime.

('werkgetreue Inszenierungen').[5] One may not necessarily consider the statement conservative, but in the context of German theatre history it was highly reactionary. The German audience had been confronted with the grittiness of naturalism in the 1890s, the violence of Expressionism in the following decades, and the experiments of Erwin Piscator and Bertolt Brecht, amongst many others, in the Weimar Republic. A return to the conventional was anything but progressive. The 1950s had a 'business as usual' flavour to them, carrying on the Nazis' unimaginative work in the theatre, with little room for innovation. Twice as many classics filled the repertoires at that time than in the 1970s. Günther Rühle views the aesthetic of the decade as 'cleansed of politics, suffused with poetry'.[6]

The conservatism of theatre direction was in harmony with the concept of the theatre's function in the post-war years, that is, of bringing the muse to a mainly middle-class audience. Germany was in a period of restoration. Former Nazis found their way back into all areas of public life, in the judiciary, medicine and politics. Rather than engaging with the catastrophe of the Third Reich, Germany was far more concerned with rebuilding the defeated nation. The hierarchies and thought structures of the *Wirtschaftswunder* (the 'economic miracle') were still authoritarian, and the German electorate continued to choose the CDU, mainly in the form of Chancellor Konrad Adenauer, until 1966. Alexander and Margarete Mitscherlich's famous study of 1967, *Die Unfähigkeit zu trauern. Grundlagen kollektiven Verhaltens* (*The Inability to Mourn. Basics of Collective Behaviour*), underlines the degree of repression required to blot out an unthinkable past. Although I am not at all trying to suggest that the German *Intendanten* as a whole were former Nazis, a certain dictatorial mindset was very much alive in their methods and practices in the 1950s.

By the 1960s the Federal Republic was back on its feet and was an economic power of international stature. In a short period it had

---

[5] Gründgens quoted by Knut Lennartz in *Theater, Künstler und Politik. 150 Jahre Deutscher Bühnenverein* (Berlin: Henschel, 1996), p. 122.

[6] Rühle, *Theater in unserer Zeit*, p. 277.

reconstructed itself, albeit at the expense of an examination of its recent past. But this was to change in the 1960s, as the children of the Second World War had the opportunity (and the economic assurance) to challenge their parents. Paternalistic *Intendanten* had preserved the theatre as a 'temple of the muses'; ideas of humanism, delivered in the grand style, were fed to the theatre-going public. Deference towards the classics was allied with deference towards the text. Bourgeois concepts of culture dominated, and kept the avant-garde at arm's length. Germany produced precious few absurdist artists and only Ionesco made any serious incursion into the repertoires in the 1950s.[7] Yet come the early 1960s, German dramatists sought a reckoning with the past in the form of documentary drama.

Rolf Hochhuth's *Der Stellvertreter* (translated as both *The Deputy* and *The Representative*) of 1963, Heinar Kipphardt's *In der Sache J. Robert Oppenheimer* (*In the Matter of J. Robert Oppenheimer*) of 1964 and Peter Weiss's *Die Ermittlung* (*The Investigation*) of 1965 took the theatrical establishment by storm (and each was staged by Piscator himself in Berlin). Documents, whether in the form of newspaper articles, official protocols or archival sources, were the foundation of a drama that actively engaged with the past and the present. The triumvirate of documentarists reintroduced a concept of political drama into the West German vocabulary, a term which not only challenged the spectator but the very structures of the theatres themselves. Politics was back on the agenda, and the generation under the microscope was the same as that running the theatres.

Another important figure in the enlivening of German-language drama was the Austrian Peter Handke. His early works undermined the very authority of the playtext. *Publikumsbeschimpfung* (*Offending* or *Insulting the Audience*) has no characters and is to be delivered by four speakers. Other *Sprechstücke* (literally 'speech plays', plays to be performed rather than acted) were to follow. Handke presented directors with texts which offered no clear instructions as to how they were to be staged. Handke is not often viewed as a 'political' writer

---

[7] Cf. Anon, 'Was wird bei uns gespielt?', *Theater heute*, 10 (1970), pp. 52–3.

(although the centrality of language, its uses and its employment in his early work make this an inescapable category) but may rather be considered a representative of a rebellious 'pop' generation. It is Handke's iconoclasm and quotations from high and low culture that locate his early work in the 1960s. His reputation as a rebel stems in part from his very public haranguing of the Gruppe 47 at its annual meeting in Princeton in 1966. The group, which was really only a loose association of writers, was primarily made up of the older generation, though it was critical of the political and social conditions of the time. Handke was still able to shake the group to its foundations and generate for himself some 'hip' publicity.

In addition, dramatists and directors were rediscovering two central representatives of the *Volksstück*[8] tradition. Ödön von Horváth (1901–38), a Hungarian who chose to live in Germany and who wrote in German, was returned to prominence in the mid-1960s, and the Bavarian Marieluise Fleisser (1901–74) was to follow a little later. Both dramatists concentrated on the lives, and more precisely the languages, of the lower strata of society during the Weimar Republic. The disjunction between the speaker and that which was spoken pointed to a political dimension: the tactical deployment of language as a weapon. Fleisser, by way of Horváth, will play an important role in the fortunes of Fassbinder and the *actiontheater*, as we will see later in this chapter.

Theatre was being revitalized by a variety of sources, yet the old guard remained intransigent. A generational conflict, so typical of

---

[8] The term is untranslatable. Literally it means 'play for/of the people', and has been translated by Michael Patterson as 'the theatre of the common man' [sic] (Michael Patterson, *German Theatre Today. Post-War Theatre in West and East Germany, Austria and Northern Switzerland* (London: Pitman, 1976), p. 88). Part of its generic difficulty is that it has changed its meaning greatly since its coinage in the eighteenth century. Originally the term denoted a play written for the common people and featured all manner of spectacle and slapstick. After further mutation in the nineteenth century, the form was revived in the twentieth as a critical examination of the lot of the common people.

the 1960s but all the more pointed in post-Nazi Germany, had ignited and was evident in all aspects of theatre production. Yet the older generation had time against it and was literally dying out. Key figures from the theatre left the stage at a most inauspicious time. Erwin Piscator and Wieland Wagner died in 1966, Heinz Hilpert and Heinz Tietjen in 1967, Jürgen Fehling in 1968, Ernst Deutsch in 1969, and Fritz Kortner in 1970. Their passing marked the end of a certain period of theatre history in Germany. In the season 1967/8 seventeen new *Intendanten* were appointed.[9]

At the end of the 1960s the West German theatre system was in crisis. Politically it was out of touch, culturally it was out of date. Most older *Intendanten* ran their theatres 'in the tradition of the autocrat'.[10] Yet moves were afoot to change the very nature of the system and they were encouraged by mass movements in society itself.

1966, politics beyond parliament, and the growth of the cultural underground

The reign of the CDU only came to a partial end in 1966. A slow-down in economic growth and a rise in both unemployment and inflation in 1965 led to the collapse of the CDU's coalition with the FDP (Free Democratic Party of Germany, the liberal party) in October 1966. Four FDP ministers left the government rather than support tax increases to finance the budget deficit. The SPD, in a bid to cast off its 'red' image, joined the CDU to form a grand coalition. Chancellor Ludwig Erhard, Adenauer's finance minister and architect of the *Wirtschaftswunder*, had led the CDU to electoral victory in 1965, but was abandoned in 1966 and replaced by the former Nazi Kurt Kiesinger in December. The

---

[9] Cf. Hans Daiber, *Deutsches Theater seit 1945. Bundesrepublik Deutschland. Deutsche Demokratische Republik. Österreich. Schweiz* (Stuttgart: Reclam, 1976), p. 278.

[10] Rolf Michaelis, 'Von den Barrikaden in den Elfenbeinturm. Aufbruch, Leerlauf, Stillstand: Die undeutlichen Jahre Schauspiel in der Bundesrepublik Deutschland zwischen 1967 und 1982', in Manfred Linke (ed.), *Theater 1967–1982* (Berlin: Institut International du Théâtre, 1983), pp. 7–25, here p. 12.

combination of a chancellor with such credentials and a government that had polled 86.9 per cent of the electorate the previous year[11] led to the formation in 1967 of the APO (the 'Extra-Parliamentary Opposition'). The APO allied itself politically with the SDS (the 'League of German Socialist Students'), which had detached itself from its parent organization, the SPD, in 1961 because the latter was not radical enough. Young people in the Federal Republic were creating a movement that forsook the major parties of Bonn in favour of more popular displays of protest and political organization. Berlin was the main focus of its activities, and the centrepiece was a massed demonstration during the state visit of the Shah of Persia in 1967. The APO gained its first martyr on 2 June 1967, when the student Benno Ohnesorg was shot dead there by a policeman. A potentially media-inspired assassination attempt on the student leader Rudi Dutschke on 11 April 1968 was to have a catalysing effect on the movement and would be felt in the *action-theater*.

The energy of the new politics was also palpable in and around the theatre system in general. The demand for democratic structures within the existing system of hierarchies was felt in the call for *Mitbestimmung* ('collective decision-making'), a topic I shall return to in chapter 4. Elsewhere the type of conflict between young and old can be understood through the example of Peter Stein and his production of Weiss's documentary drama the *Viet Nam Diskurs* at the Münchner Kammerspiele in July 1968. *Intendant* August Everding cancelled the play after three performances, when the actors collected money for the Viet Cong. The young director who would become one of the key figures of the *Regietheater* ('directors' theatre') left Munich for Bremen, Zurich and finally Berlin, where he took over the Schaubühne am Halleschen Ufer and established one of the most exciting theatres in Germany. The incident became an exemplary focus for the discontent within the system and gained a national profile through press coverage in general and, in particular, when the protagonists traded blows

---

[11] Cf. William Carr, *A History of Germany. 1815–1985* (London: Edward Arnold, 1987), p. 383.

in the opening pages of Germany's most important theatre magazine, *Theater heute*.[12]

The frustration at the older generation and the public theatre system itself led to the formation of smaller groups, independent of the state, enthused with collective structures and new dramatic forms. The growth of an underground manifested itself primarily in two directions: the *Kellertheater* ('cellar theatres', the small private theatres) and companies performing street theatre. The *Kellertheater* cannot be considered a movement as such; their approaches and programmes were too diverse. One must also remember that private theatres like these were almost as old as the Federal Republic itself. The Contra-Kreis had formed in Bonn in 1950, and smaller theatres emerged in Cologne, Düsseldorf, Stuttgart and other cities in that decade, too.[13] It was these theatres' change of emphasis in the 1960s in the face of the languishing *Staatstheater* that created a new identity for the companies. The street theatre groups, however, far more uniformly embraced the spirit of the student movement and were 'a product and a part of the protests'.[14] Although both alternative forms blossomed all over West Germany, I shall be focusing on their appearance in the Munich that Fassbinder encountered in the 1960s.

One of the first *Kellertheater*, which still exists today, was Horst A. Reichel's Theater 44. Like many others that were to follow it, this small theatre specialized in absurdist and existentialist dramas. What differentiated it from the other small theatres was its desire to ape the professional stages by charging its patrons the going rates and paying its staff and actors a living wage on a regular basis. A major development of oppositional theatre was slow in coming but had its roots in student theatre. While student groups in the late 1950s were still concerning themselves with absurdism, an interest in the recent German past and contemporary politics started to emerge

---

[12] Cf. August Everding, Wolfgang Schwiedrzik and Peter Stein, 'Was ist demokratisches Theater?', *Theater heute*, 9 (1968), pp. 1–3.

[13] Cf. Hans Daiber, *Deutsches Theater seit 1945*, pp. 306–16.

[14] Wolfram Buddecke and Helmut Fuhrmann, *Das deutschsprachige Drama seit 1945. Schweiz. Bundesrepublik. Österreich. DDR. Kommentar einer Epoche* (Munich: Winkler, 1981), p. 120.

around 1964.[15] Munich did not have a particularly strong SDS presence, but its street theatre excelled. The student theatre scene was not content to offer mere agitprop and preferred to engage wit and irony in its events and performances.[16]

The Büchner Theater, at which Fassbinder would be involved in three productions, was founded in 1965 in the cellars under a gym and fitness club at 40 Isabellastrasse. Its spirit may have been kindled by the political fervour of Büchner (in such plays as *Danton's Death* and *Woyzeck*), but the theatre in 1967 was managed by Helmut Berninger, whose interests lay far more in formal experiment. In an interview, an unnamed member of the theatre said: 'we are consciously anti-political and non-ideological, we want complex constructions devoid of motivation'.[17] Berninger wanted a theatre of language, in which the medium was treated as an artist treated paint, and he commented that he would be considering changing the theatre's name.[18] Alexei Sagerer's ProT, which took over the Büchner in 1969, pursued Berninger's aims while other theatres established in the late 1960s, like the Modernes Theater and the Off-Off-Theater, were mainly concerned with performing avant-garde texts and classic modernists. Political theatre was to be found in Munich, too. The Theater in der Kreide was opened in 1968 and the Theater am Sozialamt followed in 1969. The scene, then, was something of a mixture – it was interested in formal experiment while trying to compete with the larger, publicly funded theatres by offering an 'alternative' repertoire from the treasure troves of European modernism. Politics had a

[15] Cf. Stefan Hemler, 'Protest-Inszenierungen. Die 68er-Bewegung und das Theater in München', in Hans-Michael Körner and Jürgen Schläder (eds.), *Münchner Theatergeschichtliches Symposium 2000* (Munich: Herbert Utz, 2000), pp. 276–318, here pp. 291–2.

[16] Cf. ibid., pp. 301–3.

[17] Quoted in Nina Keller, *Report über junge Künstler in München* (Iching and Munich: Kreisselmeier, 1968), p. 91.

[18] Cf. Rudolf Waldemar Brem, 'Büchner Theater', *rupprecht-tönchen* (sic), May 1968, n.p. Brem, who became a member of the *action-theater* and a founding member of the *antiteater*, was a theatre-mad sixth-form schoolboy at the time, and this was one of three articles on theatre in Munich he wrote for the school magazine.

function, but the small Munich theatres were hardly dogmatic motors of agitprop. Their political leanings were far more subtle, in that their very dissatisfaction with the cultural status quo had led to their formation. The *action-theater* was formed in 1967 and was, as we shall see, a child of its time until Fassbinder and his supporters started to transform its direction and its philosophy.

A new (smokey) atmosphere: the early history of the *action-theater*

The *action-theater* started life as the *action-kino*. Ursula Strätz and her husband Horst Söhnlein took over the more conservative National-Kino at 12 Müllerstrasse to show art-house films, but small audiences meant that the cinema could not cover its costs. An expensive conversion was undertaken, the debts of which were to haunt the theatre for the rest of its days, and the *action-kino* became the *action-theater*. According to an interview in a newspaper article, the theatre was originally funded by a local brewery, the Klosterbrauerei, with a loan of 5,000 DM, to be repaid over two years. Further debt was underwritten by a publisher, the aptly named Dennoch-Verlag (the 'Nevertheless Publishing House'). The article's author foresaw major financial problems in that the cheap admissions prices, of 5 DM and 3 DM for concessions, could never generate enough to cover costs and repay the loans.[19] Huge debts were indeed to dog the theatre in its short existence.

The ensemble was initially populated by a group of young actors who had met and trained at a private theatre school, the Zinner-Studio. In early 1967, the group was rehearsing its opening production, *Jakob oder der Gehorsam* (*Jack or Submission*) by Ionesco. The play was premièred on 8 March, but the theatre was closed immediately for a couple of days by the city of Munich's Office for Public Order because of technical deficiencies. This was not the last intervention from the office, which would play a key role in the final closure of the theatre almost fifteen months after its debut production.

[19] Manfred Lütgenhorst, 'Kunst wird durch Bier erst schön!', *Abendzeitung*, 8/9 April 1967.

The *action-theater* itself was a smallish space with room for an audience of just over fifty. The stage was a mere eighteen square metres. The theatre's major allure was the bar, which robbed the experience of theatre of its more usual bourgeois frame. Smoking and drinking were permitted and encouraged. The idea was a novelty at the time and drew headlines such as 'A Bar and a Stage', 'Theatre in the Pub' and 'Ionesco with Beer'.[20] *Action-theater* actor-to-be Rudolf Waldemar Brem described the relaxed atmosphere of the theatre and the willingness of the actors to engage with the audience both during and after performances in his school magazine.[21] Yaak Karsunke, a critic who followed the *action-theater* and later the *antiteater* on his spot on the radio, saw an attempt to ape Brecht's wish for a theatre audience which rather resembled that of a boxing match.[22] Joachim von Mengershausen, another stalwart reviewer, who went on to make a documentary about the *antiteater*, found the atmosphere enlivening in that it had 'absolutely nothing reverent about it'.[23]

The première was mostly a hit with the press and certainly went down well with the audience – the production ran for about seventy nights. *Jakob* was directed by Erwin Reutzel, who followed Ionesco's stage directions carefully (see fig. 1). Although the production neither challenged nor undermined the playwright, it did take his suggestions seriously and translated them into engaging theatre. The masks, which eight of the nine-person cast wear throughout, and which Jack dons when he finally conforms to the will of his oppressive family, were made by Reutzel and were alive with

[20] Cf. kth, 'Mit Bar und Bühne', *Abendzeitung*, no date supplied; Jonathan Link, 'Theater in der Kneipe', *Sonntagsbeilage der Heidelheimer Zeitung*, 16 July 1967; and JK, 'Ionesco mit Bier', *Süddeutsche Zeitung*, 10 March 1967.

[21] Cf. Rudolf Waldemar Brem, '*action-theater*', *rupprechtonen* (sic), November 1967, n.p.

[22] Yaak Karsunke, '*Jakob oder der Gehorsam*', *Kulturspiegel*, Bayerischer Rundfunk, transmitted 22 March 1967.

[23] All unacknowledged references are taken from interviews conducted in the course of my research for this book. The dates of the interviews are to be found in the bibliography.

Fig. 1. Months before Fassbinder arrived, the first production of the
action-theater was *Jakob oder der Gehorsam* (*Jack or Submission*). Edgar M.
Boelke played Jack, the only character not to wear the grotesque half-masks
that drew plaudits from the critics. © Wilfried Beege

well-crafted grotesque expression. The acting was stylized and
directed 'with astonishing consistency'.[24] Reviewer Karin Thimm
was impressed by the talent and the acting skill of the company, and
the two principals were singled out for special praise.[25] Only one
critic was lukewarm in his appraisal. The theatre was 'not exactly
dilettante, but not that good either', 'not boring, but meaningless'.[26]

[24] Karsunke, 'Jakob'.
[25] kth, 'Ein kleines Wunder', *Abendzeitung*, 22 March 1967.
[26] JK, 'Ionesco mit Bier'.

24

For the most part, then, the *action-theater*'s first production was well received, with most of the critics encouraged by its energy and its philosophy of providing an alternative to the state theatres. Jörg Schmitt, who played Jack's grandfather, said that the production was consciously anti-naturalist and anti-bourgeois, 'but not political theatre in the traditional sense'. The rebellion, as at other smaller theatres, was primarily aesthetic, concerning itself with a politics of counter-culture. *Jakob* was a success, even though its choice as a debut piece was reminiscent of the other private theatres' absurdist repertoires.[27]

But the *action-theater* had new vistas. The theatre entertained a range of possibilities for its second production. Jarry's *Ubu Roi*, Gombrowicz's *Yvonne, Princess of Burgundy* and a play by William Carlos Williams were mentioned to Bernd Steets, Brecht's *Elefantenkalb* (*The Elephant Calf*), Bruckner's *Die Verbrecher* (*The Criminals*) and Pushkin's *The Stone Guest* to Manfred Lütgenhorst, and the dramatists Hans Henny Jahnn and Joe Orton to Jonathan Link.[28] The mixture of classic modernism and contemporary drama (with the exception of Pushkin) indicated a wealth of possibility but little focus. As it happened, the troupe decided to follow *Jakob* with one of the most talked-about plays of the moment, Peter Handke's *Publikumsbeschimpfung* (see fig. 2). Little is known about the production.The programme offers a photocopy of Handke's introductory note, the names of the four male speakers and only the surname of the director. The date of its first performance has been lost. Reviewer Karsunke was not terribly impressed by either Handke's text or the

[27] Schmitt told me that there was enough interest from outside to make a film of the production, recorded one night from 8 p.m. until 6 a.m. The three cameras, however, were not properly synchronized and so the film could not be edited and was never shown. He also mentioned a planned run in Strätz's hometown of Schweinfurt in June 1967. Unfortunately, the weather was so hot that one of the cast collapsed on stage and the short tour was cancelled.

[28] Cf. Bernd Steets, 'Ionesco in der Müllerstrasse', *Münchner Merkur*, 8 March 1967; Lütgenhorst, 'Kunst wird durch Bier erst schön!'; and Link, 'Theater in der Kneipe'.

Fig. 2. Words, words, words: the four speakers of Handke's
Publikumsbeschimpfung (*Offending* or *Insulting the Audience*) declaiming for
the camera. © Wilfried Beege

declamatory style of its delivery. He considered the text to be more of
a radio play that had mistakenly found its way into a theatre. And the
audience was hardly offended.[29] What the ensemble had failed to grasp
was that the play had been specifically written for the *Staatstheater*
as a polemical critique, and so a change of frame by a *Kellertheater*
deadened the impact. The *action-theater* was continuing its strategy

[29] Yaak Karsunke, '*Publikumsbeschimpfung*', *Kulturspiegel*, Bayerischer
Rundfunk, no transmission date supplied.

26

with *Jakob* by presenting stimulating contemporary drama, but without any distinctive imprint of its own. And Strätz and Söhnlein were not happy at the prospect of producing run-of-the-mill theatre.[30]

All was set to change when Söhnlein was hospitalized after an accident and Strätz was forced to find a new director for the theatre's next production. She turned to Wilhelm Rabenbauer, who was also a former member of the Zinner-Studio. As 'Peer Raben', he had been working in Wuppertal with Peter Zadek, one of the most important directors in German theatre since the late 1960s. Raben dropped everything once he got the call, something that was in breach of contract, but had initially intended to return to Wuppertal after the production. Strätz had asked Raben to do 'something new' and he decided to develop ideas based on a production of *Antigone* he had seen in 1967. It had been performed by the ground-breaking Living Theatre, which was on tour in Europe at the time. Raben was certainly enthusiastic about the production but was disappointed by the lack of integration of the text into the performance, and this provided his entry point as the rehearsals began (see fig. 3). Raben explained that during the four-week rehearsal period,

> the text of the original scenes was taken from the actors'
> memories of the version they had read. I fixed the results of
> the rehearsals and augmented them with Brecht's [prose]
> version of the myth, thus different translations and
> adaptations have informed the production . . . Deviations
> [from the texts] were not corrected.[31]

The improvised textual approach was married up with a physical theatre directly inspired by his experience of the Living Theatre. In addition, the production employed documentary elements (the numbers of war dead from 2,500 years of conflict were written in chalk on the

---

[30] Schmitt reported that rehearsals of Brecht's *Kleinbürgerhochzeit* (translated as *Petit-Bourgeois* or *Middle-Class Wedding*) were cancelled after a couple of weeks for being 'too conventional'.

[31] *Programme of Sophocles' 'Antigone', action-theater*, première 20 August 1967, n.p.

Fig. 3. *Antigone* at the *action-theater* in rehearsal, August 1967. The picture shows Heiner Schoof (with beard, upstage right), who later stabbed Marite Greiselis (face just about visible two along on his right), and Anatol von Gardner (directly on Schoof's left) among others. Gardner's accidental injury in an unrelated incident would allow Fassbinder his first role on stage at the *action-theater*; Greiselis was hospitalized after the stabbing and replaced by Hanna Schygulla at Fassbinder's suggestion. © Wilfried Beege

flats on stage, together with authentic war slogans) and engaged with the 'real world' in two ways, one of which would prove an almost fatal turning point for the *action-theater*. First, the ensemble rehearsed a battle scene with physical actions taken from the Bundeswehr's guidelines on hand-to-hand combat.[32] Second, Raben

32 Ibid.

wanted to involve 'real' people, not just actors, and recruited three local hippies to take part.

A seven-page fragment of the text shows that Raben used four actresses to play Antigone.[33] In addition, choral speeches were cut up among different groups of speakers for emphasis. Raben, as stated above, used lines of prose from Brecht's description of the myth as epic narration, a switch from drama to narrative as a means of throwing the action into relief and promoting reflection. Raben had studied theatre and music in Munich and was the most articulate and theoretically informed member of the theatre. In an interview given before the première, he told Karin Thimm that 'we are not showing the individual but the idea: resistance against arbitrary violence'.[34] Raben had thus attacked one of the mainstays of bourgeois theatre, the centrality of the individual. He preferred to shift the focus to broader issues to which individuals are forced to defer, in this case, war and state violence. The Vietnam war was an obvious point of reference.

The press gave the production a mixed reception. The link with the Living Theatre was more than apparent, and the wildness and energy, although praiseworthy, required further work. Georg Ramseger complained about the over-repetition of the ritualized choral sections and found that the battle sequences occasionally bordered on the comical.[35] Alf Brustellin concurred with Raben that the plot was secondary: 'it was about concrete agitation, shock, emotion. They played an hour of terror, hysteria, the duping of the masses, fanaticism, violence.' But all the same, 'precision was lacking'.[36] The experiment was bold but far from finished. The collective was still

---

[33] Copy in the Rainer Werner Fassbinder Foundation (RWFF), Berlin.

[34] kth, 'Brot und Wein', *Abendzeitung*, 18 August 1967. Hanna Schygulla, who joined the production far later in the run as one of the Antigones, told me: 'it wasn't about defining what you wanted to express but was rather a case of acting within a situation'.

[35] Georg Ramseger, 'Antigone im Mini-Rock', *Münchner Merkur*, 22 August 1967.

[36] Alf Brustellin, 'Kriegstänze um Sophokles', *Süddeutsche Zeitung*, 22 August 1967.

confident enough to take the production on the road, even if it was to the provincial Bavarian town of Straubing. Kurt Raab, who had come to the *action-theater* through Raben and was to become one of Fassbinder's central film actors in the mid-1970s, had used his contacts in the town. But rather than fulfilling the aspiration of playing at Straubing's *Stadttheater*, the actors played in the *Kronensaal* over the weekend of 30 September to 1 October. Not surprisingly, the unsophisticated audience did not know quite what to make of the production.[37]

Enter, stage leftish: Fassbinder joins the *action-theater*

It was at this time that Fassbinder first encountered the *action-theater*.[38] Fassbinder had trained as an actor at first with *Intendant* Max Krauss, then at the Fridl-Leonhard acting school between 1964 and 1966. He had also made two short films, *Der Stadtstreicher* (*The Vagrant*) and *Das kleine Chaos* (*A Little Chaos*),[39] had small roles as an extra at the Münchner Kammerspiele and had written two plays, *Tropfen auf heisse Steine* (*Water Drops on Burning Rocks*) and *Nur eine Scheibe Brot* (*Just a Slice of Bread*).[40] The latter, a surprisingly

---

[37] Cf. Hubert Ettl, *Kurt Raab. Hommage aus der Provinz* (Vietach: edition lichting, n.d.), pp. 49–50.

[38] This is certainly Fassbinder's contention and the accepted version. Ursula Strätz contradicts this version of events, claiming that he came to the *action-kino* (which is not unlikely, although one doubts whether he made his presence known) and attended the rehearsals of *Publikumsbeschimpfung* (which is undocumented and questionable), in Juliane Lorenz (ed.), *Das ganz normale Chaos. Gespräche über Rainer Werner Fassbinder* (Berlin: Henschel, 1995), pp. 51 and 54. Strätz is, however, a rather unreliable witness. Her version of her 'relationship' with Fassbinder (as retold most recently in Praunheim's sensationalist film *The Grinning Victims of Rainer Werner Fassbinder*) is generally held to be a figment of her imagination. There is no evidence of the claims she makes about her intimacy with him or the belief that they had met on more personal terms before *Antigone*.

[39] Both have been restored and are available on bonus discs accompanying various DVD editions of Fassbinder's films.

[40] Both were unpublished and unperformed in Fassbinder's lifetime. They were, however, discovered in his papers after his death, and their

mature play for a twenty-one-year-old, deals with the insuperable problems encountered by a director trying to make a film about Auschwitz and came third in a local drama competition.

According to his mother, Liselotte Eder, Fassbinder wanted to attend evening classes to acquire the qualification (the *Abitur*) required for university entry. He wanted to study Theatre to become a director, but she suggested he attend acting school instead.[41] Fassbinder was not overly stimulated there but met Hanna Schygulla, whom he would turn into an international film star, and Marite Greiselis, who appeared in *Das kleine Chaos*. Greiselis joined the *action-theater* and was one of the Antigones in Raben's production. She had invited Fassbinder to one of the performances, and he was transfixed. In an article for a book on Schygulla, Fassbinder wrote: 'there was something like a trance between the actors and the audience, something like a collective desire for a revolutionary utopia'.[42] In 1973, he admitted that he had not understood the political level of the production but was totally taken with its intensity, its disturbing 'uncertainty'.[43] Fassbinder was also attracted by the location of the theatre. It was not in the trendy, arty district of

premières will be discussed in chapter 5. *Water Drops* was successfully filmed by François Ozon in 2000.

[41] In Hans Günther Pflaum's documentary film, *Ich will nicht nur, dass Ihr mich liebt*, 1992.

[42] Rainer Werner Fassbinder, 'Hanna Schygulla – kein Star, nur ein schwacher Mensch wie wir alle. (Unordentliche Gedanken über eine Frau, die interessiert)', in Hanna Schygulla, *Bilder aus Filmen von Rainer Werner Fassbinder. Mit einem autobiographischen Text von Hanna Schygulla und einem Beitrag von Rainer Werner Fassbinder* (Munich: Schirmer/Mosel, 1981), pp. 169–87, here p. 175.

[43] Corinna Brocher, 'Gruppen sind ja vieles. Gespräche mit Rainer Werner Fassbinder über die Geschichte des antiteaters', unpublished manuscript, 1973, p. 3. The interviews, conducted over five nights during a journey from Paris to Almeria, are the most important documents concerning Fassbinder's relationship to the *action-theater* and the *antiteater*. The lengthy protocol, itself a fragment at over 130 pages, was compiled for an aborted book on the *antiteater*. According to Brocher, it was Fassbinder who wanted to work through the circumstances of a failed collective through dialogues, not her (email to

Schwabing, but in the city centre.[44] There was a sense that the *action-ensemble* was genuinely trying to strike out, quite literally, into new territory.

Fassbinder returned to see the production several more times and was asked to stand in for one of the actors, Anatol von Gardner, who played the Messenger, who had accidentally injured himself. Fassbinder famously fluffed his lines in his first public performance but used the opportunity to establish himself as a full member of the group, despite opposition from others who took issue with the outsider. Fassbinder's influence grew after an incident involving one of the hippies Raben had engaged: Heiner Schoof stabbed his girlfriend, Marite Greiselis, allegedly in a fit of jealousy. Schoof was arrested and sentenced to ten years; Greiselis survived the attack but remained wheelchair-bound for the rest of her life. Away from the shock of the incident and the hysterical coverage in the local and national press,[45] the company needed a replacement for the stricken actress, and Fassbinder turned to Hanna Schygulla. Again there was resistance from the group, which not only felt that another outsider was being brought in, but that the initiator was the man of whom the group was already suspicious. The attack also signalled that the *action-theater* had to grow up and take itself more seriously. Fassbinder was convinced that the group had to get rid of the hippies and the hangers-on to recruit actors who could fulfil the potential of the *action-theater*, something with which Strätz and Raben agreed (cf. Brocher, p. 14).

Raben had become a figure of importance, the house director, through *Antigone*, and Fassbinder was yet to establish himself.

the author from Corinna Brocher 17 October 2001). The interviews appear in a highly reduced form in Fassbinder, *Anarchie der Phantasie*, as 'Da habe ich das Regieführen gelernt', pp. 15–29. Further reference to the interview appears as 'Brocher' in the text.

[44] Fassbinder, 'Hanna Schygulla', ibid.

[45] The conservative press took advantage of the attack to lambast the oppositional group. Karsunke criticized the tabloid-style reporting that even made it into the quality broadsheet, the *Süddeutsche Zeitung*, on his spot on the radio (undated typescript, supplied by Karsunke).

Drawing on his musical interests and training, Raben started rehearsing Karl Orff's musical theatre piece written in Bavarian dialect, *Astutuli* (1947–8). Rehearsals were soon abandoned when the technical requirements threatened to overwhelm the still quite inexperienced troupe, and Fassbinder openly signalled that he had lost interest in the project. Strätz proposed *Leonce und Lena* by Büchner, and the novel idea of collective direction was mooted. The two principal actors, Fassbinder and Raben, were to direct the two principal actresses, Strätz and Kristin Petersen,[46] and vice versa. Although this attribution still stood on the playbill, Fassbinder's was actually the defining voice. The classic text, a comedy written between 1836 and 1837, was presented amid a sea of flowers. Leonce, the bored prince of Popo ('Bum-Bum'), is the son of King Peter, who wants his son to marry Lena, princess of Pipi ('Wee-Wee'). Both escape their parents, bump into each other on the run, fall in love and marry, unaware that they are fulfilling their parents' wishes. Leonce accedes to the throne but the ending is rather bitter-sweet.

Raben believed the theme of a 'life without work' fitted the hippie times well. Contemporary politics were also a feature of the production in the shape of pictures of the Shah of Persia, whose visit to West Germany that summer had been accompanied by the death of student Benno Ohnesorg. The device lent an uncomfortable actuality to the scene in which the masses are told how to behave at the royal wedding (see fig. 4). But along with the political satire, the *action-theater* was starting to understand the cut-up aesthetics of American pop culture. As well as quoting the Shah, the ensemble allowed the Beatles to make an appearance in the form of the song 'When I'm Sixty-Four', an ironic comment on the commitment of the young couple to each other. The production itself was quite literally a quotation, as Fassbinder began the evening by reading from his Reclam edition of the text. An announcement made just before the première on 3 October 1967 added another pop touch in that tomatoes would be distributed

[46] *Action-theater* flyers and programmes give the spelling as both 'Peterson' and 'Petersen'.

Fig. 4. *Leonce und Lena* at the *action-theater*: Fassbinder as Valerio marries the prince and princess and showers them with flowers. The set features all the actors' names. Onlookers include Rudolf Waldemar Brem (leaning above the name 'Fassbinder') and *action-theater* founder Ursula Strätz (to Brem's right) in a hat. © Wilfried Beege

before the performance to be either consumed or thrown depending on the spectator's inclination.[47] The programme shows a disordered list of the many impetuses and associations the group had brought to the text. Political terms and figures ('spent nihilism', Heinrich Lübke – the Federal President, who, like Kiesinger, was a former

[47] Anon, 'Tomaten für die Zuschauer', *Abendzeitung*, 30 September 1967.

member of the Nazi Party – and 'materialism') rub shoulders with cultural references ('Godard', 'The Rolling Stones' and 'Vivaldi') and a variety of other concepts ('structuralism', 'tristesse', 'boredom' and 'taxes'). The final word in the list, 'action', was written in capitals.[48]

The production was another partial victory. With the exception of K. H. Kramberg, who wrote, 'all the children of the world have to have read *Leonce and Lena* by Georg Büchner. But they shouldn't do it in public. The play is too good' (this was his complete review),[49] the local critics were fairly positive. Effi Horn found pertinent links between the play and the present, observed that the production went down well with the audience, but feared the latter was only being offered what it wanted to see anyway.[50] Karin Thimm also found that the production had captured the *Zeitgeist* when she considered the cast as 'figures of longing . . . who only want to perceive scraps of the real world'.[51] There was, however, a sense that the production was still not going far enough. Thimm noted that the text was being respected far more than in *Antigone* and Karsunke felt that the weaker sections showed too much reverence towards Büchner.[52] Fassbinder had not yet gained the confidence to adulterate his source texts in public but would approach the business of adaptation with guns blazing after the next production, *Hands Up, Heiliger Johannes* (*Hands Up, John the Baptist*).[53] He was, however, developing an understanding of

[48] *Programme of Georg Büchner's Leonce und Lena, action-theater,* première 3 October 1967, n.p.

[49] K. H. Kramberg, 'Büchner im Action-Theater', *Süddeutsche Zeitung,* 9 October 1967.

[50] Effi Horn, 'Büchner-Happening mit Bauchtanz', *Münchner Merkur,* 5 October 1967.

[51] kth, 'Hippie à la Büchner', *Abendzeitung,* 6 October 1967.

[52] Yaak Karsunke, 'Leonce und Lena', *Kulturspiegel,* Bayerischer Rundfunk, no transmission date supplied. Rudolf Waldemar Brem, who had got involved with the theatre through his school newspaper and appeared in *Leonce* in a minor role, confirmed to me that the text was hardly altered, with the exception of some deletions and some contemporizations.

[53] The name of the English original has been lost over time. Peer Raben assured me it was quite different.

distancing techniques in his direction. In his gossipy book on Fass-binder (to call it a biography would be a gross overstatement), Kurt Raab tells how the director instructed him to play King Peter: not as a real king, but as a petit-bourgeois parvenu would imagine a king to be.[54] The implicit directorial critique of an inevitable iden-tity signals a practical beginning of Fassbinder's interest in role and role-play.

After the trip to Straubing in October 1967 with *Antigone*, the *action-theater* looked further afield and travelled to Paris with *Leonce und Lena*, subsidized by a state grant of 4,000 DM secured by the troupe's 'treasurer', Ursula Strätz. The tour, which ran from 11 to 25 November, was a disaster. The money mysteriously disappeared and the theatre in Paris was not ready for them. There was no pub-licity and very small audiences. Friction had also entered into the theatre's dynamic when Söhnlein and a couple of others destroyed some of the theatre's seating just before the departure for France. Fassbinder believed Söhnlein felt that his theatre was being taken over by Fassbinder and his supporters (cf. Brocher, p. 31). Brem, on the other hand, noted that there was a lot of alcohol being con-sumed at the time and that damage of this sort could have had a different cause. Either way, Söhnlein and Fassbinder factions were forming, and the tensions that ensued would dog the rest of the *action-theater*'s short life. Söhnlein also had a more overtly political agenda and was not content with the more subtle political critiques currently being produced by the theatre (cf. Brocher, p. 36). One can only assume that the 'script for a short film' called *Theaterarbeit*[55] (*Work in the Theatre*) and dedicated to Söhnlein was written after *Antigone* but before the trip to Paris. The script ends with a short performance of *Jakob* in masks. 'Ursula' says that to have success in the theatre is quite acceptable, the Söhnlein figure 'Henning Rühle' (an amalgam of two leading theatre critics of the time, the *Theater heute* editor

[54] Raab and Peters, *Sehnsucht*, p. 39.
[55] *Theaterarbeit* quotes the central volume that documents and comments upon Brecht's work at the Berliner Ensemble. The typed and handwritten fragments of Fassbinder's text are to be found in the archive of the Kinemathek, Berlin. One page of the script is missing.

Henning Rischbieter and the *Frankfurter Allgemeine Zeitung's*
Günther Rühle) retorts that 'action should not be applauded'. The
short piece is an exploration of the interrelation of theatre and life,
and quotes Brecht, *Hamlet* and the *action-theater* itself.

The development into a more Fassbinder-dominated theatre
was marked by a small production that only featured members sym-
pathetic to Fassbinder. Premièred on 10 December 1967, *Hands Up,
Heiliger Johannes* was hardly a nativity play. It has only appeared in
one account of the *action-theater's* history.[56] The play was directed
by Fassbinder ally Raben, and featured Fassbinder as John the Baptist,
Kurt Raab as King Herod and Elke Koska as Salome (see fig. 5). The
play was written by Bob Burleson and had first played in San Francisco,
where it had caused a riot and brought about its author's flight from
the city. The flyer was clearly trying to capitalize on the play's scan-
dalous reputation by quoting reviewer Karsunke's contextual information presented on the radio.[57] The text, of which only a fragment
remains in the Rainer Werner Fassbinder Foundation archive, shows a
heavily eroticized treatment of the Salome story, in which Herod com-
mands John to display his sensuality and to stab himself in the eyes.
He does both and, as a consequence, loses his faith and has delusions
of grandeur. The text is not a cheap satire, rather an exploration of
religious ideals and sexuality. It is undoubtedly a play of its time, and
it does creak in places. Raben saw it as a 'provocation' and eschewed
the more physical style of *Antigone* in favour of a concentration on
the text itself. Karsunke, in what appears to be the only review, was
pleased with its challenge, even though he accepted the limitations of
the text.[58]

---

[56] Cf. the brief, inaccurate mention in Peter Berling, *Die 13 Jahre des
Rainer Werner Fassbinder*, revised paperback edition (Bergisch
Gladbach: Gustav Lübbe, 1995), pp. 54–5.

[57] *Flyer for Bob Burleson's Hands Up, Heiliger Johannes*, action-theater,
première 10 December 1967. The rare document is to be found in the
Flugblätter der Universität München, Handschriftenabteilung of the
University Library, Munich.

[58] Yaak Karsunke, '*Hands Up, Heiliger Johannes*', *Kulturspiegel*,
Bayerischer Rundfunk, no transmission date supplied.

Fig. 5. Hardly a nativity play: the *action-theater* produces *Hands Up, Heiliger Johannes* (*Hands Up, John the Baptist*) for Christmas 1967. Fassbinder played John the Baptist in *Lederhosen* and Kurt Raab's Herod wore summer-wear as suited the sandy stage floor. The actors were divided from the audience by means of a thin lattice, suggesting a prison. © Wilfried Beege

Developing an aesthetic: Fassbinder adapts and directs
Die Verbrecher and *Zum Beispiel Ingolstadt*

Hot on the heels of *Hands Up* came the production of a play already mentioned back at the launch of the *action-theater*, Ferdinand Bruckner's *Die Verbrecher* (*The Criminals*). Written back in 1928, it was premièred at the *action-theater* on 19 December 1967. After that,

Fassbinder, Raben and actors loyal to them temporarily left the *action-theater*, when Horst Söhnlein cancelled the first late-night production, Fassbinder's *Der amerikanische Soldat* (*The American Soldier*). It was due to be shown at 10.30 p.m. on 21 January 1968 and invitations had already been sent out.[59] Fassbinder and Raben searched for a suitable venue and approached Helmut Berninger, the head of the Büchner Theater. As we have seen, the theatre had a very different agenda and approach to that of the *action-theater*, but the duo managed to convince the owner to give up his venue.[60] They staged their version of Marieluise Fleisser's *Pioniere in Ingolstadt* (*Military Engineers in Ingolstadt*) of 1928[61] as *Zum Beispiel Ingolstadt* (*Ingolstadt, For Example*) on 18 February 1968 and used a couple of members of the Büchner Theater's own ensemble. One of the actors was a dramatist who would set the West German theatre alight with his

[59] Invitation for Liselotte Eder to *Der amerikanische Soldat*, undated, signed by Irm Hermann, held in the RWFF archive. Hermann was another of Fassbinder's discoveries and was brought in as an actress to the *action-theater* in November 1967. She performed for the first time in *Die Verbrecher*. Now an established actress in her own right, she was then an untrained secretary whom Fassbinder had happened upon.

[60] Money certainly played a role here. Fassbinder said that his group only received 25 per cent of the takings, something which led actors Kurt Raab and Elke Koska to leave before the fifth performance (cf. Brocher, p. 39).

[61] The play was revised twice subsequently. A production that Brecht had 'spiced up' in 1929 had to be rewritten immediately at the insistence of the police. Fleisser then returned to the text in 1968. The play, originally written in the same year as *Die Verbrecher*, is also based on a montage principle. Fleisser tells that she was encouraged to write it by Brecht, who said, 'the play doesn't have to have a proper plot, it must be assembled, like certain cars you see driving round Paris, cars that are their own model but made up of parts, which the manufacturer was able to obtain by chance, but you can still drive it!' (quoted in Marieluise Fleisser, *Gesammelte Werke. Erster Band. Dramen*, ed. Günther Rühle (Frankfurt/Main: Suhrkamp, 1994), p. 442.

dialect plays in the early 1970s, Franz Xaver Kroetz.[62] The two productions, *Die Verbrecher* and *Zum Beispiel*, exhibit common features in their direction and allow us to understand a crucial, formative period in Fassbinder's career as a director.

Neither the text of Fassbinder's adaptation of *Die Verbrecher* nor the programme, which may have shed some light on the production, is extant. Neither archives nor actors' personal collections have yielded either document. We do know, however, that the text was an adaptation rather than a 'version'.[63] The evidence is clear from two reviews of the production. Effi Horn wrote, 'it [the *action-theater*] swallowed Bruckner whole, spat out connections between the scenes, the fates of the individuals, the characters as useless – and turned the rest into the customary action-pudding (with some raisins)'.[64] Joachim von Mengershausen concurred that Fassbinder 'divested the heroes of their individuality and thus of their heroic poses by depriving them of all their illusionistic trappings and a welter of "nice" speeches'.[65] He concluded that the ideas behind the production were better than their execution but was still able to applaud the attempt at a different theatre.

Evidence of Fassbinder's willingness to change his sources radically is to be found early on, in his application for the first film school in the Federal Republic, which opened in West Berlin in 1966. Fassbinder was called to examination in May 1966 at the age of

[62] At the time, Kroetz was an ardent formalist, who eschewed the Bavarian dialect of Fleisser. It is thus possible that Fassbinder was one of the catalysts of Kroetz's fame. However, Kroetz and Fassbinder were involved in a bitter argument around the film *Wildwechsel* (*Wild Game*) in 1973. Kroetz accused Fassbinder of turning his play into pornography, a peculiar charge from an author whose work of the time included scenes of nudity and masturbation on stage.

[63] An invitation to the première clearly states '*The Criminals* after [i.e. not 'by'] Ferdinand Bruckner' and Fassbinder said that he added scenes to both *Die Verbrecher* and *Zum Beispiel Ingolstadt* (cf. Brocher, p. 42).

[64] Effi Horn, 'Verhör mit Walzerbegleitung', *Münchner Merkur*, 20 December 1967.

[65] JvM, 'Kriminelle Reflexionen', *Süddeutsche Zeitung*, 21 December 1967.

twenty-one. One of the exercises was to write a treatment for a film based on a short story, 'Der Kleine-Mädchen Fresser' ('The Man Who Ate Little Girls'). What is remarkable about Fassbinder's treatment is that it shifts the focus to a minor female character and completely forgoes the story's climax.[66] Fassbinder's method of adapting *Die Verbrecher* was similarly bold and sought to augment Bruckner's filmic dramaturgy of montage[67] by undermining the individuality of the characters. How this was achieved and what effects were being sought is revealed by an analysis of *Zum Beispiel Ingolstadt*, which took a comparable approach.

Fassbinder modified the text in a variety of ways. Possibly the most central was his decision to do away with the crowd scenes in favour of smaller dialogues. On the one hand, one can understand this as the need to accommodate his cast within the small space of the Büchner Theater. On the other, the paring-down of the scenes into two- and three-person configurations introduces a dramaturgical feature that would stay with Fassbinder for almost all his career in the theatre. Fassbinder enacts the demolition of the sovereign individual, together with its psychology, in favour of social role and the change of persona as defined by its context. The emphasis on relationships, witnessed earlier in Raben's direction of *Antigone*, has been taken up and radicalized in the joint direction of Fassbinder and Raben.[68] With the larger scenes reduced to a series of smaller interactions, Fassbinder was keen to use the space between the actors and their bodies as a means of conveying the terms of the particular relationships

---

[66] Cf. Hans Helmut Prinzler, 'The Application', in Kardish (ed.), *Rainer Werner Fassbinder*, pp. 77–84, here p. 82.

[67] The set, as envisaged by Bruckner, is a large structure with three levels. The action cuts between the various locations. Acts 1 and 3 take place in seven rooms of a large house, Act 2 in six chambers of a court.

[68] All the actors and performers I have spoken with (including Raben himself) confirm that Fassbinder was always the 'director' when both names were credited. He was the one who dealt with the actors and had a concrete idea of how the production should look. Raben, the more theoretically informed partner, played more the role of 'adviser', and offered Fassbinder his critical views.

Fig. 6. Attitudes, not characterizations: Kurt Raab, Irm Hermann and Lilith Ungerer (towards the back) strike poses for *Zum Beispiel Ingolstadt* (*Ingolstadt, For Example*) at the Büchner Theater. © Wilfried Beege

(see fig. 6). He choreographed the production and demanded an almost neutral delivery of lines that made the idea of naturalistic characterization redundant. The approach is dialectical and refuses to treat the individual as anything but an ensemble of its social relations. Such a consistently executed dramaturgical and directorial strategy contradicts the more widespread understanding of Fassbinder's decisions in the *action-theater* and *antiteater* as 'making a virtue of a necessity'.[69]

[69] Töteberg, 'Das Theater der Grausamkeit', p. 20.

Annette Sabelus offers a comprehensive and illuminating survey of Fassbinder's incursions into Fleisser's source text. She describes how he added five scenes, all of which include the minor character of Freda, promoting her to one of the female leads.[70] Freda becomes part of a trio of young women and contrasts with the others as naive and exploited. Fassbinder also cut certain scenes and modernized some of the elements. A song mentioned in the opening scene is brought up to date as a marching song a contemporary audience would recognize, for example. Sabelus also notes the movement from longer scenes into short encounters: 'it is Fassbinder's practice heartily to dismantle that which he finds, put it together afresh, and thus radically to confront it with his own political and social reality and its questions'.[71]

Fassbinder thus engaged in a process that dovetailed the businesses of adaptation and direction in order to generate concrete theatrical effects. He took apart Fleisser's (and Bruckner's) dramaturgy in order to present a sustained series of permutations, ever-changing configurations of characters on stage. His 'choreographical' direction was concerned with the supra-individual analysis of social interaction. The almost neutral tone of delivery further served to highlight the communication itself. Raben said, with reference to *Die Verbrecher*, that, 'at first Fassbinder had tried to construct the dialogues purely on the level of linguistic tension'. The centrality of language in Fassbinder's theatre, a subject to which I will continue to return, is the final strand of his nascent directorial aesthetics. In a rare theoretical explication, an anonymous note in the programme tells,

> through associative means, the production departs from the
> historical, philological and dramaturgical postulates [of
> Fleisser's original] in favour of the demonstration of complex
> processes: . . . the thought, not in concepts but images, the

[70] Annette Sabelus, *'Mir persönlich brachten sie allerhand Verdruss . . .'.*
Die Bearbeitung von Marieluise Fleissers 'Pioniere in Ingolstadt' durch
Rainer Werner Fassbinder (unpublished MA thesis: University of
Hamburg, 1996), pp. 29–34.
[71] Ibid., p. 12.

speech, not as a formal occurrence but as the mechanism of repeating models of expression which have now become commonplace.[72]

The note signals the importance of the concept of 'demonstration'. The audience is not being offered an insight into the private lives of the characters. Rather it is presented with an exemplary study, indicated by the adaptation's title, of deindividuated characters for the purpose of defamiliarizing the subject and presenting it in a new light.

A further directorial decision, which would colour future productions as well, was to have the full cast on stage all the time. This probably had a great deal to do with the small spaces in which the ensemble played, but had the effect of being both anti-illusionistic and metatheatrical. The latter dimension implies that the figures are involved in the drama of their own lives, not in a 'real' or inevitable series of dialogues driven by themselves. The deference to a text suggests that the cast is not the master of its destiny but subject to rules and behaviour whose authorship lies elsewhere.

The new perspective was lauded neither by the local press nor by Fleisser herself.[73] One reviewer damned the production with faint praise before dismissing it as 'superfluous', while another criticized the acting as boring and monotone, while nonetheless acknowledging that the audience seemed to enjoy it.[74] Karsunke, in a letter to Raben and Fassbinder, suggested that the aesthetic may have presumed a rather higher level of political consciousness in the audience than was in fact the case.[75] All the same, he approved of both the dialectical 'attitudes' of the characters and the effects of these on the delivery of the language.

[72] Programme of Zum Beispiel Ingolstadt nach Motiven von Marieluise Fleisser, Büchner Theater, première 18 February 1986.

[73] Irm Hermann accounted for the poor reaction by viewing the rehearsal process as 'the search for a form, but the form was greater than the text'.

[74] HL, 'Fleisser-Montage im Büchner Theater', Abendzeitung, 20 February 1968; and Beate Kayser, 'Langweiligkeit als Stilprinzip', Donau-Kurier, 20 February 1968, respectively.

[75] Unpublished letter from Yaak Karsunke to Peer Raben and Rainer Werner Fassbinder, 21 February 1968, Yaak Karsunke's private archive.

Fleisser had problems of her own with the production. She had read an announcement about the production in her local paper, the *Donau-Kurier*, and was scandalized that no one had asked her for the rights. The ensemble thought that they had evaded the issue by changing the title of the production, but this did not reassure the dramatist. Raben went to see Fleisser at home in Ingolstadt, but she remained implacable. When she read the *Donau-Kurier* on 13 February she discovered that the company was still going ahead with the production and initiated legal action against it, supported by the newspaper. A new deputation visited Fleisser, which, according to the source, consisted either of Fassbinder and the Berningers, Fassbinder and Raben, or Fassbinder, Strätz and Söhnlein (the least likely of the three permutations).[76] Whatever the composition of the group, Fleisser was persuaded to attend the dress rehearsal, something she undertook with her friend Therese Giehse, one of the most important German actresses of the twentieth century. The dramatist demurred, called off the litigation, and declared, 'I believe . . . that the scenic montage I saw is a valid route ['ein gangbarer Weg'] for staging this early work in a small theatre.'[77] But her qualified acceptance was not her final word on the matter. In a letter to her publishers, Suhrkamp, who had acquired the performance rights from the Desch Verlag, Fleisser wrote that the production 'left a lot to be desired'.[78] One of her criticisms, made some time after Fassbinder filmed the play as *Pioniere in Ingolstadt* in 1970, was Fassbinder's translation of the Bavarian of the original into 'Hochdeutsch', or standard German. This she considered 'banal', because to her mind Bavarian was not a dialect but a 'set of

---

[76] Cf. letter from Marieluise Fleisser to Franz Xaver Kroetz, 7 September 1973, in Marieluise Fleisser, *Briefwechsel 1925–1974*, ed. Günther Rühle (Frankfurt/Main: Suhrkamp, 2001), pp. 587–8, here p. 587; Günther Rühle in Marieluise Fleisser, *Materialien zum Leben und Schreiben der Marieluise Fleisser*, ed. Rühle (Frankfurt/Main: Suhrkamp, 1973), p. 677; and Sabelus, p. 16.

[77] Fleisser quoted in Beate Kayser, 'Langweiligkeit als Stilprinzip', *Donau-Kurier*, 20 February 1968.

[78] Unpublished letter from Marieluise Fleisser to Ursula Bothe, 31 December 1969, quoted in Sabelus, '*Mir persönlich*', p. 16.

south German verbal attitudes [Sprachstellung]'.[79] Yet she had found
certain aspects of Fassbinder's adaptation interesting. Suhrkamp had
demanded that the company send Fleisser a copy of their text by
16 February 1968. Fleisser must have read it while working on her
own new version of *Pioniere* as, for example, the marching song that
Fassbinder included is to be found in Fleisser's revised version.[80]
Fassbinder's attempts to present language as unnatural had not had
the desired effect on Fleisser. He would, however, continue with linguistic experimentation with his first major play to be performed in
public.

Refining the model: Fassbinder writes and directs *Katzelmacher*

The French avant-garde film-maker Jean-Marie Straub had been living in Munich and was something of a hero to young cineastes at the
time. He had seen and enjoyed the rehearsals of the *action-theater*'s
Die Verbrecher and decided to adapt the same author and to direct
the results at the same venue. Söhnlein now had to make an important decision: Straub, a big draw for the theatre, wanted to work with
Raben, Schygulla, Hermann and Brem, that is, the faction loyal to
Fassbinder, as well as with the director himself. Söhnlein took the
path that was best for the theatre and accepted Straub's offer. The
problem was that Straub's version of *Krankheit der Jugend* (*Diseased
Youth*) reduced an eighty-five-page, three-act play to a mere ten minutes of performance. Fassbinder offered to write a second drama for
the evening, and because of the power of his faction, he was able to
force it through. That said, Söhnlein provided *Katzelmacher*[81] with

---

[79] Letter to Klaus-Peter Wieland, 14 December 1973, in Fleisser,
Briefwechsel, pp. 597–600, here p. 599.
[80] Cf. Marieluise Fleisser, *Pioniere in Ingolstadt*, 1968 version, in Fleisser,
Dramen, pp. 127–85, here p. 129, as compared with Fleisser, *Pioniere in
Ingolstadt*, 1929 version, in ibid., pp. 187–222, here p. 189.
[81] The title, which I am leaving untranslated, is colloquial German for a
foreigner. Various theories as to its origin have been posited, but all
share the common characteristic of sexual potency.

actresses Ingrid Caven and Doris Mattes, who, at the time, were more inclined towards his views, to keep him informed.

Fassbinder now had a cast and started writing for them while rehearsing with Straub. That Fassbinder wrote *Katzelmacher* with his cast and their abilities in mind became a significant feature in his writing and directing practice. As we shall see in chapter 2, part of Fassbinder's directorial approach was to use casting as a means of avoiding psychological direction. He cast certain actors because he knew they had 'the right qualities' for the roles and consequently would not require discussions on 'motivation' and other factors Fassbinder considered superfluous. With the strengths and weaknesses of his actors in mind, he constructed his text. In addition, Fassbinder was careful to follow a dramaturgy which would reflect the collective nature of the *action-theater* (cf. Brocher, p. 43). As a result, the nine roles are of roughly equal length, eliminating principal characters and perpetuating the anti-individualistic ideology of the theatre collective. Another sign of Fassbinder's sentiments at the time was to be found on the cover of the playtext, which could be bought at the performances: 'there are no rights to this play. It is free for anyone.'[82]

Fassbinder claimed that directing *Die Verbrecher*, adapting *Pioniere* and observing Straub's work on *Krankheit* were the major influences on *Katzelmacher* (cf. Brocher, ibid.). To Fassbinder, Straub rehearsed with great precision, used a great deal of time and offered little discussion of his rationales (cf. Brocher, p. 41). The product of the work can be seen in Straub's short film of 1968, *Der Bräutigam, die Komödiantin und der Zuhälter (The Bridegroom, the Actress and the Pimp)*. The twenty-three-minute-long work includes about ten-and-a-half minutes of *Krankheit*, presumably the full or nearly full extent of his work there. The sequence is shot in the *action-theater* and comprises solely authentic dialogue from Bruckner. The reduction is so drastic that all one is left with is associative fragments, indices of relationships and action.[83]

---

[82] *Programme for Rainer Werner Fassbinder's 'Katzelmacher'*, *action-theater*, première 7 April 1968, inside front cover.

[83] The full text and some photographs of the film are reprinted in *Filmkritik*, 12 (1968), no. 10, pp. 681–7.

Katzelmacher plays a similar game but offers more in terms of context. The play follows a group of eight young people and the way in which they deal with a new *Gastarbeiter* ('guest worker'), the Greek Jorgos. *Gastarbeiter* were brought into West Germany in great numbers in the 1960s as a response to a shortage of manual labourers. By 1972 there were 3.5 million resident foreigners, or roughly 5 per cent of the population.[84] Fassbinder was the first dramatist to approach the topic and he did so in a style which was typically ambivalent: the statuses of perpetrator and victim, which are central roles in the play, do not yield to negative and positive values, respectively. In Fassbinder's eyes, all the characters are agents and victims of language.

Two versions of the drama *Katzelmacher* exist: one appeared in a numbered programme for 2 DM and one was published by Suhrkamp in 1970 (in addition to the rewritten and augmented script for the film of 1969).[85] There are few differences between the two. The first version is written in a more dialectal German with frequent elision and abbreviation. There are also slight discrepancies in a scene in which money is being discussed, but these may have been Fassbinder's attempts to keep up with inflation, as all the figures are higher in the 1970 version. One short scene is completely missing from that later version too, and it comes shortly before the end. In it, Franz, who was involved in a violent attack on Jorgos, seeks a reconciliation. He actively tries to persuade Jorgos to stay in Germany with a variety of arguments but Jorgos remains unconvinced. The removal of the scene could have been an accident, it could have been deliberate. Maybe it was too positive a portrayal of Franz, maybe Jorgos's decision to leave

---

[84] Source: Rob Burns and Wilfried van der Will, 'The Federal Republic 1968–1990: From the Industrial Society to the Culture Society', in Rob Burns (ed.), *German Cultural Studies. An Introduction* (Oxford: Oxford University Press, 1995), pp. 257–323, here p. 301.

[85] The programme may be consulted at the RWFF archive. The first printed version is Rainer Werner Fassbinder, *Katzelmacher*, in Fassbinder, *Antiteater* (Frankfurt/Main: Suhrkamp, 1970), pp. 7–30. The film script is to be found as *Katzelmacher* in Fassbinder, *Die Kinofilme*, vol. 1, ed. Michael Töteberg (Munich: Schirmer/Mosel, 1987), pp. 131–223.

is too resolute, as, by the end of the play, there is a sense of uncertainty about what is to happen once the action on stage is over.

The published play is a series of forty-nine short scenes of which forty feature two or three characters. It sketches the relationships between eight young adults from a provincial village and Jorgos. There is little plot involved, save the planning and execution of an attack on the foreigner. The action is mainly small-scale, involving situations and details rather than sustained plots. As the film version amply demonstrates, *Katzelmacher* is more about atmosphere and social attitude than action. After an expository scene of roughly three pages, only six subsequent ones last for more than half a page. The form of the piece is thus highly filmic and fragmentary. It cuts swiftly between the dialogues and offers glimpses of the characters rather than any real sense of development. The star of the work, in the absence of central characters, is the language and the relationships it constructs and mediates.

The text is riddled with sententious remarks, proverbs and clichés. Carmel Finnan shows how a biblical register in Fleisser's *Fegefeuer in Ingolstadt (Purgatory in Ingolstadt)* is replaced by a more media-derived vernacular in *Katzelmacher*.[86] She goes on to identify ritual processes that undermine any sense of individuality in the play.[87] Even Jorgos, the victim of the attack and the xenophobia of the local youth, is not immune. His linguistic courtship of Marie is driven by cliché and he reveals himself to be just as bigoted as the others when he expresses antipathy towards the news that a Turkish *Gastarbeiter* is due to work in the same factory as him at the end of the play.

---

[86] Carmel Finnan, 'Volkstümlichkeit als Alltagsritual. Der Einfluss Marieluise Fleissers auf Rainer Werner Fassbinder am Beispiel von *Fegefeuer in Ingolstadt* und *Katzelmacher*', in Ursula Hassel and Herbert Herzmann (eds.), *Das zeitgenössische deutschsprachige Volksstück. Akten der internationalen Symposions. University College Dublin 28. Februar–2. März 1991* (Tübingen: Stauffenburg, 1992), pp. 131–7, here p. 132.

[87] Ibid., pp. 136–7.

A different debate surrounds the genre of the play. The association with Fleisser, to whom both the play and the film are dedicated, and certain features of the play (its use of colloquial forms, its setting in the provinces) have led to an inquiry as to whether the play is a *Volksstück*. *Katzelmacher* was indeed written around the time when interest in the genre was much aroused. Horváth was enjoying a revival,[88] and the 'Fleisser boom' was just around the corner. The dramatist Martin Sperr had written *Jagdszenen aus Niederbayern* (*Hunting Scenes from Lower Bavaria*) in 1966, and paved the way for a new generation of *Volksstücke*.[89] Early critics, like Wend Kässens and Michael Töteberg, were keen to file *Katzelmacher* under the *Volksstück* label.[90] They contend that the new *Volksstück* turns away from the formalistic, absurdist and poetic drama that preceded it. However, the formal terseness and focus on language over character calls the assertion into question. Torsten Bügner, in a study of the new *Volksstück*, can only view the genre as a 'collage particle' in *Katzelmacher*, not a determining aesthetic.[91] A more recent scholar tends towards an opposite extreme when he claims,

> in the theatrical hyper-naturalism without the naturalist aesthetic [of the new *Volksstück*], that which is lurking beneath the surface does not come to light through a

[88] Fassbinder had originally planned to stage some Horváth but found the casts too old and too large for the *action-theater*, cf. Fassbinder on Fleisser in the *Donau-Kurier*, 23 November 1971. Raben suggested *Volksstück*-writer Fleisser, to whom he had come through his interest in Brecht. The result was *Zum Beispiel Ingolstadt*.

[89] We learn early on but only once that Franz's surname is 'Sperr', a fleeting acknowledgement of the dramatist; Rainer Werner Fassbinder, *Katzelmacher*, in Fassbinder, *Sämtliche Stücke* (Frankfurt/Main: Verlag der Autoren, 1991), pp. 63–92, here p. 68. This is the standard edition of almost all the plays and will subsequently be referred to as '*Stücke*' in this study.

[90] Cf. Wend Kässens and Michael Töteberg, 'Fortschritt im Realismus? Zur Erneuerung des kritischen Volksstücks seit 1966', *Basis*, 6 (1976), pp. 30–47, here p. 30.

[91] Torsten Bügner, *Annäherung an die Wirklichkeit. Gattung und Autoren des neuen Volksstücks* (Frankfurt/Main et al.: Peter Lang, 1986), p. 114.

dramaturgy of disclosure, nor is it interpreted socially, on the contrary, it reveals itself in lyrical and imagistic ecstasies of the imagination.[92]

One may well take issue with Lehmann's extravagant conclusion, but he is right to expunge the play from a more conventional naturalist interpretation. The use of dialect and its syntactical manifestations in such a fragmented form has led one critic to surmise that the play is 'supra-regional' and more a 'theatre of demonstration' than an accurate picture of provincial Bavaria.[93] That Fassbinder is offering a model rather than a 'slice of life' reflects the more Brechtian approach to individuals noted in Fassbinder's earlier productions.

Yet before *Katzelmacher* had even been staged, Söhnlein's political dissatisfaction with the *action-theater* was to take a far more concrete form. He destroyed the theatre's equipment in Munich and travelled to Frankfurt as one of four young people who set light to the department stores Kaufhof and Schneider on 2 April 1968. Söhnlein's accomplices were Andreas Baader, Gudrun Ensslin and Thorwald Proll. The action effectively provided the germ of the Baader-Meinhof group. However, it would be May 1970, when Baader was sprung from prison by the recently radicalized Ulrike Meinhof and four others, that marked the unofficial founding of the Red Army Faction. An interesting detail of the personnel involved in the department store attacks is that Proll was also active in the theatre. In fact, he acted in Jack Gelber's *The Connection* (1961), a play about drugs brought to prominence by the Living Theatre in New York, staged at the Forum Theater in Berlin in the 1967/8 season.[94] The discontent with the theatre and its political effectiveness and the shift to direct action serve as a useful

[92] Hans-Thies Lehmann, *Postdramatisches Theater* (Frankfurt/Main: Verlag der Autoren, 1999), p. 212.

[93] Johannes G. Pankau, 'Figurationen des Bayerischen: Sperr, Fassbinder, Achtenbusch', in Helfried W. Seliger (ed.), *Der Begriff 'Heimat' in der deutschen Gegenwartsliteratur* (Munich: iudicium, 1987), pp. 133–47, here both quotations p. 137.

[94] Cf. Senate of Berlin (ed.), *25 Jahre Theater in Berlin. Theaterpremieren 1945–70* (Berlin: Heinz Spitzing, 1972), p. 354. The Forum Theater would host several *antiteater* productions between 1968 and 1969.

index for understanding the practical politics of the disaffected at the time. The means of the theatre would, however, re-emerge at the trial that was held in October 1968. Attempts to undermine the proceedings included Baader giving his date of birth as 1789, the year of the French Revolution, and the disregard for courtroom decorum when the defendants rolled cigarettes and offered each other sweets.[95] One journalist maintained that the stunts were 'obviously rehearsed'.[96] The theatrical mode employed by the defendants actually refers back to the trial of the 'Berlin Communards', to which I shall return in chapter 2.

Back in Munich, the theatre was made good quickly and the production was premièred shortly after the destruction, on 7 April 1968. The use of an empty stage with minimal set was taken from Fassbinder's earlier directing experience. A motto – 'Freedom is the reality consciousness is prepared to allow itself' – taken from Hegel and supplied by Raben, was the only comment on the flyer (but Gunter Krää believed that the slogan was also on the stage's backdrop). Krää was one of Brem's fellow schoolmates and started acting with the troupe for *Zum Beispiel Ingolstadt*. Fassbinder was working on the principle of slowness again, which worried Krää, but he was led to understand that this was a new and different approach to performance. Fassbinder asked his cast to deliver the texts as if they were standard German, something which further defamiliarized and drew attention to the language, presenting it as a construction rather than a commonplace. Jörg Schmitt, who also acted in *Katzelmacher*, said that the style 'was not artificial' but cool and understated. Fassbinder, together with 'adviser' Raben, was refining his ideas on clarity and precision. Schmitt also reported that the atmosphere in the theatre was almost ideal. There was a sense of really being a collective, and at this time Fassbinder was still not in charge. Instead, in Schmitt's words, he was 'very cautious . . . he was the one doing the asking, not yet giving the orders'.

[95] Cf. Anon., 'Prozess ohne die Angeklagten', *Süddeutsche Zeitung*, 15 October 1968.

[96] Walter Gutermuth, 'Sie wollten sogar Zigaretten rauchen', *Abendzeitung*, 15 October 1968.

Katzelmacher found more resonance in the press than *Zum Beispiel Ingolstadt*, but there was still resistance to the new form of performance. On the positive side, Annemarie Czaschke, one of the very few commentators from outside Munich, enjoyed the emphasis on 'the power of the word', as opposed to any effort at illusionism.[97] The absence of pathos or the 'grand style' led her approvingly to compare the choreographed movements with the interaction of 'figures on an ornamental clock'. Alf Brustellin saw the company as a perfect example of the cultural spirit of the time. The indigestibility of the production was both 'hostile to culture' and 'hostile to the audience', both meant in an affirmative sense.[98] He continued with the observation that the audience was confronted with 'a kaleidoscope of attitudes [Haltungen], prejudices, passions, dreams and everyday acts of cruelty'. Here 'attitudes' is not meant as a state of mind but the physical representation of attitudes, constantly in flux and defined by the particular relationship in which any given character was involved at the time. The vocabulary is Brechtian and repeats Karsunke's comments on *Zum Beispiel Ingolstadt*. The negative criticism the play received failed to engage with the new, cooler style and was happy to consign the play to the scrapheap as a rip-off of Edward Bond's *Saved*, which had been successfully staged at the Münchner Kammerspiele, translated into Bavarian by Martin Sperr and directed by Peter Stein in his first professional production. As we shall see in the epilogue, it perhaps says something for the play's substance that *Katzelmacher* became one of the central plays after 1989, when the reunified Germany showed disturbing yet isolated signs of xenophobia.

Politics with a capital 'P': the collective devises
Axel Caesar Haarmann

If only Söhnlein were not under arrest, he might have warmed to the more overtly political production that was to follow *Katzelmacher*. Fassbinder was not extensively involved in it, but was

---

[97] Annemarie Czaschke, 'Neue Impulse von Aussenseitern', *Frankfurter Rundschau*, 24 April 1968.
[98] Alf Brustellin, 'Jenseits des Kulturbetriebs', *Süddeutsche Zeitung*, 9 April 1968.

the initiator of the piece, according to Jörg Schmitt. Student leader Rudi Dutschke had been shot on 11 April 1968 and his assailant Josef Bachmann had, it seemed, been inspired by hate campaigns conducted by the tabloid press. The SDS blamed media magnate Axel Caesar Springer, far and away the most influential publisher in post-war Germany, whose *Bild-Zeitung* dominated the conservative tabloids. The slogan 'disappropriate Springer' was one of the many phrases on the *Leonce und Lena* programme in 1967, and Fassbinder believed that a play about Springer should be devised and produced by the collective as a spontaneous project. Töteberg speculates: 'Fassbinder strikingly kept himself out' of the piece, suggesting that such aesthetic bluntness ran counter to his sensibilities.[99] Schmitt, on the other hand, told me that Fassbinder had confided to Schmitt that he was busy elsewhere. Fassbinder had no income outside the theatre and wanted to use his acting training to generate money. While the anti-state, anti-Vietnam collective was compiling and rehearsing the play against Springer, Fassbinder was acting for the Bundeswehr (the German armed forces). Fassbinder scholarship has been partly aware of such activity, but his own account is a little economical with the truth: 'I acted in films for the Bundeswehr . . . to show the poor soldiers that when they were working in the garage they shouldn't squirt the brake pads with oil, otherwise there could be a fatal accident.'[100] This is certainly possible – the imaginatively titled training film *Technische Durchsicht – Pflege von Radkraftfahrzeugen* (*Technical Inspection – the Care of Road Vehicles*) was made in 1967. Ronald Hayman claims that Irm Hermann (as Fassbinder's agent) had got him a role in a film for the army which he calls *Tonys Freunde* (*Tony's Friends*).[101] Fassbinder was indeed in the film *Tonys Freunde*, but this was not a Bundeswehr film. Instead,

[99] Michael Töteberg, 'Fassbinders Theaterarbeit. Eine Recherche im Nachlass', in Rainer Werner Fassbinder, *Anarchie in Bayern und andere Stücke* (Frankfurt/Main: Verlag der Autoren, 1985), pp. 151–64, here p. 159.

[100] Fassbinder quoted in Spaich, *Rainer Werner Fassbinder*, pp. 37–8.

[101] Ronald Hayman, *Fassbinder: Film Maker* (London: Weidenfeld and Nicolson, 1984), p. 21.

Fassbinder took his first-ever starring role on celluloid in the training film *Schuldig oder Nichtschuldig* (*Guilty or Not-Guilty*) in 1968,[102] not in his own *Liebe ist kälter als der Tod* (*Love is Colder than Death* – 1969) as is usually understood. The training film is about the civil trial of a soldier, Erwin Abel (Fassbinder), and his two accomplices. Abel is a barrack-room lawyer who thinks he knows the Federal Republic's Army Act and thus behaves insubordinately and physically attacks a superior rank in the belief that he and his cronies have evaded the Act's jurisdiction. Abel is obviously wrong and herein lies the film's educative value. Abel is sentenced to a short term in prison and has to pay costs (see fig. 7). Fassbinder's performance is quite entertaining from a contemporary standpoint, as he does his best to wriggle off the legal hook. Schmitt kept quiet about the performance all the same, and Rudolf Waldemar Brem confirmed that there would have been hell to pay if the collective had found out the 'military' reason for Fassbinder's absence.

The collective, mainly without Fassbinder, proceeded to devise a play in which material that was appropriate to their political reality was channelled into theatre. The methods of documentary drama, still a popular form at the time, even after the initial excitement surrounding the form in the early 1960s, were employed. Each performer had to collect material, and the glossy news journals *Der Spiegel* and *Stern* provided the best news coverage available. The play's title, *Axel Caesar Haarmann*, which conflates Springer and Fritz Haarmann, a serial child-murderer from the Weimar Republic, was suggested by Fassbinder and taken from *Stern*. The attempted assassination of Dutschke was the catalyst and the belief that Springer was indirectly responsible shaped the title.

The text of the play has never been discussed in the scholarly literature and was believed to have been lost, but this is not fully the case. Brem has a nineteen-page fragment and the Kinemathek in Berlin, where many of Fassbinder's papers have been deposited, holds sixteen pages of text that include a full list of the production's nineteen

---

[102] The film can be viewed at the Medienzentrale der Bundeswehr in Sankt Augustin, near Bonn.

Fig. 7. Pleading his innocence in *Schuldig oder Nichtschuldig* (*Guilty or Not-Guilty*): Fassbinder's first-ever starring role in a film came courtesy of the Bundeswehr, while the *action-theater* was working on their anti-Springer, anti-Vietnam play *Axel Caesar Haarmann*. © Bundeswehr

sections. The collective endeavour is more a revue than a play, its parts are too diverse to offer a cohesive unity. The very first scene allows the mixture of Springer and Haarmann to introduce himself directly to the audience. Obsessed with order and cleanliness, Springer is confronted by a chorus chanting 'flesh, flesh, flesh!' It then breaks into a short song which satirically varies a couplet on the Haarmann child-murders. Instead of the word 'Beilchen' ('a little hatchet') making a 'dead person' out of his victim, one finds 'Zeilchen' ('a little headline') making a 'stupid person'. The revue continues in this satirical vein and takes documentary sources as the material for satire. In the 'Prayer' scene, headlines and slogans from *Bild* are juxtaposed with the refrain 'Bild für uns', an advertising line that means both '*Bild* for us' and 'form opinions for us'. The voices chorally intone a plea for their 'right' to consume before changing the last three lines of the refrain to 'think for us'. Other scenes are rooted more firmly in documentary sources and use speakers to communicate information. Actual lines from public figures, such as the police chief of Berlin, Springer himself and Dutschke, mingle with eyewitness accounts of demonstrations, and quotations from the Federal law on disappropriation. Dramatic scenes also feature, including one set on a tram where everyone except a schoolboy is reading *Bild*. The 'youth of today' is criticized by the older readers, who say that such a state of affairs would not have occurred under Hitler. The schoolboy closes the scene with a quotation from Martin Luther King on how change begins with oneself. The conclusion to the show was Fassbinder's idea and comprises a message over the PA announcing that the theatre management has ordered the clearance of the theatre. The message, repeated three times, was augmented by Fassbinder taking to the stage and hosing the audience down with a jet.

The revue concentrated on the full gamut of issues current at the time. As well as the extensive critique of Springer and the power of the media, the group looked at Vietnam, the judiciary, the *Notstandsgesetze* (the 'Emergency Laws' of 1968) and the far-right NPD ('National Party of Germany'). The last two were of particular concern to the student movement. The Emergency Laws were actually passed after the première of the show on 30 May, but were obviously the subject of much consternation beforehand. The sweeping powers of the Act suggested a link among its opponents with Hitler's Enabling Law, which turned Germany into a dictatorship. Coupled with this were the electoral victories for the NPD in regional elections in 1967 and 1968 (when it took a massive 10 per cent of the vote in Baden-Württemberg).[103]

One scene that has not survived is the tenth, 'Brecht'. Quite how he figured is therefore uncertain, but the subtle dialectical relationships that dominated Fassbinder's work at the *action-theater* were not terribly evident in this production. What was clear, however, was the interest in the deployment of epic narration and Brechtian

[103] Cf. Carr, *History of Germany*, p. 383.

choruses as representatives of a collective, the latter a feature associated with the *Lehrstück* (the 'learning play', written mainly between
1929 and 1933). A quotation from Brecht on misunderstanding what
control meant also served as an epigraph on the playbill.[104] In one
of the final scenes, 'Geständnis' ('admission' or 'confession'), a group
chorally delivers a set of self-reproaches for not acting in the face of
due cause.[105] An initial volley of twelve short lines, all beginning with
'we', brings about a state of political consciousness. The group gives
up on argument and moves into action. The ritual aspect of the scene,
its self-accusation, may also owe something to Peter Handke.

Jane Shattuc's belief that 'the aim of the performance [of the
revue as a whole] was to ignite iconoclastic pleasure, anger, and ultimately action, not Brechtian distance and realization' only tells half
the story. Her contention that the show was based on an 'American
model' ignores both the Brechtian elements of collective dramaturgy
and the large input of documentary material, a theatrical influence
that had its roots in Kipphardt, Weiss and Hochhuth.[106] It is difficult
to call *Haarmann* pure agitprop. Its satirical bent is more subtle and
the variety of forms, from pure narrated information, through ironic
parody, to song and choral sections, make it a broad engagement with
forms of political theatre rather than a one-dimensional piece of propaganda. The show's playbill approached the event from a variety of
angles, calling it, 'The Greatest Criminal Case . . . A Reckoning . . .
Rehearsing the State of Emergency . . . A Horror-Musical'.[107] Its political colours were, all the same, eminently visible: the playbill clearly

---

[104] Cf. *Playbill for Axel Caesar Haarmann*, action-theater, première 26
April 1968. The line is 'on that which is called control, there exists a
confused opinion in some'.

[105] The scene may owe more than a passing debt to a famous speech given
by the writer Peter Schneider at a sit-in at the Freie Universität, West
Berlin, on 5 May 1967, cf. Stefan Aust, *Der Baader Meinhof Komplex*,
expanded and modernized edition (Munich: Goldmann, 1998), pp. 50–1.

[106] Jane Shattuc, *Television, Tabloids and Tears. Fassbinder and Popular
Culture* (Minneapolis: University of Minneapolis Press, 1995), both
quotations p. 96.

[107] 'Rehearsing the State of Emergency' is a reference to Michael Hatry's
play *Notstandsübung* (1968), which was another dramatic response to

tells that all the profits will be donated to the SDS's fund for legal expenses.

Annemarie Czaschke was pleased to see that political protest was not limited to the universities or the cabaret circuit, and found the collage technique a helpful means of targeting a broad range of topics.[108] The well-disposed reviewer also tells us something more about the circumstances of the production: politics in this form is essentially preaching to the converted. Krää believed that a consistent dramaturgy was not that necessary for the show because there was 'a very tight common pool of knowledge' shared by the actors and their audience. Brem explained that the audience actually flocked to the theatre after the first night; the hosepipe stunt attracted students and champagne socialists who came with umbrellas and raincoats to experience the performance, which is also confirmed by Hermann. The *action-theater*'s brand of political theatre was not something for the workers, it seems.

Audience demand extended the run from the publicized three nights in the playbill, and the theatre was invited to take *Haarmann* to a demonstration and a picket line by the SDS, according to Schmitt. Although the proceeds of the show went to the SDS, the collective turned the offer down. They did, however, take the show, together with *Katzelmacher*, to the Technical University in distant Karlsruhe. The stint was not a great success, because few tickets had been sold, just as in Paris the year before.

Undeterred, the theatre took a short story by Boris Vian as the basis for their only piece of street theatre, *Chung*. The production was directed by an assistant director from Bremen. Fassbinder distanced himself from it, calling it 'repulsive' (Brocher, p. 55), because of a sense of stagnation in the group. He saw the strength of *Haarmann* as the activation of the players through collective work but found that little had actually been achieved through the process (cf. Brocher, p. 52).

the Emergency Laws. My 'Horror-Musical' translation does not do justice to the theatre's elision of 'Grusel' (horror) and 'Musical' into 'Grusical'.

[108] Cz, '*Axel Cäsar Haarmaan*', *Frankfurter Rundschau*, 23 May 1968.

Chung was first presented on 19 May 1968 as an open dress rehearsal in the *action-theater* before it was sent out into Munich. The text has not survived and none of my interview partners was involved in it. Joachim von Mengershausen did not berate the production in a review, although he did point out that it used some fairly conventional cabaret ideas of the time.[109] Czaschke was a little more critical, finding the use of music and sound not very well thought through, among other things.[110]

Chung was to be the final production of the *action-theater*. The Office of Public Order had returned to the theatre in early May and filed a report on 15 May demanding a series of repairs to be undertaken by the 30th.[111] The items, which seem to exaggerate the danger to the public, were practically a closure order for the theatre. Public safety was far more a ruse for masking a distrust of the political content of the recent productions. Götz Haydar Aly notes that a local electrician had offered to do the repairs for free but could not meet the Office's deadline. Aly also quotes the theatre's 'technician', Gottfried von Hüngsberg, who said that everything that he could make good was made good.[112] Karsunke confirmed the story about the electrician and related a conversation with a representative of the Office on his radio slot.[113] The official told him that the theatre had a licence to exist as a theatre, not 'a political cabaret'. The touchy civic authorities seem to have overreacted to the political activities of the theatre without understanding that the theatre itself was not terribly happy with its own latest offering. It is ironic that at this time the small theatre was written about for the first time in the most important theatre

---

[109] Joachim von Mengershausen, 'Sprung auf die Strasse', *Süddeutsche Zeitung*, 21 May 1968.

[110] Cz, '*Axel*'.

[111] Report on the technical state of the *action-theater* to Willi Rabenbauer (i.e. Peer Raben) from Mr Röschert, 21 May 1968, private archive of Yaak Karsunke.

[112] Götz Haydar Aly, 'Kuckuck klebt am Action-Theater', *Abendzeitung*, 8/9 June 1968.

[113] Yaak Karsunke, 'Zur Schliessung des Action-Theaters in der Müllerstrasse am 6. Juni', *Kulturspiegel*, no transmission date supplied.

magazine in West Germany, *Theater heute*.[114] The article lauded the theatre's efforts and analysed its style. Such attention, either positive or negative, was rarely lavished upon a *Kellertheater* in that publication. All the same, the *action-theater* was closed on 6 June 1968. One may ask why Fassbinder and his allies did not do more to save the theatre. It was because they were already planning their next company: the *antiteater*.

[114] Alf Brustellin, '*Action-Theater* in München', *Theater heute*, 6/1968, pp. 44–5.

2   1968 and all that

Opposing forces: the politics of culture in 1968

The development of the Extra-Parliamentary Opposition (APO) in the
FRG, its protests and its campaigns in the wake of the Grand Coalition
of 1966 clearly did not take place in a vacuum. The very confidence of
the student movement has its roots in its social and economic conditions. As R. Hinton Thomas and Keith Bullivant observe: 'the expec-
tation of the increasing satisfaction of need and desire gave dynamic
force and revolutionary energy to impatience with things as they are,
materially, socially and politically'.[1] These are not therefore the revolutionary poor marching on the Winter Palace but (relatively) affluent
and educated young people demanding rights unthinkable a generation beforehand. David Roberts agrees and contextualizes the protests
further: '1968 appears increasingly as a watershed in the history of
the Federal Republic, for it indicated how much West German society
had become part of the Western world, how much its problems were
now those of (post-) industrial capitalism'.[2] The teenager, a product of
the rock 'n' roll boom in 1950s America and a new type of consumer
simultaneously, had the economic self-confidence to express him- or
herself and cultivate a consciousness that would not accept the views

[1] R. Hinton Thomas and Keith Bullivant, *Literature in Upheaval. West
German Writers and the Challenge of the 1960s* (Manchester:
Manchester University Press, 1974), p. 38.

[2] David Roberts, 'Introduction. From the 1960s to the 1970s: the
Changing Contexts of German Literature', in Keith Bullivant (ed.), *After
the 'Death of Literature'. West German Writing of the 1970s* (Oxford,
New York and Munich: Berg, 1989), pp. xi–xxiii, here p. xiv.

of the older generation unconditionally, and part of this awareness was political. The rebellious teen spirit was not far removed from that of university students – they themselves had been teenagers when or soon after the term was invented – whose grant-supported studies allowed them temporary independence from the economic laws of fair exchange.

The 'luxury' of protest in 1960s West Germany, sustained by the material comfort accrued during the reconstruction of the 1950s, meant that the political was able to extend beyond governance, legislation and representation at regional and national executive level. Culture was also a sphere that became increasingly important to the APO and its sympathizers. The crystallization of oppositional thought in this field manifested itself in Hans Magnus Enzensberger's polemic 'Gemeinplätze, die Neueste Literatur betreffend' ('Platitudes Concerning the Latest Literature').[3] This epoch-making essay starts from the position that literature is dying (hence the slogan most often associated with the piece, 'The Death of Literature') but that 'the demise of this literature' (Enz, p. 188) does not appear to be of much concern to anyone. The 'this' in the quotation is important. Enzensberger is not declaring the end of writing, but the death of bourgeois literature with its 'bread and circuses' functions of entertainment and the sublimation of dissent. Enzensberger is keen to historicize his findings by identifying movements in recent German history. He contends that the FRG is eager to see itself as a 'Kulturvolk' (Enz, p. 189), a 'People of Culture', in the wake of the barbarism of the Third Reich, but that the hypostatization of culture has blunted any possible effects it might generate in society. Enzensberger points to Walter Benjamin, who asserted that bourgeois publishing had managed to absorb and assimilate all manner of revolutionary material without calling itself into question. The commodification of literature had all but deprived that literature of edge or power. Enzensberger's only

---

[3] Hans Magnus Enzensberger, 'Gemeinplätze, die Neueste Literatur betreffend', *Kursbuch*, 15 (1968), pp. 187–97. Hereafter referred to as 'Enz'.

hope is the documentary, a form which, as we have already observed, was flourishing in the theatre at the time.[4] His final shot, the proverb 'in Türangeln gibt es keine Holzwürmer' ('there's no woodworm in a door's hinges') (Enz, p. 197), suggests that it is the small, obscure areas of cultural production that might prove the starting point for a new literature. The undermining of established forms of authority and their ossifying mechanisms becomes a central goal in the essay and broadly allies itself to the aims of the APO as a whole.

Enzensberger's essay has gone down in German cultural history as a defining moment in radical aesthetics, yet its fame is more *post-hoc*, and its direct influence on artists and intellectuals should be qualified. In a note at the end of the essay, Enzensberger connects his piece with other sources that had preceded him. He exposes how his thought is more an articulation and development of the oppositional *Zeitgeist* than a singular lead in the debate. Rather than a lone radical intellect, Enzensberger sees himself more as a representative voice of cultural nonconformity, tapping into arguments that were current at the time. Consequently, one may view his thought as useful for an understanding of the protests of the time, because specific knowledge of his essay, so lauded after the event, does not preclude an engagement with its theses, which were 'in the air'.

The 'death of literature' is an important context for our understanding of Fassbinder's work as both dramatist and director with the newly formed *antiteater* ensemble. His relationship with the *Klassikerzertrümmerung* ('reducing of the classics to rubble') started early, in the form of radical rewritings of Goethe, Sophocles and John Gay, as we shall see in this chapter, and would continue beyond Munich after the decline of the *antiteater* with Goldoni and Lope de Vega at the theatre in Bremen. Yet while this category is usually associated with directing practices (radical modernization and the destruction of conventional readings), Fassbinder's point of entry was the text itself, hence the connection with Enzensberger's thought. Fassbinder

---

[4] Enzensberger was to pen his own documentary drama, based on protocols concerning the Bay of Pigs fiasco of 1961 in *Das Verhör von Habana* in 1970.

interrogates the inheritance of bourgeois literature and fashions a set of responses that call its premises into question. The precise strategies of Fassbinder's dramatic practice will be discussed later in the chapter.

Another set of ideas current in West German cultural debates of the time was Rolf Schwendtner's theories on subculture, the development of nests of cultural activists concertedly working against the dominance of 'approved' cultural norms. Although his book, *Theorie der Subkultur*, was published in 1971,[5] the *antiteater* quoted from one of Schwendtner's articles in the programme for *Die Bettleroper* (*The Beggar's Opera*) in 1969.[6] Schwendtner taps into the thought of a favourite of the protest movement, the Frankfurt School philosopher and sociologist Herbert Marcuse. His *One-Dimensional Man* provided a critique of modern Western democracies and their capacity to stifle revolt through the apparently contradictory category of 'repressive liberalism'.[7] His clarion call is for an enlightened elite to mobilize the socially disaffected underclasses which have hitherto not been infected by consumerism. Together they will form the revolutionary vanguard. Schwendtner examines the conditions under which such groups might resist the dominant culture. His model, like Marx's of social structures, is pyramidal. At the peak is the 'establishment', which defines and controls culture both directly and more subtly through such instruments as the law (censorship, business and media law) and the media and culture industry themselves. The establishment is supported by the 'compact majority'. On its fringes, however, lies the opportunity for opposition, which can be either 'progressive' or 'regressive'. According to Schwendtner, the progressive structures are those which desire social change and alternatives to the existing system. Regressive groups look to the past for change

---

[5] Cf. Rolf Schwendtner, *Theorie der Subkultur* (Cologne and Berlin: Kiepenheuer und Witsch, 1971).

[6] *Programme of Fassbinder's 'Die Bettleroper'*, Witwe Bolte, première 1 February 1969, no pagination. The programme quotes Schwendtner's theories published in the oppositional magazine *Song* in 1968.

[7] Cf. Herbert Marcuse, *One-Dimensional Man. Studies in the Ideology of Advanced Industrial Society* (London: Ark, 1986), passim. Originally published in 1964.

in the present, are radically conservative in character and include neo-Nazis, for example. In the book, Schwendtner presents himself as an orthodox Marxist analyst whose ideas are concerned with the social base and its influence on the ideological superstructure of a given society.

The critique of established and conventional cultural forms through interventionist practice was the primary goal of a 'progressive subculture', and the quotations in the *Bettleroper* programme affirm such a position. Belief in the shock-value of surprise, democratic, decentralized production (collectives) and the development of concrete utopias are all mentioned. So too is the role theatre can play in the subcultural process. The programme advocates the smashing of routinized social roles and emphasizes the theatre's potential to comment on and actively modify role and role-playing implicitly through its unique sign systems. Both the Living Theatre and the *antiteater* are quoted in Schwendtner's piece. Again, the ramifications of such ideas will be discussed in more detail later in the chapter.[8]

The very nature of subculture, however, was highly contentious, especially in an age of mass communication. The problem is highlighted in the very magazine in which Schwendtner published the article that was later reproduced by the *antiteater*. In 1969 the editorial team of *Song* criticized a piece in the *Mainzer Allgemeine Zeitung* of 24 October 1969 which argued that the *antiteater*'s counter-cultural credentials had made it into the mainstream.[9] The team argues that the two categories are mutually exclusive and that such conflations totally misrepresent the meaning of subculture. That such a confusion can occur is telling and reflects the knife-edge on which radical cultural practice rests when it finds a mass audience. Thomas and Bullivant note that by their very nature, '[progressive] subcultures

[8] The other major socio-political concept of the time, *Mitbestimmung* ('collective decision-making'), will be discussed in chapter 4 as an essential prerequisite to our understanding of the management structures of the Theater am Turm in Frankfurt. Its roots lie very much, though, in 1968.

[9] Cf. The Editors, 'Subkultur. Zur Klärung eines Schimpfwortes und einer verschrieenen Sache', *Song*, 4 (1969), no. 4, pp. 3–4.

must involve political action'.[10] The extent to which the *antiteater* achieved this will be considered in the discussion of the nature of the political in drama, below, yet elsewhere in the Republic, an uncompromising social, political and aesthetic experiment was underway, which was to provide an additional source of inspiration for the Munich theatre group.

Kommune Eins (K1 as it became known) was formed in West Berlin on 1 January 1967 by a group of mostly disaffected students in a bid to 'revolutionize everyday life', as the slogan went. It lasted almost three years and closed down in November 1969. The group was already to the left of the SDS ('the League of German Socialist Students', one of the main engines of the APO) and rejected its tactics and campaigns. The communards were expelled from the movement in summer 1967. In April of that year, members of K1 became something akin to media stars in the wake of a foiled attempt to attack US Vice President Hubert Humphrey with a custard pie. The free-loving collective was an instant hit with the tabloid press and was pilloried (as the *antiteater* was, too)[11] at every available opportunity. The 'pudding assassination', as it was known, then gave way to a further, more controversial action. On 24 May 1967 members of the commune distributed a series of four flyers at the refectory of the Free University, West Berlin. The reading matter seemed to encourage readers to follow the example of a politically inspired arson attack in Brussels and to set Berlin department stores on fire themselves. The Belgian blaze claimed more than 300 lives. The authorities took the opportunity to try the communards for inciting arson. The trial began in July 1967 and the final verdicts were delivered in March 1968. The accused, Rainer Langhans and Fritz Teufel, were both acquitted; their flyers were considered to be satirical, or art-terrorism at most. A main line of defence came as a response to the Public Prosecutor's question as

---

[10] Thomas and Bullivant, *Literature in Upheaval*, p. 168.

[11] Cf. the two articles on a double-page splash, Arnim Borski, 'Ich liebe dich, ich liebe dich, ham, ham, ham' and 'Wer schenkt uns ein Staatstheater?', *Berliner Zeitung*, no date supplied, but circa the end of June 1969. The articles paint a cartoon picture of the ensemble, which is not surprising, as the tabloid was owned by the Springer concern.

to whether someone might read the flyers and set a department store on fire. Teufel replied: 'I'd have to say, no one came upon the idea to do that – except the Public Prosecutor. He, however, didn't do this but rather issued an arrest warrant.'[12]

The publicity generated by both the pudding assassination and the trial fixed an image of commune life and the permissive society that was too easy and convenient to be seriously challenged by the mass media. Both incidents at the centre of the reporting, however, help one to understand the workings of these ostensibly 'cartoon' hippie activists far better. The contrast between the stereotypical portrayals of the commune and its careful manipulation of public opinion enacts a subtle critique. In both public instances of K1 notoriety, no palpable danger was present. K1 was able to play with sensationalist perceptions and become a public parody of itself, whilst retaining the last laugh. K1's documentation of the trial, the book *Klau mich*, uses documentary material in the shape of real court protocols and copies of (sensationalist) newspaper reports. The protocols, which provide the left-hand pages for the book, are arranged, however, like a play, with the title 'The Moabit [the location of the court in Berlin] Soap Opera', a 'prologue' and other dramatic tropes. The book literally means 'nick me' or 'pinch me', and the authors maintain on the final page that they have merely stolen material and presented it to the reader (in the spirit of Enzensberger). The ironic awareness of their media personalities is revealed when they write, 'this book isn't by us because, for other people, we only exist in their minds, because they know us better than we know ourselves'.

K1, particularly during the trial, presented itself as a subcultural dynamo. It was able to expose the one-sidedness of the mass media, avoid prison, and retain its political credibility through its well-deployed use of irony. The parody of a commune was offered to those who wished to swallow it, while those enthused by its antics

---

[12] Rainer Langhans and Fritz Teufel, *Klau mich* (Berlin: Rixdorfer Verlag, n.d.), no pagination. Further references to this book are not footnoted for obvious reasons. This line, along with others around it, are quoted directly in Fassbinder's rewriting of Goethe's *Iphigenie*, which is discussed below.

were able to see beneath the surface and divine a more subversive thrust. The distinction between the appearance and a more complex interplay of a culturally political group would serve as another important influence on the *antiteater*.

Rethinking political theatre, rethinking Brecht: political theatre beyond political content

In order to apprehend the *antiteater* and its various aesthetic agendas, it is necessary not only to discuss the culture of political dissent of the time, but also what is to be understood by 'the political' in the theatre. The question cannot be addressed without reference to Brecht, the godfather of political drama in the twentieth century and an unavoidable figure in the arena of cultural production in the late 1960s.

Political theatre can, of course, be traced all the way back to the ancient Greeks. The problems they explored affected the foundations of their society, how it was ruled, how power was wielded, and how law was made. Yet the subject matter of the dramas tells half the story of the political nature of Athenian tragedy. Only once we have understood Aristotelian catharsis can we fully appreciate the socio-political functions of the plays. As Augusto Boal cogently argues, the dramaturgy that brings about the purgation of *elios* and *phobos* desires the abolition of dissent as portrayed in the conflicts of the drama.[13] While one is indeed confronted with rebels and outsiders (e.g. Antigone or Prometheus), Aristotle's ideas nonetheless argue that empathy with such figures still brings about the purgation of such excessive action by the end of the theatrical event. The politics of the plays is to be located as much in their form as in their content. A more contemporary example of the importance of the formal appreciation of a drama is Arthur Miller's classic *The Crucible*. On the surface, the play is about tolerance and the rights of the individual to self-defence in the face of mass political hysteria. The content is most worthy. The form of the play elicits the very opposite: its unbroken realism,

---

[13] Cf. Augusto Boal, *The Theatre of the Oppressed*, tr. Charles A. and Maria-Odilia Leal McBride (London: Pluto, 1979), pp. 1–50.

the supporting 'biographical' character descriptions and attempts at historical accuracy within apparent poetic licence,[14] and the emotional passion of the plotting do nothing to activate the spectator. The lack of thinking space and the intensity of the material exploit the spectator's feelings, inhibit a critical view of the content and unconsciously encourage an acceptance of Miller's theses. The tolerant subject matter is undermined by the highly constrictive dramaturgy of the play. While one may argue that naturalism cannot exclusively render an audience, especially a contemporary one, uncritical, the empathetic journey of the spectator in a play like *The Crucible* is paved by structures that seek to convince by emotion rather than reason.

Brecht's approach to a philosophy of political drama is more conscious of the contradictions between form and content, and thus tries to understand what is required of each to effect a more democratic relationship with the audience. The *Lehrstück* (the 'learning play') and epic theatre both represent consistent attempts to allow spectators (and actors, especially in the first genre) to examine the material presented through their formal arsenal of banners, distanced acting, direct address, use of narration, and the defamiliarization of the recognizable (*Verfremdung*). However, these devices, almost commonplaces in drama today, take a dialectical view of reality as their starting point, and it is here that the harmony of form and content becomes political in Brecht's theatre.

Theatre with a social thrust can, in very simple terms, be divided into the moral and the political. Although one can easily deconstruct this opposition, the two categories allow a certain clarity

---

[14] Miller's 'authenticity' is also highly problematic. His disclaimer before the start of the play, 'A Note on the Historical Accuracy of this Play', fails to deal with important issues that would reduce the sympathy one would attribute to his hero, Proctor, for example. While Miller rightly states 'this play is not history' and that Abigail's age had been raised (Arthur Miller, *Plays*, vol. 1 (London: Methuen, 1988), p. 224), he omits that it was raised from eleven to seventeen and that Proctor was sixty when he had his affair with her, not the 'middle thirties' of the description in the text (p. 238).

to be brought to the argument. If one views the world, as Brecht did, as dialectical, one develops an historicized concept of human nature. If, as Marx maintained, human beings are the ensemble of their social relations, then their 'nature' will inevitably change along with their social context. This postulate is the centre of political drama as Brecht understood it: by changing the world, one changes humanity. Moral drama is also concerned with change, but here it is with changes in attitudes, rather than in society as a whole. Ibsen's dramas, for example, do not envisage revolution but the reform of a system. The audience is encouraged to modify its thinking on certain issues, be they women's rights or the social order, not to question the socio-political frame within which these issues exist. Political drama is thus based on the prerequisite that society (and consequently human nature) is changeable, and is not rooted in changes in moral attitude which merely cover over the causes of injustice.

As we saw in the introduction to this book, commentators, often film specialists, are keen to paint Fassbinder the theatre practitioner as an Artaudian irrationalist as opposed to a 'scientific' Brechtian. Wallace Steadman Watson asserts that Artaud was the inspiration for much of Fassbinder's work in the theatre, as does Klaus Ulrich Militz.[15] Joanna Firaza is one of the few critics to discuss the role of Artaud in Fassbinder's work with care. She emphasizes Artaud and Fassbinder's interest in masks and disguise, as well as drawing attention to the function of ritual in Fassbinder's theatre.[16] On the other side of the coin, one finds many critics who argue against Fassbinder as a Brechtian in the theatre.[17] One strand of this school of thought suggests that Fassbinder's drama is simply too pessimistic to support political change because it presents an eternally vicious

---

[15] Watson, *Understanding Rainer Werner Fassbinder*, p. 57; Militz, *Media Interplay*, p. 41. As an argument, Militz uses the *action-theater*'s *Antigone*, which, as we have seen, featured Fassbinder in a bit part.

[16] Firaza, *Die Ästhetik des Dramenwerks*, pp. 106–9 and 121–56.

[17] Film critics, however, are rightly keen to identify Fassbinder's debt to Brecht in his use of *Verfremdung*, exposing socially determined role-play, and the careful observation of milieu and its effects on character.

picture of human nature.[18] Pessimism need not, however, be allied with an inability to change. I shall later be arguing that if cycles of oppression are presented historically, then there is already a temporally defined context which is open to examination. A variation on this viewpoint is offered by Klaus Bohnen, who considers the conflicts in Fassbinder's plays as more pathological than social.[19] Bohnen prefers to place Fassbinder's plays in the category of 'Gefühlsrealismus' ('the realism of feelings'), understood as the sensual confrontation with the characters as opposed to their dialectical analysis.[20] Irmbert Schenk also maintains that contradiction in Fassbinder's characters is more 'ontological and existential' than dialectical, but Schenk is still able to acknowledge a trace of Brecht in Fassbinder's definition of some characters as social beings.[21]

The second argument against Fassbinder as a Brechtian in the theatre partially takes up Fassbinder's own denials of the influence in interviews. As well as Fassbinder's comments on the *Lehrstück*, quoted in the introduction, Fassbinder distanced himself from Brecht elsewhere, too, linking him with coldness and abstraction.[22] Militz is keen to use Fassbinder's own remarks to support his anti-Brechtian reading.[23] Here, however, we might wish to shift our view to Fassbinder and the state of Brecht scholarship in the late 1960s and early 1970s.

---

[18] Cf. Laura Sormani, *Semiotik und Hermeneutik im interkulturellen Rahmen. Interpretationen zu Werken von Peter Weiss, Rainer Werner Fassbinder, Thomas Bernhard und Botho Strauss* (Frankfurt/Main et al.: Peter Lang, 1998), p. 197. Sormani is referring to *Das Kaffeehaus* in her chapter, but the argument can easily be extended to many of Fassbinder's dramas, as we shall see.

[19] Bohnen, '"Raum-Höllen"', pp. 141–62, here p. 156.

[20] Ibid., p. 161.

[21] Irmbert Schenk, 'Widerspruchsbehandlung bei Rainer Werner Fassbinder am Beispiel von *Katzelmacher, Bremer Freiheit* und *Nora Helmer*', *TheaterZeitSchrift*, 33/4 (1993), pp. 163–80, here p. 166.

[22] Cf. Thomsen, 'Conversations with Rainer Werner Fassbinder', p. 88.

[23] Militz, *Media Interplay*, p. 20.

Fassbinder's view of Brecht as emotionally remote is derived in part from the failures of Brecht scholarship at the time. The reception of Brecht's theory and practice shifted greatly in 1972, when Rainer Steinweg published his book on the *Lehrstück*.[24] As a result of intensive archival work, Steinweg was able to assemble a 'theory' of the form based on several hundred fragments dispersed throughout the archive in the erstwhile East Berlin. One such fragment states quite clearly: 'when, with the best will in the world, I couldn't do anything more with a theatre of empathy, I constructed the *Lehrstück* for that quality'.[25] The *Lehrstück*, the genre that had been most often attacked for its cold, propagandistic thrust within Brecht's dramatic oeuvre, was revealed as a site of emotional and political education. Brecht the sensualist was starting to emerge, but too late for Fassbinder. There is also evidence from Fassbinder's closest associates that Fassbinder had more time for the, by then, unfashionable playwright and theorist than he let on. Ingrid Caven, an actress in Fassbinder's theatre and his wife for a short period, recalls that Fassbinder loved the Brechtian tradition.[26] In addition, Fassbinder's closest theatrical partner, Peer Raben, with whom Fassbinder directed on several occasions, confirms that Fassbinder was well aware of Brechtian theory.[27] Raben had studied theatre for a time in Munich and had seen productions at the Berliner Ensemble. He had discussed Brecht's ideas with Fassbinder, who found them useful and wanted to develop them practically.

Brecht was (and often still is) portrayed as a monster of reason, a cold and distant dramatist who wanted the audience to think

---

[24] Cf. Rainer Steinweg, *Das Lehrstück. Brechts Theorie einer politisch-ästhetischen Erziehung* (Stuttgart: Metzler, 1972).

[25] Brecht quoted in Rainer Steinweg (ed.), *Brechts Modell der Lehrstücke. Zeugnisse, Diskussion, Erfahrungen* (Frankfurt/Main: Suhrkamp, 1976), p. 172.

[26] Cf. Ingrid Caven in Lorenz (ed.), *Das ganz normale Chaos*, p. 84.

[27] As in chapter 1, all unacknowledged references are taken from interviews conducted in the course of my research for this book. The dates of the interviews are to be found in the bibliography.

but not to feel, to be constantly aware of the artifice of the theatre, and not to be seduced by empathy and illusionism. Brecht's famous division between the 'dramatic theatre' and the 'epic theatre' is often deployed to justify this view but little attention is paid to the footnote that stressed that he was not dealing in oppositions but 'changes in accent'.[28] Brecht's is a theatre of oscillation; the spectator has to empathize with the characters for some of the time – how interminably dull the evening would be otherwise! How could one otherwise feel for the plight of Gruscha in *The Caucasian Chalk Circle*, or suffer the losses of Mother Courage? Yet how could one understand that Gruscha's 'good' act of saving an innocent child might threaten her own life, or that Mother Courage can never win because she never learns? The 'cold' Brecht is a convenient misinterpretation, as is that of his rational optimism. To return to the *Chalk Circle* again: when Azdak decrees that Gruscha is the child's mother, he advises her to flee the city because it is still not safe for her to stay. He, too, disappears in the following, brief celebration. The dialectics of motherhood and justice have not been resolved and there is no happy ending. So, when Militz says that in Fassbinder's theatre one 'thinks *and* feels',[29] he is in fact arguing for rather than against the Brechtian influence.

As we have already seen from his work as a director at the *action-theater*, Fassbinder focused on relationships by deindividualizing his characters and revealing their dependency on social codes and structures. Group scenes were shunned in favour of small two- and three-person interactions. The modification of attitude through the variation of group dynamics was introduced in *Die Verbrecher* and *Ingolstadt*, then developed in the writing and direction of *Katzelmacher*, which revealed a fascination with permutations of encounters between characters. Fassbinder was to develop these qualities, but away from the constraints of the *action-theater*. Its closure in June

[28] Bertolt Brecht, footnote to 'Anmerkungen zur Oper *Aufstieg und Fall der Stadt Mahagonny*', in Brecht, *Grosse kommentierte Berliner und Frankfurter Ausgabe*, vol. xxiv (Berlin and Frankfurt/Main: Suhrkamp, 1991), p. 78.

[29] Militz, *Media Interplay*, p. 24, his emphasis.

1968 opened the vista on a theatre collective that would be more in keeping with Fassbinder's ideas of theatre, performance and politics.

What's in a name? The establishment of the *antiteater*

Fassbinder, Raben and those loyal to them within the *action-theater* were not slow to exploit the opportunity offered by the intervention of the Office of Public Order in June 1967. There were primarily two reasons for the break with Ursula Strätz and the rest of the ensemble. The freedom from the structures of the *action-theater* was a clear motivating factor, particularly with reference to Horst Söhnlein's faction, but it was also important to escape from the huge debts of the theatre as well, by establishing a company afresh.[30] The new group, which was exclusively comprised of *action-theater* performers, was reluctant to give up the name too quickly, though, as its reputation was growing. Peer Raben said, 'we believed we were the legitimate successors to the *action-theater*. Originally, we even wanted to continue to perform under the *action-theater* banner but Ursula was having none of it.'[31] The search was on for a new name.

The origin of the choice of '*antiteater*' is uncertain. But whether it was Raben or Fassbinder who coined it, the title was evocative, if not entirely transparent. It was significant that '*antiteater*' began with a small 'a'. Counter to conventional German orthography, which capitalizes nouns, the group resisted such arbitrary 'authority' and continued to provide itself with a link to the similarly lower-case *action-theater*. The omission of the 'h' from 'theater' signalled additional nonconformity and lent the name a distinctive visual component.[32] In 1971, effectively after the demise of the *antiteater*

---

[30] Cf. Fassbinder in Corinna Brocher, 'Gruppen sind ja vieles. Gespräche mit Rainer Werner Fassbinder über die Geschichte des *antiteaters*', unpublished manuscript, 1973, p. 60. Hereafter referred to as 'Brocher'.

[31] Peer Raben quoted in Raab and Peters, *Sehnsucht*, p. 110. Fassbinder concurs in Brocher, p. 60.

[32] Bernd Eckardt maintains that Doris Mattes suggested that the 'h' be deleted, in Bernd Eckardt, *Rainer Werner Fassbinder. In 17 Jahren 42 Filme – Stationen eines Lebens für den deutschen Film* (Munich: Wilhelm Heyme, 1982), p. 76. Jörg Schmitt, in an interview with the author, asserted that it was his idea.

ensemble, Fassbinder asserted: 'what I was doing wasn't *antiteater* but theatre. *antiteater* was just a name, like a theatre being called the Schillertheater,' but this rather understates what would prove to be both a shrewd marketing concept and a bane.[33]

antiteater tapped directly into the oppositional feelings of the time, and thus the very name could ensure publicity and interest from those who preferred their culture with a rebellious edge. Yet the group was not opposed to 'theatre', of course. As Raben, the most theoretically adept of the group, put it in a documentary shot in 1969: 'above all, the name points to the structure and programme of our theatre ensemble. The rejection isn't directed against the theatre *per se* but against the social function it has had in the last 200 years.'[34] The group had tried to denote this stance by refusing to hyphenate the 'anti' and the 'teater', according to Fassbinder (Brocher, p. 61), but to little avail. The name was an excellent publicity tool, but the potential for misunderstanding led to disappointment among the radical left and those seeking wholly experimental forms. Such political narrowness in the interpretation of the ensemble's name may have been behind the small protest that accompanied the première of *Iphigenie*. Agitprop-hungry students disrupted the opening of the show and sought politics in the content at the *antiteater*.[35] What they failed to grasp was the radical form of the piece, discussed below, as political and the way in which it attacked the grandest figure of German bourgeois culture, Goethe.

The *action-theater* had hardly been closed when the *antiteater* announced its existence to the world later in June 1967 in the Pokeo-Keller, Munich. Although there is some disagreement in the secondary literature, the ten original members of the *antiteater* were Fassbinder, Raben, Rudolf Waldemar Brem, Irm Hermann, Gunter Krää, Doris Mattes, Kurt Raab, Jörg Schmitt, Hanna Schygulla and

---

[33] Thomsen, 'Conversations with Rainer Werner Fassbinder', p. 85.

[34] Peer Raben in *Ende einer Kommune* by Joachim von Mengershausen, first broadcast 2 February 1970.

[35] Cf. kth, 'Krawall auf Tauris', *Abendzeitung*, 28 October 1968; or r, 'Iphigenie im Drahtkorb', *Münchner Merkur*, 29 October 1968.

Lilith Ungerer.[36] The group represents all those centrally involved in Fassbinder's last major project with the *action-theater*, *Katzelmacher*, with the exception of Ingrid Caven (whose relationship with the group was not fully committed at this stage) and the inclusion of Kurt Raab, who had decided he wanted to ally himself with Fassbinder and not Strätz.

Anti-psychology, or Fassbinder the director

That the group was very close to Fassbinder is informative as to the director's approach to his actors, something which hardly changed throughout his career in both the theatre and the cinema. One of Fassbinder's greatest talents was his ability to understand the strengths and weaknesses of his actors. As a result, many of his productions were highly dependent on good casting.[37] His judgement of character, aptitude and potential enabled him to develop a particularly unpsychological approach to his actors. The accounts of this facility are unchanging among his associates. Raben reported that to Fassbinder, 'the actor should remain the person he [sic] is on stage. He should import the ideas of the person he's playing into his own personality.'[38] Brem speaks of a 'blind understanding' between the director and his cast: 'he only had to correct the nuances'. Schygulla gives several insightful perspectives on Fassbinder's practices: 'he had always "under"-stretched us . . . he wasn't a perfectionist . . . His grace was taking that which he had been offered.' Elsewhere she said that his style was 'to say little, but that "little" works'.[39] The 'little' is described by Hans Günther Pflaum in a book on Fassbinder's film-making techniques.

---

[36] The discrepancy rests on the inclusion of Ingrid Caven in the roll call. Eckardt, for example, includes both her and Hans Hirschmüller in his list (Eckardt, *Rainer Werner Fassbinder*, p. 75), and omits Krää. Hirschmüller had nothing to do with the *antiteater* until 1969, and Caven gravitated towards it for their production of the *Bettleroper*.

[37] As we shall see in chapters 3 and 4, some of Fassbinder's lower points as a director may be traced back, at least in part, to miscasting and the unavailability of quality actors.

[38] Peer Raben in Lorenz (ed.), *Das ganz normale Chaos*, p. 67.

[39] Schygulla, *Bilder aus Filmen*, p. 29.

The comments, however, apply equally well to Fassbinder's work as a theatre director:

> He describes attitudes [Haltungen], but doesn't act them out, he never takes up an actor's position to show him what's expected; everything appears to develop with a minimum of effort. All this hangs together with the central pillars of Fassbinder's working methods: he already tried to avoid moulding actors at the casting stage.[40]

Pflaum observed the qualities already noted in chapter 1. Fassbinder was content not to bother himself with the reductive limitations of psychology and rather let the interactions of his characters and their social environments generate their own tensions. In an extensive interview with Wolfgang Limmer, Fassbinder declared, 'anything that's based in reason [alles Vernünftige] is of no interest to me'.[41] In this sense, Fassbinder does indeed ally himself with Artaud as he is not concerned with convenient rational exegesis – but there is more to the rejection of reason than just that. By avoiding explanation and pat interpretations of his characters, Fassbinder was able to capture the complexities of particular situations. His technique of taking the actor and allowing him or her to appropriate the perceived traits of the character created a dialectical tension in performance. This can be heard, in part, on an audio collection that was compiled in 1972. *antiteater's Greatest Hits* is mainly an anthology of the music that accompanied both the early theatre and film work. Yet there are excerpts of dialogues, in which there is clear evidence of acting at a remove, 'quoting' the character rather than being it.[42] The role-playing implicit in this acting style intimates Brechtian

[40] Hans Günther Pflaum and Rainer Werner Fassbinder, *Das bisschen Realität, das ich brauche. Wie Filme entstehen* (Munich: Hanser, 1976), p. 89.

[41] Fassbinder in Wolfgang Limmer, *Rainer Werner Fassbinder, Filmemacher* (Reinbek: Rowohlt, 1981), p. 58.

[42] Cf. the two-CD collection *antiteater's Greatest Hits*, particularly disc one, track three, in which Fassbinder and Schygulla perform the 'leave-taking scene' from the *Bettleroper*.

mutability, in that the actor presents him- or herself *and* a character. The audience observes how the actor has created the character, not that the character is a fixed point, the inevitable and seamless fusion of one human being with a role. Fassbinder's directing style *ipso facto* involves a critique of 'the natural' by portraying characters as fictions, roles played by actors. There is no suggestion that there is an unbreakable link between the actor and what is being portrayed and thus no link between character and an inescapable psychology or set of traits. The emphasis on relationships and attitudes defines the characters as functions of their situation. This insight is central to a political understanding of Fassbinder's writing and direction for the theatre.

Theatre on the move: the *antiteater*'s first productions

The new ensemble might have had a catchy name, but it had nowhere to perform. While the idea of not being tied to a particular venue was attractive and well in keeping with a 'guerrilla' approach to theatre, it obviously caused great problems logistically. The *antiteater* initially wanted to return to the Büchner Theater, which had hosted the *Ingolstadt* production. This was not, however, possible because the theatre was then working with the Modernes Theater, and its leader, Uta Emmer, wanted nothing to do with Fassbinder's troupe. With students causing havoc with protests and sit-ins, the *antiteater* negotiated a short stay in Munich's Akademie der Künste (Academy of the Fine Arts) to perform its first production, the little-known Peter Weiss play *Wie dem Herrn Mockinpott das Leiden ausgetrieben wird* (*How Suffering Was Driven Out of Mr Mockinpott*). The satirical and episodic tale of one man's journey from gaol to heaven and the superficial easing of his woes through conformity would open the production history of the *antiteater*.

Fassbinder stated that the play's title had attracted him and Raben, as they were both interested in the idea that suffering as a concept could be viewed positively (cf. Brocher, p. 57). Raben admitted that the play unfortunately presented the opposite of what they had hoped for, but rehearsals had already begun and a venue had been secured. Fassbinder co-directed the play with Jörg Schmitt. Gunter

Krää confirms Schmitt's account in an interview for this book that the latter was responsible for only about 10 per cent of the direction, although he also contributed a new ending. The more left-wing conclusion was, by Schmitt's own admission, 'awful', but was the only major tampering with the text.

The pre-publicity for the production showed just how schizophrenic the group's identity was at the time. An early flyer announced that the *action-theater* of Munich would be performing a double-bill of *Mockinpott* and *Katzelmacher*.[43] Neither performance dates nor venue were given. A later flyer exploited the novelty of a production of the play (although it was originally written in 1963, it was reworked in 1968) and the popularity of Weiss in West Germany at the time. It also used the *antiteater* name for the first time, albeit carefully stressing that it had arisen from the ashes of the *action-theater*. Most remarkable, perhaps, was the assertion that the group desired to make 'predominantly socialist theatre'.[44] The programme itself was similarly willing to trade on both the *action-theater* name and the *antiteater*'s strange decision to ally itself with a party-political agenda. The name '*antiteater*' was written in the left-hand column, the right-hand one was followed by '= ensemble of the *action-theater*', '= socialist theatre', '= information', and four lines of '= . . . . '.[45] The dots at least allowed for further developments, and to judge from the production's reception, these were necessary.

The show opened on 10 July 1968 and would play for a further two nights, before being transferred to the Büchner Theater (the Modernes Theater had moved on by then). Kurt Raab played Mockinpott, and he was supported by an ironized 'chorus of angels'. Raben told me that Fassbinder and Schmitt's directorial focus was on the 'wie' ('how') of the play's title: the production was 'like a *Lehrstück* . . . a demonstration of a process'. The anti-realistic aesthetic had the effect

---

[43] This rare item is to be found in the Flugblätter der Universität München, Handschriftenabteilung of the University Library, Munich.

[44] *Second Flyer for Peter Weiss's 'Wie dem Herrn Mockinpott das Leiden ausgetrieben wird'*, Akademie der Künste, première 10 July 1968.

[45] *Programme of Peter Weiss's 'Wie dem Herrn Mockinpott das Leiden ausgetrieben wird'*, Akademie der Künste, première 10 July 1968.

of turning the production into a fairytale of sorts and this was picked up by reviewers. Joachim von Mengershausen called it a 'summer winter's tale' and was critical of the production's lack of edge and the deference made to the text.[46] The work was too unimaginative, he continued, except for the portrayal of the government in the style of the three wise monkeys as deaf, dumb and blind prostitutes.[47]

The next project was to involve greater risks and was based on Alfred Jarry's infamous and revered *Ubu Roi*. Schmitt tells that his falling out with the ensemble came as a result of this project. He had wanted to do the same with *Ubu* as Charles Marowitz had done with *Hamlet* in London. He wanted to reduce the text down to its absolute essentials and to cut and paste the speeches in a bid to generate a new relationship to a familiar play. Schmitt wrote a radically shortened version that only required ten actors, and wanted Fassbinder to play the lead. Raben and Fassbinder disagreed with Schmitt's plan and suggested playing two versions, but Schmitt felt that this was against the collective spirit of the group. Schmitt put his foot down and the matter was put to a vote. Schmitt lost by four to six, withdrew his text and left the ensemble.

The fragment of *Ubu Roi* held in the Fassbinder section of the Stiftung Deutsche Kinemathek in Berlin is certainly not the version used for the *antiteater*'s première at the Büchner Theater on 2 August 1968. The forty-page typescript shows evidence of directorial remarks (such as 'contemptuous' or physical details such as 'with his hat and coat') but is not an adaptation of the text.[48] The script may have provided an initial impetus but the production that was to follow bore little resemblance to Jarry. The *antiteater*'s source rewrites *Macbeth* as the inept rebellion of Ubu, an oafish egomaniac, against his king and its disastrous but comic consequences. The play's 1896 première

---

[46] Joachim von Mengershausen, 'Ein sommerliches Wintermärchen', *Süddeutsche Zeitung*, 12 July 1968.

[47] The members of the cast and crew I interviewed all agreed that the show did little to launch the ensemble and that audiences were small throughout its short run.

[48] Cf. Alfred Jarry, *Ubu Roi*, Fassbinder collection, Stiftung Deutsche Kinemathek, Berlin.

in Paris caused a riot through its use of bourgeois-baiting shock tactics, but the *antiteater* found itself aping Jarry more closely than it would have expected in 1968.

Orgie Ubuh (*Ubuh Orgy*, the 'h' was added by the cast) was the show that would establish the *antiteater*, but for reasons that went beyond its artistic merits. As the programme stated, 'the performers themselves have written the text and have the right to use it freely'.[49] The idea was to use the energy and iconoclasm of Jarry's play but to redirect it within a petit-bourgeois milieu. According to Raben, the production was made up of little parlour games that grew in intensity until the characters try to start an orgy but do not really know how to do so. The scene ended in chaos with real glasses thrown around the stage, while Kurt Raab performed a striptease to the chorus of the slaves from Verdi's *Nabucco*. The devising process that led to the final production marked a return to the pop-bricolage of the *action-theater*'s production of *Leonce und Lena*. Items of high and low culture were plundered and deployed within the show. Extracts from Kafka rubbed shoulders with the Rolling Stones and the shout, famous in the FRG, of 'gooooooal!' from the football commentator Herbert Zimmermann on his country winning the 1954 World Cup. This motif situated the action amid a mood of West German national regeneration in the wake of the Third Reich.[50] Fassbinder called the production 'nasty' but 'very amusing', Raben preferred to see it as 'rather wild' (Brocher, p. 69). The attempted orgy appears to have lacked the clarity and the discipline Fassbinder had brought to his *action-theater* direction.

[49] *Programme of the antiteater's 'Orgie Ubuh'*, Büchner Theater, première 2 August 1968. Although one might assume the line is a pre-emptive measure against accusations of copyright infringement, the text bore very little formal similarity to *Ubu Roi*.

[50] This short quotation is significant as it marks the 'readmission' of West Germany into the commonwealth of nations. Fassbinder was to reuse it in his film *Die Ehe der Maria Braun* (*The Marriage of Maria Braun*), his first international hit, in 1978. The audio clip ends the film and leaves the spectator in little doubt that Germany has regained respectability. Film critics have never, however, noted that Fassbinder was redeploying a motif originally used to the same critical ends in 1968.

The première was famously stopped in mid-performance for obscenity by the Büchner Theater's head, Helmut Berninger. Raab's striptease was the trigger.[51] The *Süddeutsche Zeitung* quoted Berninger as saying that he was 'against anything that was obscene or political on stage'.[52] (Yaak Karsunke was to counter that if that was Berninger's view, then he could never stage Büchner's *Danton's Death* in the Büchner Theater.)[53] Berninger's linking of the obscene and the political is indicative of the mainstream conservatism of the period.[54] The exhibition of the body sinned against a social morality that guarded certain political attitudes. Berninger's reaction was met by a chorus of 'Deutschland über Alles' from the actors, which sought to emphasize the wider implications of such conformist morality and politics.[55]

The production itself had been multi-medial. Songs, records and projection were used to situate the petit-bourgeois family within a commodified environment in which even desire and pleasure had a market value. Karsunke admired the socio-political network established in the play but argued that making the unsavoury characters into objects of satire was politically unsound, as they, too, were victims of the system. *Orgie Ubuh* was, however, mainly well received, but it was the 'scandal' of the première and the coverage it generated

[51] The pornography that was projected onto Irm Hermann's chest is another mooted cause, suggested by Brem in Thomas Koch, *Rainer Werner Fassbinder als Theaterregisseur* (unpublished MA thesis: Ludwig-Maximilians-Universität, Munich, 1994), p. 5 of the Appendix. Reviews of the première contradict this version of events. Live nudity has a far more powerful effect than its cinematic reproduction.

[52] Urs Jenny, 'Saubermann greift durch', *Süddeutsche Zeitung*, 5 August 1968.

[53] Yaak Karsunke, 'Das "antiteater" gastiert mit *Orgie Ubuh* im Theater 44', *Kulturspiegel*, Bayerischer Rundfunk, no transmission date supplied.

[54] Brem said the rebellious *Zeitgeist* of 'provocation and the breaking of taboos' was an influential factor in *Orgie Ubuh*.

[55] Cf. Bertram Bock, 'Orgie findet nicht statt', *Abendzeitung*, 3/4 August 1968.

that established the *antiteater*'s presence on the Munich scene, and indeed beyond the city when a syndicated report of the incident made it into other regional newspapers. It was there and then that, according to Schmitt, 'the legend was born'.

The unexpectedly short run did, of course, pose major problems for the ensemble as to where they were to perform. Relations with Strätz were still frosty and her *action-theater* was still closed down. Horst A. Reichel cancelled a show at his own venue, Theater 44, to allow the *antiteater* to perform *Ubuh* the following night, but this hardly solved the problem. The troupe looked further afield and found the backroom of a local pub, just a stone's throw from the university. The Witwe Bolte was to become the *antiteater*'s base and home for the next six months.

Destroying the classics: *Iphigenie auf Tauris von Johann Wolfgang von Goethe* and *Ajax*

The arrangement with the Witwe Bolte at 87 Amalienstrasse in the Schwabing district of Munich was simple. The *antiteater* would have almost unlimited access to the space as long as they kept the bar open to generate revenue for the owner. The only exceptions to this were Thursdays, when the venerable literary group *Katakombe* already had a regular booking. Although the *antiteater* had secured the Witwe Bolte in August in the wake of the *Ubuh* venue crisis, it would be the end of October before the usually prolific ensemble would offer its first production in the new theatre space.

The main problem was finding actors. Many of the *antiteater* founders had either left or were otherwise engaged (two of them, Brem and Krää, were still at school and devoted time to their final-year studies). In the light of the personnel problem, the plan to rewrite Goethe's *Iphigenie auf Tauris* (*Iphigenia on Tauris*, itself a rewriting of Euripides' text) was, in principle, a good tactic: the original only required five actors. Fassbinder cobbled together a small cast of two friends and a friend of a friend, together with Raben and Raab. Raab baled out, but a chance encounter with an old acquaintance from boarding school finally provided Fassbinder with his cast (cf. Brocher, p. 72).

84

While *Orgie Ubuh* joined *Die Verbrecher* and *Pioniere in Ingol-stadt* as another example of Fassbinder's adulteration of a classic text, it was not an example of a *Klassikerzertrümmerung* ('reducing of the classics to rubble') as such. Jarry's play was anarchic and chaotic enough; the rewrite did not challenge that facet of the source. *Ubuh* was rather a radical translation of an original into a very different present-day setting. *Klassikerzertrümmerung* was far more concerned with taking an original and questioning its premises, be they thematic or formal. As we shall see in the next chapter, this practice was primarily located in the field of the direction of classic texts under the sign of the *Regietheater* ('director's theatre'), which was itself only a nascent practice in 1968. Fassbinder's treatment of Goethe was far more, then, a response to the cultural climate of the day as articulated by Enzensberger than jumping on a *Stadttheater* bandwagon, because he was destroying a text at source rather than using the techniques of direction. Fassbinder's 'originality' had already been displayed earlier that year when he wrote the first play about a *Gastarbeiter*, *Katzel-macher*. His formal invention would be further evident in *Iphigenie* and later dramas.

Iphigenie auf Tauris von Johann Wolfgang von Goethe,[56] to give the play its full title, is a far more complex piece than Watson's

[56] Although there are two printed versions of the text (one in the standard edition of Fassbinder's plays and another printed to accompany the production of the play during Fassbinder's stint at the Theater am Turm in 1974), there are two further versions. One is held at the Fassbinder Foundation in Berlin, the other is an actor's copy, supplied to me by Brem, who was in the touring cast in the same city, Christmas 1968. Details and deviations in the Foundation text indicate that it is probably a very early version. It has none of the stage directions found in the standard edition, which are derived from the Witwe Bolte production, whereas Brem's copy does and conforms more or less to the standard edition, although there are some important variations. I shall therefore be referring to Brem's version for the following analysis, as it is almost certainly identical to the text used earlier at the Witwe Bolte. Quotations, where possible, will be taken from the standard edition for the sake of the reader's clarity.

dismissive evaluation of it as 'a topical political satire' allows.[57] *Iphigenie* is called a 'metadrama' by Michael Töteberg and this is an accurate description of the play, in that it presumes a familiarity with Goethe's original in order for an audience to appreciate its critical force.[58] The level of reflection is implicit in the title: the inclusion of Goethe's authorial name already sets up the attack on such authority in the writing by contextualizing the object of criticism: Goethe and his bourgeois humanism.[59] Goethe's drama is usually considered his first work of classicism, which heralded a shift away from the rebellious and iconoclastic works that associated the younger Goethe with the *Sturm und Drang* ('storm and stress') movement and an engagement with a cultured tradition. In Goethe's play we find an ultimately felicitous humanism that triumphs over the barbarian King of Tauris, Thoas, who grants his Greek (and therefore civilized) captive, Iphigenie, her freedom. Notions of truth and love convince Thoas that he must relinquish the woman, whose 'enlightened' influence over him had previously led him to end the practice of ritual sacrifice of all strangers in the land. The plot is driven by the arrival of Iphigenie's brother, Orest, and his companion, Pylades, who help to convince Thoas to release his prisoner, despite his love for her.

Fassbinder sums up the moral of the play in a line given to Arkas, Thoas' underling: 'in Rainer Werner Fassbinder's school exercise book, it says *Iphigenia on Tauris* is a drama about the magnanimity of the mighty. Neues Realgymnasium, 1962' (*Stücke*, p. 97). In 1968 'the mighty' were anything but magnanimous to the APO and its sympathizers.[60] The Berlin Police Chief Duensing had authorized the use of extreme force in dealing with demonstrators at the anti-Shah rally in June 1967, with the tactic: 'we shall treat the demonstrators like a liver sausage: we'll stab them in the middle so that the ends

---

[57] Watson, *Understanding Rainer Werner Fassbinder*, p. 52.

[58] Töteberg, *Rainer Werner Fassbinder*, p. 38.

[59] Fassbinder was to use the same device later in his film *Fontane Effi Briest* which implicated the author, Theodor Fontane, and his milieu in the problems of the work from the outset.

[60] Indeed, this was also the case in Goethe's day. In this sense his version is consciously utopian.

have to burst out'.[61] The courts had acquitted Karl-Heinz Kurras, the police officer who had shot dead the student protester Benno Ohnesorg at the same demonstration. The Grand Coalition had passed its Emergency Laws, and even the *action-theater* had been forcibly closed by the authorities. The magnanimity of which Goethe wrote was still in short supply. The time was ripe for a reconsideration of Goethe's political ethics.

Fassbinder almost totally removes all plotting in his short version. The assumed knowledge of the characters allows them to function more as representatives of various positions on the theme of power and social control. Fassbinder also employs polyphonic delivery, so that as many as four characters might be speaking at the same time, forcing spectators to select an aural focus for themselves. The dynamism of a plot-based drama gives way to what one might call a politicized appropriation of Beckett's static dramaturgies, in that Fassbinder's 'talking heads' are engaging with contextualized, analytical explorations of their own social positions. The characters hardly communicate with each other, rather the audience is exposed to the open conflict of developed and developing stances. Iphigenie's first speech, for example, is an associative text that creates an impression of her existence on Tauris rather than a detailed insight into her psychology: 'grief, tears, love, freedom, suffering, longing, blue, red, crying, music, light, grief, blue, red, music, light' (*Stücke*, p. 96). Although there is some dialogue, the dominant form in the play is the monologue, of characters talking to themselves and the audience. The lack of development of Thoas through humanistic education and the unremitting nature of his cruelty is felt at the play's conclusion. Arkas tries to remember the final words of Goethe's play, in which Thoas speaks of his admiration for Orest, who is supposed to depart with his sister Iphigenie, and bids 'fare well' to the Greeks.[62] But that reconciled ending is not permitted in Fassbinder's version, and Arkas, Orest,

---

[61] Quoted in Aust, *Der Baader Meinhof Komplex*, p. 57. The line is also to be found as a documentary quotation in Brem's copy of *Axel Caesar Haarmann*.

[62] Johann Wolfgang von Goethe, *Iphigenie auf Tauris* (Stuttgart: Klett, 1980), p. 64.

his lover Pylades[63] and Iphigenie simultaneously deliver despondent monologues before the lights go out.

Fassbinder also uses intertext to modify the dramaturgy of the piece. He quotes directly from the Goethe original for a long monologue which is delivered by Orest and echoed in a derisory fashion by the rest of the cast. The section is important because it comes after Orest's seizure in III i in Goethe's play. The seizure, the emotional climax of the five-act original, purges Orest of his despair and sense of persecution, and gives him the positive resolve to conclude the business nobly. The mockery of the speech is part of Fassbinder's broad attack on Goethe, his sentiments and his language.

Elsewhere, Fassbinder continues his intertextual strategy and quotes directly from Mao and Erika Runge, whose *Bottroper Protokolle* are a collection of documentary interviews about life in the town of Bottrop.[64] There is also direct reference to the K1 trial, taken from the *Klau mich* documentation, with Thoas playing the judge, Schwerdtner, and Pylades taking material from both defendants, Teufel and Langhans. The sentences passed by the judge in Brem's script are far more generalized than the detailed prison sentences that follow the dialogues in the standard edition (cf. *Stücke*, p. 111). Thoas, Arkas, Iphigenie and Orest say, 'Nine months prison without parole, ten years penitentiary, workhouse, concentration camp, etc.' Whatever satire one might find in the use of the K1 trial, which tried to present the law as an ass, the inclusion of concentration camps reminds us of the monstrous punishments designed by those in power in the earlier version.

Fassbinder is wont to translate lines into foreign languages, too. English and French are the ones he uses most frequently, possibly reflecting the globalized world in which the production takes place, possibly tying in with a contemporary pop aesthetic, too. A more deliberate use of a foreign tongue is found in a stage direction in Brem's

---

[63] The transformation of Orest and Pylades into a gay couple as opposed to loyal friends is another example of Fassbinder's social provocation.

[64] Erika Runge, *Bottroper Protokolle. Vorwort von Martin Walser* (Frankfurt/Main: Suhrkamp, 1968). A section from 'Erna E., Hausfrau' on p. 49 informs Iphigenie's speech in *Stücke*, p. 104.

script that tells Pylades to speak the following lines in Czech: 'Who is entitled to freedom. Who is entitled to rights. What does friendship mean. What does goodness mean . . .'.[65] The use of Czech was particularly resonant at the time. Alexander Dubček's reformist socialist government had been ousted by Russian tanks following the Prague Spring of 1968, and so the conscious use of a Slavonic language, whose literal meaning is unlikely to have been picked up by very many spectators, would, all the same, signal the political events that were taking place on Germany's doorstep.

As discussed earlier in this chapter, the broad political implications of drama are far more concerned with form than content. Fassbinder's *Iphigenie* is more than just a satire on humanist cultural values, or the wanton destruction of a well-loved classic. It creates space for diverse discourses on the nature and the wielding of power, without being shackled to the demands of a plot that was already familiar to the audience. Fassbinder thanked his hero Jean-Luc Godard on the cover of the programme, and the form owes much to filmic cuts that offer montage as an alternative to the harmony of a tightly plotted play.[66] The intertextual references contextualize the events on stage and rob them of any sense of 'timelessness'. While there is certainly a humorous dimension to the play, its pessimistic denouement does little to leave the spectator with a warm glow, and rather challenges the audience to find a better way to deal with authority than to turn in on oneself. Fassbinder's own example, the dismantling of Goethe, is one solution.

The production itself in the Witwe Bolte was alive with music, as all but the Foundation version of the script suggest. Raben wrote most of this, and was aided by the *action-theater*'s resident technician, Gottfried von Hüngsberg, who composed ambient and

---

[65] This detail appears to confirm that Brem's is the original stage version. Johannes Riebranz, who played Pylades, was in fact a Czech. When Brem played Pylades in Berlin, he was able to use his knowledge of Russian to deliver the lines in that language.

[66] Cf. *Programme of Rainer Werner Fassbinder's 'Iphigenie auf Tauris von Johann Wolfgang von Goethe'*, Witwe Bolte, première 25 October 1968.

Fig. 8. This picture of *Iphigenie* was taken from the 1974 production at the
TAT, and features Irm Hermann as Iphigenia and Kurt Raab as King Thoas.
The cage was, however, a feature of the original 1968 production in Munich.
© Rainer Werner Fassbinder Foundation

discordant electronic material.[67] Karin Thimm praised the musical dimension for its 'atmosphere and . . . passion', and Urs Jenny applauded the way the *antiteater* distinguished itself from the more staid modernist and absurdist 'avant-garde-ism' of the other private Munich theatres.[68] What is noteworthy, however, is that parts of the production were filmed for national television by the Hessischer Rundfunk programme *Titel, Thesen, Temperamente*.[69] The extract shows both the tiny Witwe Bolte stage, little more than a small podium, the fixed pub tables surrounding it and a raised gallery that looked down onto the stage. Iphigenie sits on a garden swing hammock surrounded by a tubular-steel and chicken-wire cage (see fig. 8). The acting is cool and distanced, and when, for example, Thoas and Pylades quote the courtroom dialogue from the K1 trial, they are actually reading the texts from pieces of paper rather than pretending the material is an homogeneous part of the script.

Critics were broadly positive about the production. Karsunke considered it 'a brilliant scenic reflection on the role of an affirmative culture' and concluded, 'whoever wants to find out how we can (and must!) play the classics today should take to the Amalienstrasse'.[70] Urs Jenny was enthusiastic but admitted that the production was not quite firing on all pistons.

Iphigenie also went to West Berlin on Christmas Eve 1968 and played at what might be considered the *antiteater*'s holiday home, the Forum Theater. The brief stay marked the beginning of a relationship that included more invitations in 1969 and the *antiteater*'s final

---

[67] This may be heard on the *antiteater's Greatest Hits*, disc one, track four, 'On Aulis'.

[68] kth (i.e. Karin Thimm), 'Krawall auf Tauris'; and Urs Jenny, 'Enteignet Thoas', *Süddeutsche Zeitung*, 31 October 1968.

[69] Broadcast on 17 November 1968, the section was entitled '*antiteater* – Experiments in Munich' and lasted a little over fourteen minutes. This national profile, however small, probably stems from the *Orgie Ubuh* 'scandal' which, through a syndicated report from the Associated Press, made it to larger papers such as the *Mannheimer Morgen* and *Der Rheinpfalz* (cf. Koch, *Fassbinder als Theaterregisseur*, pp. 20–1).

[70] Yaak Karsunke, '*Iphigenie auf Tauris von Johann Wolfgang von Goethe*', *Kulturspiegel*, Bayerischer Rundfunk, no transmission date supplied.

project together, *Werwolf*. The reception was not entirely warm: the reviewer Günther Grack found the evening incoherent and entitled his article 'Unholy Night'.[71] The assertion, propagated later, that the performance was an affront to Berlin's bourgeois sensibilities does not seem, however, to hold water. Kurt Raab in his sensationalist memoirs recounts that his first line as Orest was 'I wanna fuck you.'[72] Grack did refer to the obscenity he found in the performance, but the Forum Theater, as its list of premières clearly shows, was an avant-garde theatre, unlikely to attract the audience sketched by Raab.[73]

Although *Iphigenie* was followed by a production of Peter Handke's *Hilferufe* (*Cries for Help*), I have chosen briefly to examine Fassbinder's next adaptation of classical material for the sake of contrast, and to return to Handke a little later in the chapter. *Ajax*, a version of Sophocles' tragedy, was presented on 9 December 1968 together with *Der amerikanische Soldat* (*The American Soldier*), the short piece that was cancelled by Horst Söhnlein in January of that year at the *action-theater*. Staged as a beery meeting of soldiers in Bundeswehr uniforms at their regular table in a pub, *Ajax* went down badly, even with staunch supporters such as Karsunke and Mengershausen.[74] The latter said it reminded him more of 'student high jinks', a view shared by Verena Reichel, who said it was more 'farce than discomfort'.[75] Fassbinder, too, was not happy with

---

[71] Günther Grack, 'Unheilige Nacht', *Der Tagesspiegel*, 28 December 1968.

[72] Raab and Peters, *Sehnsucht*, p. 113. The line appears in no edition of the text. Such details are retold and embellished elsewhere, such as in Berling's gossip-ridden book, *Die 13 Jahre*, p. 68.

[73] Cf. Senate of Berlin (ed.), *25 Jahre Theater in Berlin*. The plays staged from 1967 to 1970 were mainly a mixture of absurdism, modernism and those with overtly political themes.

[74] Cf. Yaak Karsunke, '*Der amerikanische Soldat* und *Ajax*', *Kulturspiegel*, Bayerischer Rundfunk, no transmission date supplied; and Joachim von Mengershausen, 'Grabgesänge für Helden', *Süddeutsche Zeitung*, 11 December 1968.

[75] Verena Reichel, 'Klamauk statt Unbehagen', *Abendzeitung*, 11 December 1968.

the play (cf. Brocher, pp. 76–7) and felt that the text and the ensemble needed more time for development in rehearsal.

As yet, we are unable to evaluate the Witwe Bolte text, because it has been lost. The standard edition is the text Fassbinder reworked and hoped to develop in rehearsal for a production in Basle which was abandoned in the 1970/1 season.[76] The typescript in the Fassbinder Foundation acknowledges Raben and Fassbinder as the authors, has a tentative cast list and contains the crucial handwritten note: 'changes to the text during rehearsals are expected'.[77] One can only speculate, then, as to why the original *Ajax* was such a flop, but I would hazard two main arguments. First, Sophocles offers more 'resistance' to the adapter than Goethe. The latter is a much-loved member of the bourgeois literary canon, whose humanist values are far easier to connect with and thus to criticize, because his age heralded Fassbinder's own. The *antiteater* tried to tar Sophocles with the same brush of cultural authority, at least in its publicity flyer, which announced: '*Ajax* is the first of Sophocles' plays to have been awarded a prize from the state'.[78] Sophocles' time is far more distant and far more difficult to relate to our own than Goethe's. The psychological dramaturgy of the late eighteenth century is far removed from the more collective

[76] Cf. usc, 'Basler Schauspielpläne 1970/71', *Neue Zürcher Zeitung*, 26 June 1970, which announces that *Ajax* will be presented in a new version and promises to be 'the most interesting experiment in style of the season'. Reasons for the failure of the production to reach the stage are not known, but Fassbinder's intensive film and theatre work elsewhere was probably a contributory factor.

[77] It can be safely asserted that this version is not the same as the Witwe Bolte original due to another sheet in the Foundation archive. The handwritten opening to *Ajax* is written on the back of a page of script for the film *Whity*, which was made in 1970. The corrections made to the text correspond with the typescript for Basle, which shows the Swiss version postdates the handwritten one.

[78] This is another example of the rare items held in the Flugblätter der Universität München, Handschriftenabteilung of the University Library, Munich, as are the flyer and the promotional sticker for *Hilferufe* mentioned below.

understanding of an individual in ancient Athens, thus making Sophocles' figures harder to appropriate. Second, the same flyer begins with the slogan 'Sophocles is a Fascist'. When one reads this and the reviews that accuse the production of schoolboy humour, one may surmise that the general intellectual level of the piece was somewhat wanting. Sophocles deserved better than easy sloganeering and cheap gags to generate the same counter-cultural effects as with *Iphigenie*.

The drama factory: the fevered productivity of the *antiteater*
The *antiteater* was conspicuous by its prolific work rate; it managed to produce more quickly than the other *Kellertheater* and almost all its productions were based on new writing. As already noted, not only was *Ajax* the second production within six weeks, but it was presented along with the short play *Der amerikanische Soldat* as a double bill, and was preceded by a production of Peter Handke's *Hilferufe* (*Cries for Help*), which was premièred on 17 November 1968. According to Fassbinder, the production of Handke's play was more a bid to woo crowds with a popular iconoclastic playwright than an aesthetic engagement with innovative dramaturgy (cf. Brocher, p. 82). The play is a short experimental piece for an undefined number of actors. The unattributed speeches almost all end in the word 'no', which represents the inability of the speaker(s) to ask for help. By the end, the word 'help' is finally spoken but is repeated so much that it becomes meaningless.

Raben directed and a six-person cast, including Hermann, Fassbinder and Raben, tried their hands at Austria's brightest star. The text of the production reveals almost no change from Handke's four-and-a-half page original; the minor deviations are probably secretarial errors rather than conscious adulterations.[79] This was not a textual adaptation, although the performance itself very much interfered with the original, as we shall see below.[80]

[79] The typescript of *Hilferufe* is to be found in the Fassbinder collection, Stiftung Deutsche Kinemathek, Berlin.
[80] The four-page copy is a fragment. Handke's final lines, in which the play's speakers finally reach the word 'help' are missing from the

A sticker campaign announced the production to the potential audience and a flyer quoted three approving reviews. The *antiteater* was praised for its inventiveness and its ability to generate lively performance from a protean text. All the same, Fassbinder recalled that the audiences were not huge, and the play was not all that enjoyable to be in (cf. Brocher, p. 83). Karsunke gave possible reasons for this. He identified Handke as a navel-gazer, out of step with the political issues of the day, as someone who was more concerned with overly interpreting himself than the situation of people in society.[81] On the other hand, he enjoyed Raben's direction and ideas. Fassbinder continually interrupted the proceedings through a microphone, adding words such as 'action', 'breakfast', 'Springer' and 'Goethe' before allowing the ensemble to return to the text. The climax of the piece, the call for help, was represented by signs held up by the performers, and Fassbinder complemented them by holding up Coca-Cola placards. Although Karsunke praised this ironic move, Handke actually suggests that the performers 'can drink Coca-Cola during the piece' in his notes to the play, so the idea may have come from here.[82] Karsunke called the *antiteater*'s ideas 'funnier and more powerful' than Handke's original text but found that the play itself was too insignificant. With reference to *Iphigenie* he considered, 'one has to knock away classical plaster with a hammer, a pin is all one needs for a soap bubble'.

Read from today's landscape of complex detective movies and knowing nods towards older examples of the genre, *Der amerikanische Soldat* is a none-too-special thriller vignette, which is almost totally unrelated to Fassbinder's film of the same name, shot in

document, which ends at the base of its fourth page. Karsunke's review of the production includes reference to the finale: cf. Yaak Karsunke, '*Der amerikanische Soldat* und *Ajax*'.

[81] Yaak Karsunke, '*Hilferufe* von Peter Handke im *antiteater*', *Kulturspiegel*, Bayerischer Rundfunk, 18 November 1968.

[82] Peter Handke, 'Untitled [Notes to *Hilferufe*]', in Peter Handke, *Stücke*, vol. 1 (Frankfurt/Main: Suhrkamp, 1972), p. 92.

1970.[83] The play tells of a professional killer, Vinz,[84] who spends most of the short play waiting to receive his next contract. When it arrives he is joined by two others who are sent to support him. Chris gets on his nerves by continually asking Vinz about the job, Tony has a silent part throughout. The twist comes at the end, when the cold killer discovers that his target, Terry Franciosa, is a woman. He is unnerved and demands more money. Chris pulls a gun on him and tells him they will continue as usual. Vinz shoots Chris, Tony shoots Vinz, and the play concludes with Tony putting his pistol in Chris's hand (see fig. 9).

As stated in the programme, the plot is lifted from Irving Lerner's film *Murder by Contract* and in many ways is secondary to the rituals that pervade the text.[85] Vinz is directed to train for the hit and to narrate his daily routine throughout the play. Relentless exercise and endless waiting define his day. The central focus is his preparation for murder within the context of the Chicago underworld. The play's repetitive structures, away from the simple plot and the occasional character detail, create an atmosphere of emptiness and obsession. The play's title points to the wider picture: the play obliquely refers to Vietnam, in which soldiers confronted unknown victims, waited and trained for days on end before the call eventually

---

[83] Although Michael Töteberg notes some similarities in Fassbinder's first draft for the film, which were later excised – cf. Töteberg, 'Nachwort', in Töteberg (ed.), *Fassbinders Filme*, vol. ii (Frankfurt/Main: Verlag der Autoren, 1990), p. 247.

[84] The typescript in the Fassbinder Foundation does not diverge from the printed version, except for the occasional pencil replacement of the name 'Vinz' with 'Franz'. Franz, a name used by Fassbinder himself as a pseudonym when editing his films and as a character name in much of the cinema work, alludes to Franz Biberkopf, the flawed hero of Alfred Döblin's novel *Berlin Alexanderplatz*, who was a figure of identification for Fassbinder.

[85] Cf. *Programme of Rainer Werner Fassbinder's 'Der amerikanische Soldat'*, Witwe Bolte, première 9 December 1968. Pinter's *The Dumb Waiter*, which was widely performed in West Germany in the early 1960s, may have also proved an influence, although there is no formal acknowledgement of this in the programme or any utterances made by the *antiteater* group.

Fig. 9. Kurt Raab and Peer Raben are menaced by Fassbinder as the 'American soldier', Vinz. This picture was taken during rehearsals of the aborted production in January 1968: the latticework from *Hands Up, Heiliger Johannes* can still be seen, locating the scene in the *action-theater* and not the *antiteater*. © Wilfried Beege

came.[86] The production was certainly better received than its partner on the double bill, *Ajax*.[87]

[86] There is also a Vietnam connection in the film *Der amerikanische Soldat*. Ricky, the contract killer of the title and the 'soldier' of the title, is also a veteran of the Vietnam war.

[87] Cf. Annemarie Czaschke, '*antiteater* gegen Sophokles & Co', *Frankfurter Rundschau*, 13 December 1968; and Mengershausen, 'Grabgesänge', who, although pleased by the production, was still unhappy at the problems generated by a rushed rehearsal schedule.

In the context of a dirty war, the play presents an interesting comment on the business of the professional killer, be he a gangster or a soldier. Yet even without the link to Vietnam, which is never made explicit, the short work still processes one of Fassbinder's favourite themes, the execution and variation of daily rituals predicated upon violence or oppression. We have already seen these in *Katzelmacher*, and here Fassbinder changes the focus to the individual and not the group. The sublimation of personal satisfaction into a diet of exercise and waiting provides possibilities for contemporary production which might stress the durational and obsessive over the details of plot.

The theatrical energy seen before Christmas 1968 dissipated slightly afterwards, and the next *antiteater* première, *Die Bettleroper* (*The Beggar's Opera*) took place on 1 February 1969.[88] By all accounts this was a great success. Although *Orgie Ubuh* packed the house, *Die Bettleroper* did so not in the wake of a scandal but on its own merits. Particularly in a German context, it is difficult to look on *The Beggar's Opera* without referring to Brecht and Weill's *Die Dreigroschenoper* (*The Threepenny Opera*), but this is precisely what Fassbinder tried to do in his adaptation. He returned to John Gay and decided to modernize the fable, included the odd direct quotation and mainly followed Gay's plotting. Fassbinder retained the main plot, which involves the marriage of Polly Peachum to the highwayman Macheath against her parents' wishes. It also includes Macheath's penchant for prostitutes and the gaoler's daughter, Lucy Lockit, which brings him into conflict with Polly. In Gay, Macheath is finally apprehended and is taken to the scaffold, but a kindly player changes the ending and Macheath is spared. Fassbinder leaves his Macheath, Mecki, to rot in gaol as he is not seen in the final three scenes. His absence brings loneliness and despair to the rest of the cast and by the end all bark like dogs.

---

[88] Peter Berling opines that the reason why there was no activity in January was that Fassbinder had fled Germany after a raid on a gay sauna, in Berling, *Die 13 Jahre*, p. 69. Berling's book, which is often factually incorrect and prefers to sensationalize rather than analyse, offers no evidence for this claim. The following production, *Preparadise Sorry Now*, was premièred six weeks after *Die Bettleroper*, but there is no suggestion that Fassbinder was 'on the run' then.

But this was not the radical reworking of Goethe that Fassbinder had undertaken earlier in the season, and one would find it difficult to call the treatment a *Klassikerzertrümmerung*. Rather, the original is regarded with a certain amount of respect as opposed to the irreverence and criticism directed towards *Iphigenie*. The political backdrop is altered so that Gay's extended satires of the eighteenth century give way to the ridicule of bar-stool Bolshevism and romantic attempts to set up a commune. The cast is reduced to fit the small and unstable *antiteater* personnel: only two whores remain and Macheath's gang is non-existent.

The acting in the production, as is evident from the reviews, exemplifies Fassbinder's distanced style. An excerpt from the original production, recorded live, may be heard on the *antiteaters Greatest Hits* CD, disc one, track three, where Hanna Schygulla shows her ability to present emotion as a quotation, rather than merely acting it out. Mengershausen praised the acting style and concluded that the roles were 'no longer to be consumed', they required active engagement to fathom their complexities.[89]

Music was provided exclusively by Raben, and an example of it can be heard in the excerpt on the CD mentioned above. The 'pop' style of the music reflected the more relaxed and lighter air of this piece, something of a change for the *antiteater*. The many songs in the play, another feature taken from Gay, required musical accompaniment. In the Witwe Bolte production, three people played seven instruments. The drums were played by a new member of the team, Harry Zöttl. Rechristened Harry Baer by Fassbinder in the credits of the film version of *Katzelmacher* later that year, Zöttl was to become a key figure in Fassbinder's films rather than in the theatre. He was a schoolmate of Brem's and filled a gap when the original player, Ralph Enger, was taken ill.

The scenes were still primarily centred on two or three people owing to the problems with space (see fig. 10). This lent the production another playful dimension; the actors were like animals,

---

[89] Joachim von Mengershausen, 'Mecki, der gammelnde Marxist', *Süddeutsche Zeitung*, 3 February 1968.

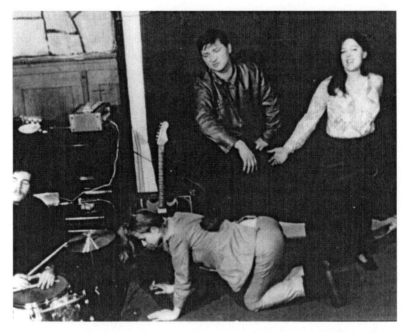

Fig. 10. Fassbinder on top: live music and a 60s take on John Gay for *Die Bettleroper* at the *antiteater*. Hanna Schygulla is on all fours, while Ursula Strätz looks on. © Rainer Werner Fassbinder Foundation

defending their small pieces of territory. The animal theme was also present in the closing lines of the play where the cast descended to the level of dogs and the final lines instructed the principals to bark. This has been used on occasion to support the irrationalist reading of Fassbinder's plays, as when Töteberg claims that this is 'an étude à la Artaud'.[90] What is forgotten here is that it is Peach, Fassbinder's Peachum, who initiates the 'chorus'. In an earlier scene, he had barked away to the two whores, playing the role of an obedient dog. The mass return to an animal state may, of course, indicate a will to cast off sentience or to expose the untamed in the characters, but alternatively, it may refer back to Peach's first manifestation of the canine and thus denote a more conscious movement into submission and role-play. The play is not without metatheatrical narration and

[90] Töteberg, 'Das Theater der Grausamkeit', p. 22.

use of role-playing elsewhere. Czaschke, in her review of the production, said that the *antiteater* was indeed filling the Witwe Bolte as if the Living Theatre were there, a group she, however, found 'too irrational, as opposed to the *antiteater*'.[91] Her remarks suggest that the finale was not exactly a bestial Artaudian orgy.

The text today is not particularly inspiring. Its satires on communal living and middle-class revolt are obvious, and Bavarian dialect is used for laughs rather than for critique as in *Katzelmacher*. Despite the play's occasional forays into the commodification of human feelings, it is far more a work of its time, in that its modernized subject matter is too well rooted in the upheavals of 1968 and its wake.[92] All the same, it was a big hit at the time and helped to raise the theatre's profile. According to Fassbinder, Kurt Hübner, the *Intendant* of the theatre in Bremen, paid *Die Bettleroper* a visit (cf. Brocher, p. 92), and this was to change Fassbinder's theatrical fortunes greatly, as we shall see in the next chapter.

Historicized pessimism: *Preparadise Sorry Now*

Fassbinder followed *Die Bettleroper* with one of his most controversial, most discussed and most performed plays, *Preparadise Sorry Now*, which was premièred on 17 March 1969 in the Witwe Bolte. The play has generated dispute for both the subject matter selected and its coldly formalistic dramaturgy. Fassbinder takes the English Moors Murders of 1963–5 as his focal point but polemically contextualizes the sadistic murder of children within a culture of oppression and exploitation. 'Ian Brady' and 'Myra Hinley' are Fassbinder's means of exploring the nature of violence and cruelty in contemporary society. Fassbinder deliberately changes the real name Hindley to Hinley and that of one of their young victims, Kilbride, to Killbridge subtly to suggest that he is not dealing in real events in the play. David Smith, who was Hindley's brother-in-law and who informed the police of the

---

[91] Annemarie Czaschke, '*Die Bettleroper* als Subkultur', *Frankfurter Rundschau*, 6 February 1968.

[92] Although Firaza does remind us that it is a text that demands performance to do it justice (cf. Firaza, *Die Ästhetik des Dramenwerks*, p. 16).

couple's crimes, is replaced by the character Jimmy. All the same, the very subject matter led to the cancellation of the Manchester and Salford dates of a British tour of the play in 1972 – the audience at venues so near to the moors themselves were not ready for the play.[93]

Raben had asked Fassbinder for a play that could only be realized through performance, one that would have no intrinsic value on the page (cf. Brocher, p. 85). Fassbinder's response was to present Raben, who directed the première, with nothing but four clusters of scenes that could be staged in any order, as long as 'the dialogues between Ian and Myra [were] the centrepiece of the dramaturgy' (*Stücke*, p. 192). Fassbinder's formal invention reached a new level with this answer to Raben's request. The filmic montage aesthetic of *Katzelmacher* and its variation in *Iphigenie* was allowed to reach its logical conclusion, the almost limitless permutation of autonomous scenes.

The first group of scenes consists of six narratives, not attributed to a speaker, which tell part of the story of Ian Brady. Fassbinder took these sections almost word for word from a German translation of Emlyn Williams's book *Beyond Belief*, when it was serialized in the radical journal *konkret*.[94] One should note that the name 'Ian Brady' does not undergo the same treatment as Myra Hindley, John Kilbride or David Smith. This points back to Fassbinder's documentary source for the texts; Fassbinder lifted the texts almost verbatim and retained the real name to acknowledge this. The second group,

---

[93] Cf. Töteberg, 'Das Theater der Grausamkeit', p. 33. Elsewhere, Töteberg notes that the play also caused a scandal in Nuremberg in 1985 (cf. Töteberg, *Rainer Werner Fassbinder*, p. 42). Hindley and Brady still cause controversy today; the UK tabloid press's treatment of the former's death in November 2002 was as rabid and hysterical as at any time during her life. The front cover of *The Sun* on 16 November was titled 'The Devil' and began: 'At last, Myra is where she belongs . . . HELL CHILD killer [sic] Myra Hindley is rotting in hell at last.'

[94] Cf. Emlyn Williams, *Beyond Belief: A Chronicle of Murder and its Detection* (London: Pan, 1968). Töteberg points out that Fassbinder only read the second instalment of the serialization in the 21 October 1968 number, pp. 36–9 (cf. Töteberg,' Das Theater der Grausamkeit', p. 33). This is somewhat typical of Fassbinder's restless creativity.

like the next two, are given French names by Fassbinder. The 'pas de deux' are nine fictitious dialogues between the murderers. The final two include Jimmy. The third group consists of fifteen 'contres', scenes which feature titles such as 'L+M-H' or 'H+K-I'. The letters signify anonymous characters,[95] two of whom gang up against the third in everyday and more extraordinary encounters: two army officers humiliate a corporal, for example, or two doctors discuss unnecessary medical experiments carried out on a now mute patient. The scenes are all very short, and the nine typescripts at the Kinemathek in Berlin reveal that none of them extends beyond one page. It is possible that Fassbinder set himself the formal challenge of articulating a conflict within the dimensions of one page to keep the scenes short and poignant. That the headings 'pas de deux' and 'contres' are taken from ballet indicate that Fassbinder is more interested in relationships than in the individuals involved in their performance, something underlined by the abstract attributions in the 'contres'. The final grouping is the 'liturgiques', 'remembrances of liturgical and cultic cannibalistic texts', as Fassbinder puts it (*Stücke*, ibid.). The typescripts in the Kinemathek clearly mark the scenes as religious 'masses' and are all reminiscent of church rituals. The scenes emphasize the more masochistic sides of Christian worship and often mention blood and sacrifice. Fassbinder commented on these scenes in an interview following a production of the play by Raben in Stuttgart in 1970: 'the Catholic church hasn't only built up an enormous power base for itself but it also demands unconditional submission'.[96]

The potential for assembling the disparate scenes into a whole is seemingly limited by the chronology of events in the narrative sections and in the 'pas de deux', but on closer investigation this is not the case. The play does not offer a full history of the Moors Murderers and therefore requires no temporal straitjacket. The importance of Brady and Hinley lies in their exemplary role as an end point

---

[95] The H and the I may be interpreted as Hinley and Ian if one so desired, but the situations in which the figures appear bear no resemblance to the Moors Murders strand.

[96] Sibylle Maus, 'Die Gesellschaft ändern – aber wie?', *Stuttgarter Nachrichten*, 30 January 1970.

of the viciousness that structures the 'contres' and underlies the 'liturgiques'.

The endless permutations have given rise to the belief that the play is concerned with an understanding of violence as eternal, an integral part of the human condition.[97] The play was dismissed in the German Democratic Republic, as well, for its lack of social dimension. Dieter Krebs, who wrote the afterword to the only edition of Fassbinder's dramas in the GDR, argued that the play was merely a 'messing about with form'.[98] Wolfgang Seibel, too, seems to share the view that the violence is left uncontextualized; 'it [the repetition of the "contres"] stresses that there is no escape from that which is being depicted and heightens the depiction itself. Everything is repeated, everything stays the same.'[99] Yet he continues, 'the openness of the structure does not suggest the absence of direction, diversity does not suggest arbitrariness'.[100] Seibel argues that because situations and not individuals are presented, Fassbinder is focusing on violence as a social phenomenon. Töteberg agrees when he identifies Brecht lurking behind the Artaudian rituals of violence.[101]

The Brechtian emphasis on relationships within a social context is also located in the language Fassbinder deploys in the various groups of scenes. In her analysis of the play, Dagmar Ralinofsky focuses on Brady and Hinley and notes that their use of German is somewhat peculiar. In the text, both speak a stilted and unnatural German.[102] This is linked to the Nazi associations that inform their

---

[97] Cf. Militz, *Media Interplay*, p. 58.

[98] Dieter Krebs, 'Kamikaze oder Die lange Angst des Rainer Werner Fassbinder', in Rainer Werner Fassbinder, *Katzelmacher Preparadise Sorry Now Bremer Freiheit Blut am Hals der Katze* (Berlin: Henschel, 1985), pp. 170–87, here p. 179.

[99] Wolfgang Seibel, *Die Formenwelt der Fertigteile. Künstlerische Montagetechnik und ihre Anwendung im Drama* (Würzburg: Königshausen and Neumann, 1988), p. 174.

[100] Ibid., p. 175.

[101] Töteberg, 'Das Theater der Grausamkeit', p. 29.

[102] Denis Calandra's excellent translation of the play also renders their dialogues in awkward English, in Fassbinder, *Plays* (New York: PAJ, 1985), pp. 127–59.

relationship. Brady develops an obsession with Nazi history and names Hinley 'Hessie' (*Stücke*, p. 200), a reference to Hitler's deputy, Rudolf Hess. Ralinofsky interprets the language of their dialogues as flawed attempts at learning German and understands '[their] language is a scheme of imitation of a reality which no longer exists'.[103] She argues that their identities can only be understood as imitated ones, they are shams who use language in a bid to impose some kind of unity on their personalities.[104] But Ralinofsky is keen to pursue Fassbinder's linguistic usage further. She investigates the use of proverbs as universalizing strategies and the impersonal pronoun 'one' as a normative device for the formation of an identity.[105] We can conclude, then, that language is being deployed in the play to generate normality and a sense of unchangeability, whilst being exposed as a construct. The manufacture of the universal is presented to the spectator for his or her analysis, a Brechtian approach rooted in *Verfremdung*.

The social contexts, primarily located in the man-made institution of the church and the situations of the 'contres', also help to historicize the violence and argue against a universal picture of human cruelty. The 'contres' confront the audience with recognizable scenes of conflict and brutality. They are all presented in naturalistic language and thus evoke scenes as filmic snapshots taken from life, yet the characters are only ciphers, the speeches are attributed to letters rather than names. Power relations, focusing on the monetary and the sexual, point to the deformation of interpersonal relationships as having its roots in structures which are not innately human. Fassbinder combines the abstract, that is, the nameless characters, with the concrete, that is, the situations, in a way that makes the

---

[103] Dagmar Ralinofsky, *Die Gestaltung zwischenmenschlicher Beziehungen im Drama der Moderne. Tradition und Mutation* (Frankfurt/Main: Peter Lang, 1976), p. 47.

[104] Cf. ibid., pp. 45–6. Hanna Schygulla, who appeared in the original Witwe Bolte production, confirmed Ralinofsky's theory when she told me that the performers of Brady and Hinley were asked by Raben to feign English accents in performance.

[105] Cf. ibid., pp. 62 and 57.

anonymous figures on stage functions of the situations and not vice versa. The pessimism, which is unremitting, is contextualized, otherwise Fassbinder could have resorted to more abstract portrayals of conflict, such as the allegorical strategies of medieval morality plays. Fassbinder takes a dialectical view of violence; its sustained presentation reflects the unlikely prospect of a change in the social or political system in the FRG, not humanity's inability to live more peacefully.

There are also two important extra-textual influences on the play. The first is signalled by its title. *Preparadise Sorry Now*, an English neologism, directly takes issue with the more utopian hopes of the Living Theatre's *Paradise Now* production, which suggested that paradise was indeed achievable in the present. Fassbinder is keen to dismiss this reading, but not on the grounds of it never being realizable. Rather he sees the current climate, as defined by the dominance of dehumanizing social structures, as irreconcilable with universal happiness. The other source for the play is the *Volksstück*, which was discussed in greater depth in chapter 1. Torsten Bügner considers the 'contres' and 'pas de deux' as 'the abstraction of the new *Volksstück*'.[106] He continues that the linguistic contradictions in the short scenes owe something to the cleavage in the *Volksstück* between the speaker and the spoken.[107] One may infer that Fassbinder has taken his understanding of the genre, already radicalized in *Katzelmacher*, and distilled it even further, so that the cross-section of society becomes a rapid succession of impressions. There is no need to work on a rounded representation of social types; their abbreviated quotation transfers the emphasis from character to relationship, and redirects the *Volksstück* aesthetic towards the mechanisms of social interaction.

The original production featured five performers who took on the many roles implicit in the script.[108] In addition, Fassbinder played

---

[106] Bügner, *Annäherung an die Wirklichkeit*, p. 121.

[107] Cf. ibid., p. 122.

[108] Fassbinder recommends a cast of five as a minimum and thirty as optimal (*Stücke*, p. 192).

the narrator of the scenes taken from *konkret*. The play's two subtitles, '54 Scenes for a Future Anarchy' and 'The Brutal Game of Elevation and Humiliation – The Liturgy of a Crime' (*Stücke*, p. 720), both omitted from all printed versions,[109] point respectively to the political (a world without capitalist order) and the fictional nature of the play. The set consisted of five oil drums, one per performer, a rubbish dump of human relations. The smallness of the performance space became all the more claustrophobic because movement was severely limited by the drums. Stylization was used exclusively to create a distance between the familiarity of the scenes and the relational dynamics that robbed them of psychological depth.[110]

Raben also chose to double the 'contres' so that each one was performed twice. The same strategy was used in Stuttgart, as well, and Fassbinder commented on that production that 'these scenes are already too tense due to their directness. Through repetition, they stop being just theatre.'[111] Joachim von Mengershausen was struck by the centrality of the language in the Munich production and saw it as the prison within which Brady and Hinley had enclosed themselves. He did, however, criticize the distanced acting style, believing that 'it has the effect of making things dry and didactic, and thus more improving than unsettling'.[112] More contact was required between the stage and the auditorium. In a later review, when the *antiteater* came to Berlin with the production, the reviewer was impressed by the power of the 'less is more' aesthetic.[113] The reception seems in part to have been a matter of taste, but it demonstrates Raben's insistence on withholding

[109] They appear in the apparatus of the *Stücke* volume and not in the actual text.

[110] Schygulla told me that the distance between herself and the role allowed her to ask, 'Is that me? No, I'm not like that. Or am I?' She reflected on herself as an actress of the generation after Auschwitz.

[111] Sibylle Maus, 'Die Gesellschaft ändern'.

[112] Joachim von Mengershausen, 'Bitterböse Moormörder', *Süddeutsche Zeitung*, 19 March 1969.

[113] RSt, 'Faktographie eines Verbrechens', *Der Tagesspiegel*, 11 April 1969.

easy identification in favour of a more complex cerebral and emotional engagement with the material.

Fassbinder and Raben were so fascinated by the text that they took it to two professional stages in 1970, once the *antiteater* had effectively ceased to exist. The production in Darmstadt (première 27 January 1970) was, according to Raben, very similar to the *antiteater* original. The reviews again criticize the production's didacticism, but also praise the acute stylization.[114] The Stuttgart première, which followed Darmstadt by a mere two days, was quite different. Raben chose to stage the play 'more wildly', as a sort of dark 'celebration' in which flowers adorned the stage. Raben wanted to burst out of the 'closed' nature of the Munich and Darmstadt productions. He had lines sung and used a more playful irony to disorientate his audience, thus problematizing the moral dilemmas of the play all the more.

Preparadise builds on Fassbinder's more innovative dramatic practices, which he began with *Katzelmacher* and developed through *Iphigenie*. Its radically free form dispensed with conventional dramatic conceptions of the time in that its elements could be arranged as a director saw fit. The play, as mentioned earlier, is one of the most performed in Fassbinder's oeuvre, and this owes much to the protean nature of its dramaturgy. *Preparadise* marks another high point in Fassbinder's work as a playwright and reflects his ability to create new forms and to furnish them with a sharpness of linguistic detail that had already characterized his other major plays.

Not with a bang: the demise of the *antiteater*

If one reads the cast lists of the *antiteater*'s productions, there is little to suggest a stable ensemble. Of the ten founding members, Fassbinder and Raben were the only constants. Others had left or had other commitments which meant they only appeared sporadically in the productions. The *antiteater* had an identity problem, and this was evident in its final productions.

The Witwe Bolte, itself one of the few stable elements for the company, was temporarily relinquished when the larger *Stadttheater*,

---

[114] Cf. Georg Hensel, 'Monster-Modelle', *Theater heute*, 3/1970, p. 14.

the Münchner Kammerspiele, offered the *antiteater* its studio theatre, the Werkraum, for a production in June 1969. August Everding, the *Intendant* of the Kammerspiele, had wished for a more regular relationship with the local group that was attracting national attention, but the nature of that arrangement was too constricting according to Fassbinder (cf. Brocher, p. 86). Everding considered the company to be an enlivening factor in West German theatre because of its energy and its imperfections. He saw the quality of the work as a critique of the 'Leistungsgesellschaft', which roughly translates as 'a society based on achievement'.[115] The *antiteater* took *Die Bettleroper* and a new play, *Anarchie in Bayern* (*Anarchy in Bavaria*), to the Kammerspiele. *Die Bettleroper* was received well, whereas *Anarchie* garnered a mixed bunch of reviews.

According to Fassbinder (cf. Brocher, p. 86A), he wrote *Anarchie* after shooting his first full-length film, *Liebe ist kälter als der Tod* (*Love is Colder than Death*). The filming in April 1969 explains the gap in the *antiteater*'s production history, and the role of filming in general over the coming years would continually shift the emphasis of Fassbinder's work in the arts.

Anarchie is a satire on the difficulties of adjusting to life after massive social upheaval. The anarchist revolution in Bavaria is easily made and has already been achieved by the third of the twenty-two scenes: Bavaria cuts itself off from the FRG and declares its independence. Life in the new society is far more difficult and the play is mainly concerned with the attitudes and mindsets of the old system, represented by Familie Normalzeit ('the Normality Family') in the face of a new one. The problems are illuminated in the flyer that accompanied the production: '*Anarchy in Bavaria* is directed against a revolution "on the quick", and pleads for a "long march", a revolution in the consciousness of the revolutionaries and the citizens.'[116] The 'long march' quotes student leader Rudi Dutschke (rather than

---

[115] Everding's opinions can be heard on the *antiteater's Greatest Hits*, disc one, track two.

[116] *Flyer for Rainer Werner Fassbinder's 'Anarchie in Bayern'*, Münchner Kammerspiele, première 14 June 1969.

Mao) and his belief that a lasting social revolution could only take place over time as opposed to being forced by violence and sudden legislative overkill.

The text itself is incomplete. Its published version is missing the final two scenes, the 'Occupation Speech', which was delivered by Fassbinder, and the 'Conclusion'.[117] In addition, there is an important piece of dialogue missing in the nineteenth scene that appears in the typescript in the Kinemathek, Berlin. The omitted passage refers back to an earlier scene in which the new authority suggests the new republic's most serious punishment: banishment to the FRG. The passage deals with a murderer who has killed a child and is threatened with expulsion. It also plays with ideas of surface normality and inner criminality. The conclusion has, however, been preserved on Joachim von Mengershausen's documentary, *Ende einer Kommune* (*End of a Commune*), to which I shall return below. The sequence is centred on the ritual repetition of the mantra 'and – go – stop – kill – freedom', all delivered in English. The realization of liberation through violence is a motif that presents itself in several of Fassbinder's works.

The flyer called the play a 'revue', and this indeed describes its form. It is more 'scenes from a revolution' than a tightly plotted chronicle. The characters also help dislocate the 'realism' of the piece. Fassbinder uses typologized names such as The Great Chairman, The Mother of all Whores and The Child Killer, but also more suggestive ones like Married With a Car, Old Romantic Love Female (and Male), and Phoenix Normality. The allegorical figures present clashes of ideology as numbers in a revolutionary revue. While Firaza is right to state that 'the play is a satire on the fixation on order and authority, which excludes any form of change or resistance', we should linger on the ways in which the satire is articulated.[118] Fassbinder's fascination with language is again evident in his observation of linguistic forms

---

[117] A complete 'map' of the scenes and their performers is found in the play's programme.

[118] Joanna Firaza, 'Flucht vor Mimesis: Rainer Werner Fassbinders *Anarchie in Bayern*', in Sascha Feuchert (ed.), *Flucht und Vertreibung in der deutschen Literatur. Beiträge* (Frankfurt/Main: Peter Lang, 2001), pp. 239–48, here p. 243.

and their relationships to modes of action. The scene 'Revolution in the Loudspeaker' reproduces the clichés and cadences of government-sponsored radio, criticizing the insurgence in Bavaria. Two revolutionaries enter during the announcement and hand the speaker a new text, which merely continues the clichés whilst superficially changing the content. The 'Speech of the German Chancellor' also targets ideologically driven linguistic abuse. Fassbinder substitutes the real Chancellor, Kurt Kiesinger, with a version of Franz Josef Strauss, the prominent Bavarian conservative, whose own dreams of becoming chancellor were later dashed in 1980. The Chancellor reuses or slightly modifies Nazi phrases in the scene, as when he exhorts the new republic to come 'Home to the Federation!' (*Stücke*, p. 307) which echoes Hitler's call for annexed lands such as Austria to come 'Home to the Reich'. The Chancellor's use of Nazi phrases shows that his mindset has not moved on from that period. Yet despite the sensitivity of the satire to the language of revolution, the targets are not terribly subtle and the play as a whole is more rooted in its time, just like *Die Bettleroper*. The play does not exhibit the formal flexibility of *Katzelmacher* or *Preparadise* which has allowed them to resonate beyond their original contexts.

The première itself was marked by tightly choreographed movement and arrangement of the actors to emphasize the nature of the conflict between the old and the new. The large stage of the Werkraum was divided into seven sections to signify changed locations because there was no actual set to speak of.[119] Music and dance were used to suggest the link between the slush of popular culture and the closed minds of the figures on stage. The feeling among the critics, however, was that the *antiteater* was out of its depth. They felt that the stage of the *Stadttheater* was simply too big, and that the use of space exposed the troupe's inexperience of such venues (see fig. 11).[120] The obviousness of Fassbinder's satirical critique also drew brickbats of

[119] The hand-drawn groundplan was lent to me by Rudolf Waldemar Brem and may also be viewed in the Kinemathek in Berlin.

[120] Cf. Urs Jenny, 'Chaos macht Spass', *Süddeutsche Zeitung*, 16/17 June 1969; and Alf Brustellin, 'Heisse Plattheiten', *Stuttgarter Zeitung*, 20 June 1969.

Fig. 11. *Anarchie in Bayern* (*Anarchy in Bavaria*) gave the *antiteater* its first chance to perform on a large, well-equipped stage. The bare set may well have emphasized the artifice of the production but it also pointed to the penurious state of the company's finances. © Rainer Werner Fassbinder Foundation

its own from the same and other critics.[121] The praise was for the performers whose approach was considered robust and lively, but the lingering feeling was that the material itself offered too little 'resistance' and thus made for an evening that did not engage with its subject matter in a thorough or complex way.[122] The *antiteater* returned to West Berlin later in 1969 to perform the play at the Forum Theater, where the reviews were little different from those in Munich.

The ensemble was in Berlin at the end of June for the Berlin Film Festival, at which the German entry was Fassbinder's *Liebe ist kälter als der Tod*. Later, during a trip to Paris, Brem suggested that the next film project should be a version of *Katzelmacher*

[121] Cf. Hans Bertram Bock, 'Nacht der langen Messer', *Abendzeitung*, 16 June 1969; or Dietmar N. Schmidt, 'Gescheiterte Kommune', *Die Welt*, 27 June 1969.

[122] Jenny, 'Chaos macht Spass'.

(cf. Brocher, p. 94). Although Fassbinder was casting the *antiteater* actors in his films, his stage stars, with the notable exception of Hanna Schygulla, were not, at this time, being groomed for the screen. Fassbinder's absences from the Witwe Bolte allowed other members of the ensemble to try their hand at direction. The results were not entirely successful.

In late July 1969, Kurt Raab directed his version of Schiller's classic *Don Carlos*. Although Raab would win plaudits later in his career as a director at the Theater am Turm in Frankfurt, he presented something of a ham-fisted *Klassikerzertrümmerung* in Munich. The focus was on 'securing the relations of power between youth and the older generation'.[123] The action was reduced to the way power was exercised within the Spanish court, although visual gags were also employed. The production was set in a tenement kitchen and the relationship between Carlos and the Marquis of Posa was little more than an unsubtle gay affair. By his own admission, Raab said he was working 'in the manner of Fassbinder', something the reviews bear out, although the quality of the reproduction was somewhat lower.[124] Raben called the production 'unconsidered'. There was, however, a second element to the evening, *Gewidmet Rosa von Praunheim* (*Dedicated to Rosa von Praunheim*), based on Praunheim's film *Rosa Arbeiter auf goldener Strasse* (*Red Workers on the Streets of Gold*), in which two East German citizens find the streets of West Berlin paved with nothing but misery. The short dumb show was directed by Fassbinder against a musical background of Mozart and Elvis. In a note in Mengershausen's review, which lauded the wordless piece, he regretted that the Witwe Bolte was to start charging the company rent, a sign that the *antiteater* would soon have to face up to new financial and logistical problems.

After Raab, Brem saw his chance to take the director's chair. He chose *Herr Peter Squenz* (*Mr Peter Quince*), Andreas Gryphius's baroque comedy after *A Midsummer Night's Dream*. Although there

[123] Joachim von Mengershausen, 'Für R. von Praunheim und F. von Schiller', *Süddeutsche Zeitung*, 23 July 1969.
[124] Raab, *Sehnsucht*, p. 138.

is no documentary evidence to confirm the date, it would seem that the première was a rushed one, most probably following *Don Carlos* in July 1968.[125] The short run of three nights does not seem to have generated any press reviews. The comments from the actors themselves reveal that there was little merit in the production. Brem complained that he was simply unable to get good performances out of his actors, Fassbinder called it 'not worked through and unfermented' (Brocher, p. 101), and Raben found it little different from 'student theatre'. Fassbinder at least admired Raab's *Carlos* for following the *antiteater* sensibility because it had 'a style of its own' (Brocher, p. 102).

The final 'independent' production was given in September 1969. Ursula Strätz, who had appeared in *Die Bettleroper, Anarchie* and *Carlos*, adapted Wedekind's *Lulu* plays and directed her version, *Lulluhh*. Dubbed a 'nudical' by one reviewer,[126] the acting was generally considered to be of a high standard, but was again let down by the weaknesses of the adaptation. There were no teeth to the production and it is difficult to ignore the similarities to the reception of *Anarchie*. *Lulluhh* was performed as a double-bill with the *antiteater* favourite *Orgie Ubuh*, but there was a definite sense that the company was flogging at least a dying horse.

All of the above productions featured *antiteater* regulars, but, with the exception of *Gewidmet Rosa von Praunheim*, Fassbinder is conspicuous by his absence. Although the acting skills in the productions were continually praised, direction and dynamism were lacking. The attempts at quick fixes lacked focus and the *antiteater* was exposed as a first-rate ensemble that could achieve little without the creative input of Fassbinder or Raben. By September 1969, Fassbinder had been seconded to the Bremer Theater, as we shall see in the following chapter, and his cinematic ambitions were beginning to find the

---

[125] Fassbinder reports that it was after the first shoot for Schlöndorff's *Baal*, in which Fassbinder played the lead, and before the filming of *Katzelmacher* in August (cf. Brocher, p. 101).

[126] Ernst Günther Bleisch, 'Neuer Lyrikerjob: Tango tanzen in der Witwe Bolte', *Münchner Merkur*, 8 September 1969.

means through which they could and would be realized. The *antiteater* was to perform one last time in the Witwe Bolte, an export of a production from Bremen. Yet before we follow Fassbinder as he began to establish himself as a theatre director of national stature, we should not forget the *antiteater*'s last stand, *Werwolf* (*Werewolf*).[127]

Harry Baer told me that the project had started out as his plan for a film script but Fassbinder's influence turned it into a play. The idea was for the two to write scenes, 'each one for itself' according to Baer, and for Fassbinder and Baer to work independently of each other. The joint writing process was supposed to set the tone for the collective development and direction of the scenes. The hope, to return to a model of shared production, did not last long. The actors, Raab, Hermann, Ungerer, Baer and Peter Moland, sought a director in Fassbinder and not a facilitator for collective work. Hermann maintained that 'everyone was looking for a boss'. Fassbinder refused the role and insisted on developing the co-operative process in order for the group to develop (cf. Brocher, p. 115).

The germ for *Werwolf* was the story of a young man who had become a mass murderer in the middle ages. The Enlightenment impulse behind the writing was to contextualize the story. As Fassbinder put it: 'we were trying to make quite clear why we thought that someone would become a murderer in the fifteenth century. That is, in a time when you don't become a murderer through mass media like the TV or magazines, but possibly as a protest against society' (Brocher, p. 114). The dialectical investigation was to take place in the free montage form of *Preparadise*.

The programme reports that the idea was discussed on 12 November 1969, that the play was completed on 2 December, and that rehearsal started in earnest thereafter.[128] The production was

---

[127] As we shall see, the *antiteater* banner was to be raised on occasion in 1970 and one final time for the production of *Blut am Hals der Katze* in 1971, but it would be difficult to call the group a company as such.

[128] Cf. *Programme of Harry Baer and Rainer Werner Fassbinder's 'Werwolf'*, Forum Theater, Berlin, première 19 December 1969.

Fig. 12. A sheep in wolf's clothing: as this picture shows, there was little dynamism in the *antiteater*'s final full production, *Werwolf*, at the Forum Theater, Berlin. Repetitious rituals and stasis marked the show as one that garnered very little praise. © Frank Roland Beeneken

premièred at the Forum Theater on 19 December 1969, owing to a paying Christmas booking at the Witwe Bolte. That the production came to Munich for one weekend at the beginning of February 1970, and to the Kammerspiele at that, indicates that the *antiteater*'s theatrical links with its hometown and its regular venue were all but severed. The speed of the production process was fast, but not unusually so for either Fassbinder or the *antiteater*. The collective project, however, failed miserably.

Extended use of ritualized movements and prayers against a background of scenes that did not have the same thematic cohesion as *Preparadise* or *Katzelmacher* before them made for confusion and fatigue in the audience (see fig. 12). Again, the lack of direction led to critics accusing the ensemble of going through the *antiteater* motions, as it had with the minor productions that preceded the première.[129] The botched combination of ideas was summed up by Hellmuth Kotschenreuther as 'Oberammergau plus Grand Guignol plus Marxist environmental theory'.[130]

The failure of the production and the fault lines it exposed meant, as Fassbinder said, that 'it was no surprise that we had nothing to do with the theatre for a long, long time afterwards' (Brocher, p. 115). The *antiteater* was a spent force. Its final productions traded on its reputation and an approach to theatre that was unable to move on. The real split with many of the old ensemble started with *Werwolf* and reached a climax during the filming of *Whity* in April 1970.[131] The problems were nonetheless visible in Mengershausen's documentary, *Ende einer Kommune*.

The film, shot during the bulk of 1969, was to chronicle the fortunes of an ensemble Mengershausen admired. The director told me that he thought he was making a film about a 'radical left-wing theatre group' but found that history had overtaken him. The documentary followed the *antiteater* from *Anarchie* in Munich via the Berlin Film Festival to Bremen and featured *cinéma vérité*, interviews and Raben delivering his thoughts on what the *antiteater* stood for straight to

---

[129] Cf. Karena Niehoff, 'Schaf im Wolfspelz', *Süddeutsche Zeitung*, 22 December 1969; or Lucie Schauer, 'Der Mensch – des Menschen Wolf', *Die Welt*, 22 December 1969.

[130] Hellmuth Kotschenreuther, 'So strapaziert man das geduldigste Publikum', *Abendpost*, 29 December 1969.

[131] Fassbinder's letter written to what was left of the *antiteater* ensemble and other members of the cast of *Warnung vor einer heiligen Nutte* (*Beware the Holy Whore*), 14 September 1970, expresses the end point of the collective endeavour. *Warnung* was an attempt to film the filming of a film, based on the none-too-favourable experiences making *Whity*. The letter reflects on the inability of the group to work on 'claims on the matter [collective production], which have not been fulfilled (or are not fulfillable) in the course of time'. The appellation, 'Dear Friends or Comrades or whatever', signals an irony or a cynicism in Fassbinder, depending on one's view. The letter was shown to me by one of its recipients, Rudolf Waldemar Brem.

camera. The documentary was not popular with Fassbinder, Raben or most of the rest of the group. Fassbinder was given to believe that Mengershausen was going to allow the *antiteater* some say over the final edit of the film. This was not the case, and when it was first transmitted on 2 February 1970, the continuity announcer had to read out a disclaimer written by Mengershausen stating the differences in editorial opinion and the fact that the group was opposed to the broadcast. Fassbinder did not like the way he was portrayed in the film as a linchpin, as the central figure. Raben objected to the lack of documentation of important processes that gave what he considered to be a distorted view of the collective. It is difficult to determine whether this was the case. Mengershausen was not a sensationalist film-maker who wanted to expose the antics of a left-wing theatre group, but it may have been that the sequences in which the collective visibly frays were not offset by more felicitous moments.

The *antiteater* was certainly caught at a fascinating point in its life cycle. The earliest material comes from the optimism surrounding the production of *Anarchie* in Munich. The viewer also sees Fassbinder rehearsing his actors in the same play for a tour in Bremen, Fassbinder answering his critics at the Berlin Film Festival and viewing a rehearsal of his play *Das Kaffeehaus* in Bremen. The most fascinating sequence, however, is the final one, in which the ensemble reflects on its working methods and its identity. The desire to define itself as a collective and the contradictions involved in the process present a group on the verge of collapse. It is likely that the discussion was filmed in late October 1969, just before a touring performance of *Anarchie* in Bremen, two months before the *Werwolf* debacle.

Fassbinder had achieved much with the *antiteater*. It had given him a forum to develop both his playwriting and directorial skills. His willingness to engage with forms that owed much to the editing practices of the cinema made certain of his plays sharp and fresh, and they endure today in the repertoires of theatres both in the German-speaking countries and further afield. Where he was less successful, there is still evidence of a closeness to linguistic detail which would accompany his writing for many years to come and which would be adapted to the different genres he would approach, as we shall see in chapter 3. But the *antiteater* also had its limitations; its anarchic freedom came at a price. A lack of sustained funding meant that the ensemble fluctuated and the precariousness of their 'regular' venue meant that a talent like Fassbinder would almost inevitably find himself drawn to the luxurious apparatus of the *Stadttheater*.

3 Beyond Bavaria

A new impulse: the emergence of *Regietheater* and the theatre in Bremen

Surveying the West German theatre scene in the mid-1970s, Michael Patterson wrote: 'if there are any stars in the German theatre, then they are the directors'.[1] The modern German theatre system that emerged with the Weimar Republic and was divided by the coexistence of two states on German soil during the Cold War was well funded and decentred, as discussed in chapter 1. These two defining qualities have had a number of effects that have distinguished the German theatre from others in Europe. One of these was and is the raised profile of the director in the creative process at the expense of the more usual regard for leading actors. Although one still finds popular actors as centres of attention, there is little doubt that directors hold sway in the German theatre today as they have for several decades.

Highly subsidized theatre has allowed directors to challenge the sanctity of the text since the early years of the Weimar Republic. Leopold Jessner's version of Schiller's *Wilhelm Tell* in December 1919 was followed by a string of productions that called accepted readings of classic and canonical plays into question. Erwin Piscator also contributed to the tendency with a ground-breaking reinterpretation of Schiller's *Die Räuber* (*The Robbers*) in September 1926. Freed from the pressure to sell tickets and fill theatres, directors could interrogate the text in innovative ways. Radical approaches and striking styles were defined by the influence of the director rather than that of the text or

---

[1] Patterson, *German Theatre Today*, p. 8.

the cast. The director became the main draw. The decentralized nature of the theatre system, discussed in chapter 1, also helped to marginalize the cult status of the actor. Although there were and certainly are stars, a factor that is linked to the German film and television industries, actors found it hard to establish themselves in their own right. Character-actors are fêted for their interpretations in theatres where the influence of the director is more covert and where financial factors lead to less experimental, safer and more naturalistic production aesthetics. In the director-centred system, however, the actors, although frequently praised in reviews, become more a function of the directorial style than interpreters themselves. The decentred nature of the system has the effect of making it doubly difficult for an actor to attain national standing. Not only does the actor have to shine in one theatre among many, but he or she also has to eclipse the director's production. When major directors change their (geographical) position, it is almost customary for them to take to their next engagement those elements of their troupes with whom they have had the most productive relationships. Well-regarded actors often follow the directors who made them, and it is not uncommon to hear some of the major German actors referred to as 'Peymann actors', 'Zadek actors', or, as was, 'Fassbinder actors'.[2] *Theater heute*, the premier theatre magazine in Germany, is still wont to draw attention through its headlines to directors rather than actors on its front pages today.

Even though the immediate post-war situation in West German theatres was not experimental in any concerted sense – we remember Gustaf Gründgens' comments on being faithful to the text, quoted in chapter 1 – the director was still the dominant figure. Gustav Sellner, Saladin Schmitt and Gründgens were nationally regarded keepers of the classical tradition and were major figures whose

---

[2] In fact, there are actors today who were so central to Fassbinder that they are still referred to in such terms. Hanna Schygulla is one of them, regardless of her achievements after Fassbinder's death. And when Kurt Raab, for example, became West Germany's first 'star' AIDS victim in the late 1980s, he was always regarded as a 'Fassbinder actor' in the coverage, even though the director died in 1982 and had broken with Raab in 1977.

reputations have eclipsed almost all those of the actors they worked with. Yet, come the 1960s, as we have already seen, all was not well with either the *Stadttheater* or the *Intendanten* who ran them. Theatres were not delivering the sort of productions that reflected the substantial changes in the fabric of West German society. That is, most theatres were not. A hitherto unremarkable theatre in Bremen, in the north-west of the FRG, would reactivate the impulses of the Weimar Republic in the early 1960s and help to redefine the nature of theatrical production in West Germany as a whole.

It was in 1962 that Gründgens left the theatre in general and the *Intendanz* of the Schauspielhaus Hamburg in particular, and Kurt Hübner took over the theatre in Bremen. This coincidence marks a symbolic movement in the West German system, as we shall see below. Hübner was possibly the most important person in the system in the 1960s, although it was not primarily as a director that he established his reputation as one of the great German theatre reformers. Having served as *Intendant* in Ulm for three years, he was appointed in the same capacity to the little-known Bremer Theater to start in the 1962/3 season. Bremen enjoyed little prestige at the time: its subsidies were low and the quality of its productions had never put it on the FRG's theatrical map. With Hübner at its helm, the institution gained a national profile that made it one of the most important theatres in West Germany until 1973, when Hübner was ousted by the machinations of local politics.

Hübner's genius lay in his ability to gather together some of the most imaginative, creative theatre workers and provide them with the means to explore their art in ways that were largely unfettered by financial or aesthetic constraints. The two partners who accompanied Hübner from Ulm were the director Peter Zadek and the set designer Wilfried Minks. Peter Palitzsch, one of Brecht's collaborators at the Berliner Ensemble, was also part of the early team, but Hübner's decision to appoint Zadek and not Palitzsch *Oberspielleiter* (roughly: 'head director') set the tone for the work that was to follow in that Hübner opted for the creativity of Zadek instead of the politics of Palitzsch. As Peter Iden notes: 'Hübner's programme was always emphatically anti-ideological. He placed importance on the autonomy of the work of art and of the artists whom he, with a keen sense for their innovative worth, brought to Bremen.'[3] This is not to say that the Bremen theatre produced apolitical art for art's sake – its political function was far more formal, in that it changed modes of perception and thus challenged existing and accepted structures of meaning.

In the first phase of its new life, driven by the energy of Zadek and Minks, the theatre probed the classics and engaged with new writing. Zadek's family had fled the Nazis in 1933 and lived in exile in England. Zadek, having studied briefly in Oxford, trained as a director under Tyrone Guthrie at the Old Vic in London in 1946. Having worked for the BBC and experienced English rep, he directed the world première of Genet's *Le Balcon* in London in 1957, which, despite the author's vociferous protests, became a great success. Zadek returned to Germany a year later with a wealth of experience acquired from a very different theatrical environment. His first production at Bremen, Brendan Behan's *The Hostage*, set the tone for a new attitude to theatre in that elements of popular culture were mixed with a serious engagement with the play's subject matter. Zadek's freshness of approach would reach its apogee in his production of *Measure for Measure* (1967). Zadek's interpretation of the play still counts today as one of the great productions of the century in Germany. Begun as an attempt to treat Shakespeare realistically, the process presented 'the discovery of a body language', which produced an eminently 'unliterary theatre'.[4] The treatment of the text, wrote Rolf Michaelis, resulted in 'a shock and "happening" theatre in the style of a "comic-strip revue"'.[5] He continued that this production marked the beginnings of the rebirth of the German *Regietheater* ('Directors' Theatre').

The production was designed by Minks, whose influence in German theatre is equivalent to that of Brecht's friend and colleague

---

[3] Peter Iden, *Die Schaubühne am Halleschen Ufer. 1970–1979* (Munich and Vienna: Carl Hanser, 1979), p. 19.

[4] Anonymous commentary on Peter Zadek's *Measure for Measure*, in Burkhard Mauer and Barbara Krauss (eds.), *Spielräume – Arbeitsergebnisse. Theater Bremen 1962–73* (Bremen: Theater Bremen, 1973), p. 171. Volume hereafter referred to as '*Bremen*'.

[5] Michaelis, 'Von den Barrikaden in den Elfenbeinturm', p. 8.

Caspar Neher. Minks pushed the boundaries of representational sets and moved into more associative spaces. He altered the nature of the theatrical space and thus changed the audience's experience of the productions therein. Set design became 'a challenge to the director', an autonomous sign-system, removed from its more conventional role of supporting or complementing a production.[6] Günther Rühle understood the role of the actors in a Minks set as either living props or live defiance of their environment.[7] *Regietheater* as a whole reprocessed theatrical signs in all their forms, be they acting style, lighting, sound or set, in order to offer resistance to standard consumption of the text. The challenge to more harmonious and established conventions was political by its very nature in that it refused to accept orthodoxies left unquestioned in other theatres.

But Zadek was not the only director capable of rewriting the rulebook in Bremen. Possibly the most celebrated reinterpretation of a classic was Peter Stein's *Torquato Tasso*, a production based on Goethe's play about the Italian poet, which was premièred in March 1969.[8] Although Rühle points out that Stein owed much to the highly developed acting ensemble and to the approaches taken to the classics in previous productions by other directors at the theatre, he nonetheless concludes that the production was a landmark in the FRG's theatrical history.[9] Stein's direction activated a play considered to be all but unstageable owing to its lengthy speeches and lack of action, and processed it in the light of the debates in and around 1968 about the efficacy of art in a class society. Iden maintained that the production was 'pervaded by a deep scepticism towards art and the possibility of the theatre having any sort of effect'.[10] The production

[6] Erich Emigholz, 'Erst lauter Namen, dann ein Begriff', in *Bremen*, pp. 244–55, here p. 246.

[7] Günther Rühle, 'Der Wille, der Spass, die Phantasie und die Kunst', in *Bremen*, pp. 232–43, here p. 235.

[8] Cf. Johann Wolfgang Goethe et al., *Torquato Tasso. Regiebuch der Bremer Inszenierung*, ed. Volker Canaris (Frankfurt/Main: Suhrkamp, 1970) for a full version of the director's script and additional materials.

[9] Cf. Rühle, 'Der Wille', p. 235.

[10] Iden, *Die Schaubühne*, p. 24.

demonstrated the level of intervention available to a modern director without his wilfully destroying the original. Erich Emigholz summed up the creative thrust of the theatre in Bremen by asserting that, 'it isn't the dead (poets) who are making theatre that is to appear today, but the living'.[11]

Regietheater, according to Rühle, developed in two broad directions in the late 1960s and 1970s. One direction 'leads back to an unformalized freedom and spontaneity of the elementary bedrocks of the theatre', a category into which he placed Zadek.[12] The other direction 'desires the most extreme intellectual concentration, which claws its way behind the surface of appearances and which is predicated upon the distinctive, emphatic image of itself with lofty magical or intellectual contours'.[13] *Regietheater* was both sensual and cerebral, plumbing the text for impulses that went beyond the bourgeois functions of the theatre, such as providing cultured entertainment or education for its audience.[14]

Back in Bremen, the first phase of that theatre's rise came to an end with the departure of Zadek in 1967. The second began with Hübner's shrewd replacement of his missing star with a welter of new talent. Hübner's research and experience led him to appoint new directors, who included Peter Stein, Klaus Michael Grüber, Hans Neuenfels, Hans Hollmann and Rainer Werner Fassbinder, all of whom were to influence the FRG's theatre with their differing yet enlivening approaches over the next decades. Hübner set himself the task of locating young directors, even though he may have found them 'uncomfortable' to work with because of their views.[15] Yet for all his administrative and indeed creative flair, Hübner was still an

---

[11] Emigholz, 'Erst lauter Namen', p. 244.

[12] Günther Rühle, *Anarchie in der Regie? Theater in unserer Zeit*, vol. II (Frankfurt/Main: Suhrkamp, 1982), p. 119.

[13] Ibid., pp. 119–20.

[14] The past tense is used to here indicate that *Regietheater* itself has evolved over time. Current impulses in directors' theatre have moved away from their earlier incarnations, primarily in the development of a postdramatic theatre.

[15] Emigholz, 'Erst lauter Namen', p. 248.

Intendant who would not have his authority undermined, as we shall see in chapter 4, when we consider the notion of *Mitbestimmung* ('collective decision-making').

Hübner's 'acquisition' of directors also demonstrates the central value and power of this profession in the West German system. Given the emphasis on the centrality of the director which had been established in the second decade of the twentieth century, perpetuated during and in the wake of the Third Reich, and redefined in the FRG at the end of the 1960s, the job was at a premium in theatres hungry to raise or uphold their reputations. Although directors would normally work under contract for an *Intendant* (if they were not the *Intendant* already), a growing number found themselves in such demand that freelance or guest directors could pick and choose where they worked and for how long. Fassbinder, never one to be tied to very much for very long, was one such director. In this chapter we shall follow him as he established himself as a director of national stature in Bremen, through commissions in Nuremberg and Darmstadt, to West Berlin, where he directed one last time for Hübner.

Welcome to the machine: Fassbinder as adaptor and director of *Das Kaffeehaus* in Bremen

Hübner took a hands-on approach to developing his team and travelled all over the country in his search for new talent. Precisely what Hübner saw of Fassbinder's at the *antiteater* is unclear. Fassbinder maintained that Hübner had been to *Die Bettleroper* and was impressed by his adaptation of a classic text (cf. Brocher, p. 92). Hübner himself told me that he had seen *Iphigenie* in October 1968. Either way, Fassbinder was first commissioned by Bremen to adapt a play, not to direct it. Fassbinder remembered that he was first offered a play by Sean O'Casey, which would be used by Zadek, but that those plans came to nothing (cf. Brocher, p. 92). Fassbinder then agreed to adapt a different play, Carlo Goldoni's *Il Bodega del Café* (*The Coffeehouse*).

Before we examine Fassbinder's treatment of the text, we should first consider why Fassbinder made the move from the subcultural *Kellertheater* to the apparatus of the mainstream *Stadttheater*.

One reason is obvious. The chance to work at one of the pre-eminent stages of the country was clearly attractive. The enhanced resources and the exposure would help Fassbinder both in his work in the theatre and consequently in the cinema. In an interview, Fassbinder said that the bourgeois public in West Germany snobbishly rated the theatre far more highly than its parvenu competitor, the cinema.[16] By making his name in the older medium, he had more chance of being taken seriously in the younger one. In addition, the *antiteater* itself was losing steam, as was apparent from its productions in the summer of 1969, and a new creative stimulus was needed. Although the company actually began to stabilize its membership around that time, Fassbinder's continued absence from Munich meant that the cast was being deployed in films rather than in the theatre.

Yet the move to Bremen might also have had other material causes, based on the ability of the *Stadttheater* of the time to eliminate almost all competition from the private sector through its financial power. The *Stadttheater* realized in the 1960s that their lavishly expansive stages were not suitable for the chamber plays that were emerging, or for plays that required a more differentiated relationship to space than grand stages were able to afford. In the building boom of the 1960s and 70s, West German theatres thus invested heavily in workshops, studios and chamber theatres.[17] The *Stadttheater* had managed to trump the small private theatres by offering audiences a more intimate experience of theatre without having to sacrifice quality. Hans Daiber maintains that by 1975 private studio theatres had become all but meaningless.[18]

---

[16] Cf. Thomsen, 'Conversations with Rainer Werner Fassbinder', pp. 85–6.

[17] Cf. Daiber, *Deutsches Theater seit 1945*, p. 308.

[18] Cf. ibid., p. 316. However, he does also register the response from the private sector, the growth of 'freie Theatergruppen' ('free theatre groups') on p. 399. Rolf Michaelis notes how these groups have enlivened the scene by not being tied to a particular space but accepts that they nonetheless serve the system because they find it hard to live independently of its facilities (cf. Michaelis, 'Von den Barrikaden in den Elfenbeinturm', p. 20).

Fassbinder was not the only member of the *antiteater* personnel to make the move to Bremen. Hans Hirschmüller, a co-founder of the *action-theater* in 1967 and subsequently a performer in *Anarchie* and Fassbinder's early films, had a full acting contract as of the 1969/70 season. So Fassbinder already had a familiar face in the ensemble. Not that that was overly necessary for an adaptor: Fassbinder had to engage with a playwright rather than a group of actors.

Goldoni's comedies revolutionized Italian theatre in the eighteenth century. Their social and moral dimensions led to comedies which could be critical of current attitudes, moving away from the formal restrictions of the dominant *commedia dell'arte* styles yet without banishing them completely. *Il Bodega del Café* (1750) is set in Venice at carnival time and revolves around Don Marzio, a Neapolitan gentleman, whose gossiping distorts situations and betrays the other characters. The various plot lines are set against the backdrop of the eponymous coffeehouse with its owner Ridolfo, and the casino next door, run by the less than saintly Pandolfo. The monetary theme of winnings and debts pervades the comedy and by the end, Ridolfo's honesty triumphs as he is instrumental in the reconciliation of the play's conflicts, Pandolfo is sent to gaol for using marked cards, and Marzio is forced to leave Venice by the other characters. In a final enlightened moment of *anagnorisis*, Marzio realizes it was his slanderous tongue that caused his downfall and leaves the stage in sadness.

Although Fassbinder retained the main characters and the broad structures of the piece, whose title he preserved in translation as *Das Kaffeehaus*, he made several important changes. The centrality of money is emphasized by the introduction of a comic and anachronistic device in which any mention of Italian currency is automatically converted into dollars, pounds and marks by whoever is the conversation partner at the time. The device is used a grand total of forty-one times during the play, something criticized by reviewers of the original production as over-egging the pudding.[19] It is certainly

---

[19] Cf. Karin Güthlein-Fritzsche, 'Zur totalen Langeweile umfunktioniert', *Nordwest-Zeitung*, 12 September 1969; or Jost Nolte, 'Seltsam in den Schlag gespielt', *Die Welt*, 12 September 1969.

true that the joke wears off after a few airings, yet it is its persistence that shapes the architecture of the play and the device is clearly not designed to garner laughs at every mention. The opposition of culture, represented by the coffeehouse, and finance, represented by the casino next door, is collapsed by Fassbinder through the centrality of money and the coffeehouse's interaction with the casino, whence its clientele come to recuperate. The young servant-cum-waiter Trappola is a minor role in Goldoni. Fassbinder turns him into Trappolo, a one-time gold prospector in Arizona who has returned to Venice to live a simpler life. He bails out the incorrigible gambler Eugenio with some of his savings and has his money fraudulently reappropriated by Marzio, who says he will invest it on the stock exchange for Trappolo. The fraud is allowed to stand unchallenged because of social class – no one believes that Marzio would behave so dishonourably, especially as Trappolo does not have a receipt. Marzio the gentleman trumps Trappolo the servant, and the company is happy to cement the oppressive status quo. Ridolfo, too, is mainly interested in the business of running a coffeehouse rather than presenting a model of social virtue. On top of this, Pandolfo looks to Eugenio to become a partner in the casino because he wants Eugenio's wife, Vittoria, to act as a 'hostess' to keep the gamblers interested at the tables. Vittoria is happy to oblige; it is her husband Eugenio who opposes the move. He dramatizes the contradiction of a cash-crazed addiction to gambling and a morality which will not let a wife use her femininity for financial gain. By the play's conclusion, Pandolfo is satirically spared incarceration because he is so much in debt to the city of Venice that it cannot afford to imprison him. His ironic 'happy end' is augmented when Eugenio gives permission for his wife to play her role in the casino because the price is right. The introduction of new contradictions has led Laura Sormani to argue that Fassbinder carries Goldoni's reforming spirit into his own times, viewing the process of adaptation as dynamic and never-ending.[20]

Fassbinder is also keen to make a link between the proprietary financial relationships on stage and those of an interpersonal

---

[20] Cf. Sormani, *Semiotik und Hermeneutik*, p. 213.

nature. Just as in the Goldoni original, there is a subplot that involves Flaminio Ardenti, who has fled his wife Placida, come to Venice, adopted a pseudonym (Count Leander) and taken a lover, the former prostitute Lisaura. Goldoni has Leander reconciled with his wife by the benevolent Ridolfo. Although the same happens to the couple at the very end of Fassbinder's version, the reconciliation is based upon dependency rather than love. Placida is unable to throw off Leander's shackles and the last words of the play are tinged with an unsettling air of need and despair. The inability to escape the tentacles of capital is mirrored in Placida's inability to liberate herself from a cheating husband.

Fassbinder's major stylistic intervention was in his treatment of the language of the play. His attention to linguistic detail, as seen previously in the artificial Bavarian of *Katzelmacher*, the awkward German of the English characters Brady and Hinley in *Preparadise* or the satirical reproduction of political discourse in *Anarchie*, was directed here towards the syntax of the baroque. The text is kept highly synthetic by Fassbinder's use of archaic sentence structures and dated linguistic usages, something which is regularly juxtaposed with the anachronisms of the monetary conversions and details such as cowboy-style duels, which occur twice in the play. The calculated way in which money colonizes the characters and the action of the play in Fassbinder's version leads Sormani to conclude that the equally twisted language of *Das Kaffeehaus* is no longer reliable for communication.[21]

Fassbinder had delivered a *Klassikerzertrümmerung* more than equal to his reworking of *Iphigenie*, although it used very different dramaturgical means. Fassbinder's thoughts on the business of adaptation were articulated in one of his rare incursions into the theoretical, written shortly before his death in 1982. Fassbinder noted, with reference to his adaptation of Genet's novel *Querelle*:

> Contrary to popular opinion, filming literature does not
> legitimize itself at all through the best possible translation
> of one medium (literature) into another (film). Filmic

[21] Cf. ibid., p. 217.

interaction with a literary work cannot find its justification in optimally realizing the images that the literature suggests to the reader . . . Only with the clear attitude that questions literature and language, or analyses the content and attitudes of the writer, with an imaginative relationship to the literary work which is recognizable as personal and not through an attempt to 'realize' literature is such a film made legitimate.[22]

It would not seem unfair to swap the language of the cinema for that of the theatre to understand that Fassbinder's attitude to adaptation had changed little over his creative career. Fassbinder refuses to transfer one medium into another because of the impossibility of a universal response to the source: 'the images that literature suggests to the reader' are defined by that reader's personal associations with language. This leads Fassbinder to the centrality of the adaptor's critical subjectivity. The adaptor is not, however, given free rein, as Fassbinder is keen to emphasize. It is the adaptor's questioning of relationships and attitudes that provides the germ for further development into the autonomous realm of a different genre. The adaptor is thus caught in a dialectic that not only involves his or her interaction with the source, but the source's interaction between its own and its target medium. Fassbinder's recognition of both processes signals a sensitivity to his media that meant that even the filming of a stage production for the small screen required subtle yet fundamental changes (*Das Kaffeehaus* was filmed for television in 1970). Fassbinder did not believe that one could simply export one medium in the vain hope that it might work in another.

Back in Bremen, Fassbinder's appointment to the position of adaptor was to have far wider implications for Fassbinder than the initial brief would suggest, and these were instigated by the director who was originally working on Fassbinder's play. Alois Michael Heigl started rehearsals with actors from the Bremen ensemble in the summer of 1969. Fassbinder paid the rehearsals a visit, together with

---

[22] Rainer Werner Fassbinder, 'Vormerkungen zu *Querelle*', in Fassbinder, *Filme befreien den Kopf. Essays und Arbeitsnotizen*, ed. Michael Töteberg (Frankfurt/Main: Fischer, 1984), pp. 116–18, here p. 116.

some of his *antiteater* colleagues. The initial work had pleased him, but a trip a couple of weeks later showed Fassbinder a director in difficulties. Heigl worked with a sham naturalism that simply ignored the stylization implicit in the text and was searching for meaning behind the text rather than letting the unspoken text emerge by itself.[23] Fassbinder's dissatisfaction is clear and can be seen towards the end of the *Ende einer Kommune* documentary. He makes suggestions to Heigl and criticizes the conventional way of dealing with the actors.[24]

Fassbinder was installed as the new director and it was in this capacity that he made the acquaintance of Margit Carstensen, who was playing Vittoria. Carstensen was to become Fassbinder's new star, eclipsing Hanna Schygulla in the theatre if not in the cinema. Again Fassbinder displayed his sensitivity to the qualities an actor brought to performance when he preferred to keep Schygulla as his film star and have Carstensen as his leading lady on stage.[25] According to Carstensen, once Fassbinder took over the production he began to change things 'with quite minor suggestions' rather than a radical conceptual rethink. His main strategy was to regroup the actors into the two- and three-person arrangements of the script and to ask for a general direction that all the actors presented their characters as 'loving and unfathomable' ('liebevoll und abgründig'). This was a tenor Carstensen identified in most of her theatre work with Fassbinder and it reveals crucial points about Fassbinder's understanding of character in the theatre. The word 'and' instead of 'but' in the phrase demonstrates Fassbinder's love of complexity. This simple directorial

[23] Hirschmüller, who played Trappolo, confirmed that Heigl had 'no point of entry' to the language and style of the play.

[24] Joachim von Mengershausen told me that Fassbinder had only been there a couple of days before Heigl was relieved of his position by Hübner.

[25] Carstensen can, however, be seen as the lead in *Die bitteren Tränen der Petra von Kant*, *Martha* and *Chinesisches Roulette*, just as Schygulla was still an important part of the theatre work. But each female lead was cast predominantly in the other genre, accentuating each woman's particular talents.

Fig. 13. The icing on the cake: *Das Kaffeehaus* premières in Bremen against an intriguing backdrop, designed by Wilfried Minks. Fassbinder refined his directorial technique to deliver something of a shock for audiences who had come expecting a lighter interpretation of Goldoni. © Rainer Werner Fassbinder Foundation

premise positions the figures between desire and a realm beyond mere psychological explanation, one which opens up a discourse away from the individual that includes the political. The emotional content of the phrase cannot be denied, so the audience is invited to question the social situation itself and its prerequisites as a site of change.

The production of *Das Kaffeehaus* opened the season in Bremen on 10 September 1969 under the co-direction of Fassbinder and Raben. Raben, as discussed in chapter 1, played the role of the advisor, offering constructive criticism, while Fassbinder worked through his concrete ideas of staging. The set, designed by Minks, combined a pop motif with an empty, white, avant-garde stage (see fig. 13). A giant cream gateau towered over the actors, and sat atop an equally over-large glass cake-stand. One slice had already been taken. The question as to whether everyone would get their share was posed visually from the outset. Above the stage was an illuminated ticker-tape display that reproduced the stock-market rates converted by the characters. To the sides of the stage, two blown-up Dürers depicted Adam and Eve; the Fall had clearly taken place on stage. All the major items on stage except for the giant cake and its stand had been recycled from earlier productions at the theatre, including Stein's *Tasso*. The idea of taking what had gone before and refunctioning it in the adaptation was emblematically communicated to the regular Bremen theatre-goer. All nine actors stayed on stage for the complete performance, with eleven chairs available for their comfort.

If the audience had expected a light Italian comedy with morally unambiguous characters, it was to receive a shock. The predominant mood of the production was melancholic. Naturalism was all but eschewed in the name of a mannered and dampened set of relationships. Wilhelm Herrmann approvingly called it: 'a spoken concert . . . a Goldoni produced like a Chekhov'.[26] Another positive response came from Dietrich Stubbendorff, who wrote: 'Michael König [Eugenio] offers a masterful achievement in the "underplaying" demanded by the direction'.[27] Hermann Dannecke praised the style as one 'of a hardly surpassable artificiality'.[28] Other reviewers were less well inclined to the experimental production and mirrored the split audience. But even the critical commentators occasionally had to admit there was an '"admittedly cold" fascination'.[29] From today's perspective, it is difficult to view the performance style as anything but a strident step in the direction of the 'postdramatic', the term coined by Hans-Thies Lehmann and elaborated upon in his book *Postdramatisches Theater*.[30] Lehmann sketches a theatre

[26] Wilhelm Herrmann, 'Play Goldoni mit Dürers Adam und Eva', *Münchner Merkur*, 12 September 1969.

[27] Dietrich Stubbendorff, 'Fassbinders Kaffeehausgespräche', *Hannoversche Allgemeine*, 12 September 1969.

[28] Hermann Dannecke, 'Umfunktioniertes Kaffeehaus', *Rheinischer Merkur*, 19 September 1969. The later quotation is from the same source.

[29] HH, 'Aus dem Lebenskuchen', *Abendzeitung*, 12 September 1969.

[30] Cf. Lehmann, *Postdramatisches Theater*.

beyond representation, a theatre of language in which text floats freely above denotation and is able to tap into associations among the audience. Although Fassbinder and Raben were still allied in some way to the representation of a set of plots and the characters that inhabited them, the style, in its unhurried melancholy, presented a lack of communication on stage, offering the texts to the audience rather than to the other characters. Hermann Dannecke noted: 'everyone remained narcissistically enclosed in themselves'.[31]

Fassbinder, who was still only freelancing in Bremen and had not yet been through the experience of *Werwolf*, continued to maintain a link with the *antiteater* in Munich. But rather than writing a new play for it, or even directing one, Fassbinder redirected the Bremen version, as clearly spelt out in the production's programme.[32] The programme also reproduced an expository text found in the Bremen programme and printed four favourable reviews of the Bremen production. Even the casual reader could appreciate how Fassbinder's allegiances were changing.

That said, Fassbinder did not shirk his responsibility to the actors and transposed the production with care and attention; the reviews were positive. The *antiteater* audience presented a more sophisticated body, having been party to the experiments that had already taken place in the Witwe Bolte. Its response, too, was affirmative, as its expectations differed from those of the *Stadttheater* theatregoers in Bremen. The reviews also articulate the differences that still existed between the *antiteater* actors and those of the *Stadttheater*. Armin Eichholz praised the collective strength of the ensemble playing, and was pleased to be unable to discern a star turn.[33] Another reviewer felt the production was, 'not a farce but a kind of mass, an

---

[31] Dannecke, 'Umfunktioniertes Kaffeehaus'.

[32] Cf. *Programme for Rainer Werner Fassbinder's 'Das Kaffeehaus'*, Witwe Bolte, première 14 October 1969. The première's elusive date is taken from an invitation to the production found in the Fassbinder Foundation archive.

[33] Cf. Armin Eichholz, 'Bei den H-Entfernungen in der Amalienstrasse', *Münchner Merkur*, 16 October 1969. Carstensen confirmed this reception and said that the Bremen production was 'more individual'.

unending, extended and occasionally static ritual of language and gesture, rigidity and theatrical force'.[34] The production toured Stuttgart
in March 1970 and played for one day in Bielefeld that June. Despite a
mixed review in Stuttgart, Jürgen Offenbach admired the 'honesty' of
Fassbinder's theatre: 'there was no false empathy being played here,
and none expected from the audience, where pity is illusory anyway'.[35]

On 1 November 1969 there was a unique coming-together
of the *Kellertheater* and the *Stadttheater*. Kurt Hübner offered his
new director a one-day festival, the *Showdown*. Fassbinder had chosen the English name. The packed day started at eleven o'clock, when
Fassbinder's first film, *Liebe ist kälter als der Tod*, was shown
in a small local cinema. The *antiteater* then performed *Anarchie* in
Bremen's main house at one. The film version of *Katzelmacher* graced
the screen at half past three, a discussion followed in the theatre at half
past five, and a performance of the Bremen *Kaffeehaus* at eight o'clock
rounded off the extravaganza. Not surprisingly, the critics found it a
mixed day, with its highs (*Das Kaffeehaus*) and its lows (*Anarchie*).[36]
The professionalism of the *Stadttheater* seemed to outshine the naive
charm of *antiteater*. The writing was on the wall for the latter. Yet
even the *Werwolf* project did not prevent Fassbinder from filming
Das Kaffeehaus in Cologne for WDR television in January 1970. Two
members of the Bremen cast, Carstensen and Hirschmüller, joined
antiteater actors to perform a slightly altered version of the production
in a bare, white studio, adorned only with chairs. The film, broadcast
on 18 May 1970, captures the languid, melancholic air of both productions and gives at least a flavour of what was happening in Bremen
and Munich at the time.[37]

---

[34] ab, 'Die kraftlosen Rituale von Geld und Liebe', *Süddeutsche Zeitung*,
17 October 1969.

[35] Jürgen Offenbach, 'Gemeinde-Abend', *Stuttgarter Nachrichten*, 2 March
1970.

[36] Cf. Peter Iden, 'Rituale und Spiele aus anderen Spielen', *Frankfurter
Rundschau*, 6 November 1969; or Jürgen Schmidt, 'Fassbinderei',
Stuttgarter Zeitung, 6 November 1969.

[37] Peter Seibert offers a useful contrast between the stage and screen
versions of the play in 'Rainer Werner Fassbinder: Film wie

A growing reputation: Fassbinder confronts
the *Intendanten* on stage

The move away from Munich had raised Fassbinder's profile both in the media and the upper cultural circles of the FRG. His debut production in Bremen had been widely reviewed, and the honour of having his own festival at one of the most important theatres in West Germany before he was even twenty-five was not to be treated lightly. The theatre had also nominated Fassbinder for a Gerhard Hauptmann prize, which he was awarded in December 1969 for *Katzelmacher*. The *Förderpreis* was designed to nurture young writers and was worth 3,000 DM.[38] By 1970, Fassbinder had directed four feature-length films, two of which would later win Federal Film Prizes. He was to make a further seven films in 1970. Fassbinder's productivity was an object of envy. And the reference point for journalists for much of his achievement at that time was his extensive work with the *antiteater*, whose very sellable name did little to deflate a burgeoning mythology of a hyper-productive *enfant terrible*. Fassbinder had arrived in the public consciousness.

It is difficult to say precisely why the *antiteater* was invited to the AGM of the Deutscher Bühnenverein in Essen. The association, made up of the FRG's *Intendanten*, was hardly a hotbed of avant-garde experimentation. But regardless of whether it was a bid to seem 'contemporary' or a genuine attempt to engage with alternative forms of theatre, the result was the almost universal rejection by the delegates of the proffered performance. The *antiteater* decided to revive a production that pre-dated its existence, Fassbinder's first attempt at directing solo at the *action-theater*, *Die Verbrecher* (*The Criminals*) by Ferdinand Bruckner. The première took place on 8 June 1970, the first day of the meeting. The forty-five-minute production with eleven actors made few compromises. Its pared-down,

---

Theater – Theater wie Film', in Inga Lemke (ed.) with Sandra Nuy, *Theaterbühne – Fernsehbilder. Sprech-, Musik- und Tanztheater im und für das Fernsehen* (Anif/Salzburg: Müller-Speiser, 1998), pp. 103–17, here pp. 113–15.

[38] Cf. RM, 'Hauptmann-Stipendien', *Frankfurter Allgemeine Zeitung*, 11 December 1969.

choreographed arrangement of dialogue fragments cut little ice with the audience, and it was received in much the same way as it had been in 1967. The programme, which offered a perspective of sorts on the performance that was to follow, stated:

> One has to forget the work as the description of a milieu and follow a purely formal stimulus, which exchanges an artificial setting for a most artificial reality, a conglomeration of all the clichés about crime. What perhaps emerges from this for the spectator is a confrontation with the impatience of the middle class, which is starved of perspectives on social and political standpoints by its established impasses, and with the ideologically muddy mediocrity of our West German present.[39]

The critic who quoted this section went on to say that the confrontation promised took place in the post-show discussion rather than on the stage. The *Intendanten* were not amused, yet some of the reviewers were more understanding of Fassbinder's refusal to offer the spectator an easy ride. Ulrich Schreiber, for example, welcomed the controlled deliveries, which evinced a certain beauty, and acerbically concluded that Fassbinder was offering an aesthetic for an active audience.[40] The production seems to have been recorded on audio tape.[41] The two tracks available for contemporary appraisal amply illustrate the care and attention with which the production was directed. The control, timbre and timing of the two-person exchanges cleave word and emotion apart, so that the emotion is still audible without the typical signifier of a charged or heightened voice.

[39] Quoted in Hans Schwab-Felisch, 'Verbrecher und Verhöre', *Frankfurter Allgemeine Zeitung*, 11 June 1970.

[40] Ulrich Schreiber, 'Kunst als Ware – wahre Kunst', *Handelsblatt*, 16 June 1970.

[41] There are two short excerpts on the *antiteater's Greatest Hits* CD (disc one, tracks nine and eleven). One of these features Margit Carstensen, whom Fassbinder had only met earlier in 1969, well after the demise of the *action-theater*. The voices also reverberate, which again suggests a live stage recording.

To accompany the première, the Deutscher Bühnenverein published an interview with Fassbinder in the June number of its organ, *Die deutsche Bühne*, in which Fassbinder engaged with the cultural-political issues of the day. He also discussed his position within the theatre system. At least Fassbinder was under no illusions about his role: 'I have already received many commissions and offers from the *Stadttheater*. I am clearly not a risk for them any more. Naturally I have the function of an alibi for the apparat'.[42] The *Stadttheater* had assimilated and integrated him, yet the reception at the AGM indicates that Fassbinder was still able to provoke within the subsidized system's parameters.

Fassbinder's belief in his relative impotence within the *Stadttheater* echoed the Tasso of Peter Stein's production in Bremen, but Fassbinder was never fully able to break with the political possibilities of drama or film. The role of art in politics was a central theme of *Die Niklashauser Fart* (*The Journeye to Niklashausen*), which Fassbinder filmed in May, a month before the *Verbrecher* production in Essen. It opens with an interesting catechism in which The Black Monk, played by Fassbinder, quizzes his two accomplices, Antonio and Johanna, about revolutionary strategy:

> THE BLACK MONK: Are they [revolutionaries] allowed to
> stage a revolution?
> JOHANNA: That is impossible.
> THE BLACK MONK: Are they allowed to make use of
> theatrical effects, for example, to agitate more effectively?
> JOHANNA: Yes. Of course. Yes.[43]

The dialogue offers a perspective on the functions of art and its limitations within a political context. It is not art's duty to feign reality or to deform it but to allow itself to be deployed in the name of change.

---

[42] Fassbinder quoted in Gernot Raue, '"Was man kapiert, ist wichtig". Ein Gespräch mit Rainer Werner Fassbinder', *Die deutsche Bühne*, 6 (1970), pp. 112–13, here p. 113.

[43] Rainer Werner Fassbinder, *Die Niklashauser Fart*, in Fassbinder, *Fassbinders Filme*, vol. II, ed. Michael Töteberg (Frankfurt/Main: Verlag der Autoren, 1990), pp. 125–55, here p. 128.

Art's subservience to agitation may be satirical in the exchange but if agitation is understood as the offer rather than the dogmatic articulation of a political impulse, then art can help to mould reality by suggesting alternatives. Fassbinder was never an artist who believed that worthy sentiments would bring about a revolution. Rather, by using the system to present different realities, he was at least engaged in a dialogue which deviated from the given order of the time.

In between the filming: *Das brennende Dorf* and *Pioniere in Ingolstadt* in Bremen

Fassbinder's extensive film commitments curtailed his theatrical activity for much of the rest of the year. *Der amerikanische Soldat* (*The American Soldier*) was filmed in August 1970 and *Warnung vor einer heiligen Nutte* (*Beware the Holy Whore*) that September in Italy. Work started on a film version of *Pioniere in Ingolstadt* (*Military Engineers in Ingolstadt*) in November, but beforehand Fassbinder let Raben direct a new adaptation in Bremen.

Das brennende Dorf (*The Burning Village*) was another commission and was written in a variety of locations (Munich, Madrid, Fuerteventura, Las Palmas and Paris) between December 1969 and March 1970.[44] The play is Fassbinder's rewriting of Lope de Vega's *Fuente Ovejuna*, a drama written in the early 1600s about political power and social revolt, based on historical events in 1476. In the original, the village of Fuente Ovejuna is terrorized by the arbitrariness of its ruler, the Commander. He abducts Laurentia, a local woman who spurns his advances, just after her wedding, and imprisons her new husband, Frondoso. This is the final insult which leads to the murder of the Commander. When Ferdinand, the King of Spain, investigates the incident, he finds that no one will own up to the murder. When asked who killed the Commander, the village replies with one voice, 'Fuente Ovejuna.' Overcome by the solidarity of the community, he pardons the village *en masse*.

As we have already observed in Fassbinder's treatment of *Iphigenie* the magnanimity of the mighty was not an idea he could

---

[44] Cf. Rainer Werner Fassbinder, *Stücke*, vol. III (Frankfurt/Main: Suhrkamp, 1976), p. 45.

easily accept. He was no less critical in this adaptation, and his major change to the plot comes at its conclusion. The Spanish court, which had been portrayed as capricious, unserious and contemptuous of its subjects throughout by Fassbinder, is presented with the collective perpetrators. But rather than admiring the will of the village, the King orders their collective execution. The villagers advance on the court and eat the royal couple and their retinue alive.

There are other changes too. Fassbinder introduces an itinerant student who is appalled at the Commander's rule and suggests that the village use Gutenberg's printing technology to organize its resistance more effectively. There are also a host of anachronistic details which wrench the play out of its historical milieu. When the villagers gather to plan their response to the abduction of Laurentia and the imprisonment of Frondoso, they give the salute of the Spanish anarchists. When Laurentia arrives, bloodied and violated, she demands revenge and rebels against her father's plea for a more measured response by saying, 'I spit in your liberal face' (*Stücke*, p. 483), thus using a contemporary political insult, the accusation of liberal reform as opposed to radical revolution. Sexuality is also accentuated in Fassbinder's version. The Grand Master, another ruling figure, is openly gay and has an entourage of youths. When some of their number fall in battle he laments the future pleasure now denied to them. In addition, Laurentia is told in the stage directions that when relating the circumstances of her rape by the Commander, she must also communicate that she enjoyed the ordeal (see fig. 14). Such controversial direction is another part of an approach that helps to render the actions on stage ambivalent.

Christian Braad Thomsen reads the adaptation through the Freudian lens, as he often does in his book on Fassbinder, and relates the concluding violence to *Totem and Taboo*. He believes: 'The Burning Village can be interpreted as an analysis of this myth', in which the father figure, the Commander, is devoured by his sons, the villagers.[45] This certainly sheds light on the cannibalism of the play, a motif which is signalled very early in the character of Laurentia,

---

[45] Thomsen, *Fassbinder*, p. 56.

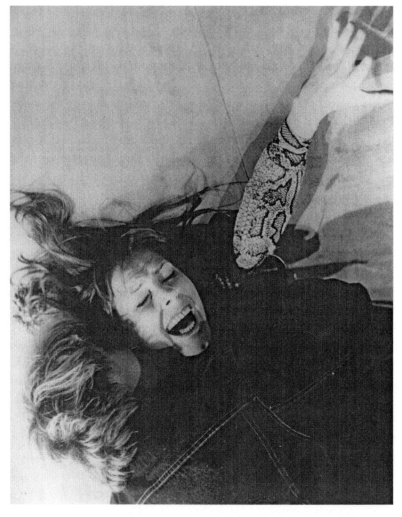

Fig. 14. Margit Carstensen, Fassbinder's most important discovery in Bremen, plays Laurentia in *Das brennende Dorf* (*The Burning Village*). © Rainer Werner Fassbinder Foundation

who is keen to taste human flesh. Yet Fassbinder's play involves a political discourse which goes beyond Thomsen's assertion that the play is also about terrorism and the degeneration of a revolt 'into mad destructiveness'.[46] At the meeting to decide what is to be done in the wake of the abduction, the politics of revenge are discussed. The male, liberal line is discursively associated with reason; the calls for the hanging of the Commander with 'manic women and hysteria' (*Stücke*, p. 482). Male 'reason' uses rhetoric rather than argument to eliminate political dissent. Morality is also revealed as politically determined, such as when the bourgeois Laurentia mocks the prostitute Jacinta as her respectable father would. Only later in the play, once Laurentia has gained political insights into the solidarity of the oppressed through suffering abuse, can she understand the broader picture, and she accepts Jacinta as a fellow comrade.

For the première in Bremen on 7 November 1970, Raben deployed a large cast and was offered a grand space by Minks, the set designer. The stage had four levels. The Spanish court sat upstage throughout. An orchestra performed the extensive musical score in front of them. The space between the orchestra and the edge of the stage was for the scenes away from the court, and a staircase rose up from the orchestra pit to allow the villagers to approach the court in the final scene. The backdrop to the production was an inverted baroque image on which the sky was where the earth should be, suggesting cosmic disharmony. Two giant statues of saints flanked the stage, each holding a sword and a book. One reviewer interpreted the objects as the utopian resolution of the poles of 'intellect and power'.[47]

Raben chose to stage the play in an operatic style. His knowledge of the form meant that his decision was not made on a whim, and the use of music and an orchestra helped to transform the play

---

[46] Ibid.

[47] Wilhelm Herrmann, 'Amoklauf der Dörfler', *Weser-Kurier*, 9 November 1970. The opposition refers to a term articulated by Heinrich Mann in a fragment on Frederick the Great of Prussia, and has often been used as a reference point in debates on political leadership since its publication in 1960, ten years after Mann's death.

into something more artificial and less realistic. The music was to contrast with the historical period on stage and thus the composer imitated Hindemith and other modernists to add anachronistic tension. Raben was satisfied with the actors he was using but found that a corporeal style eluded many of the professionals from Bremen in the cast. He had wanted 'gentle exaggeration' that fitted the operatic tenor of the production.[48] The actors were not required to perform 'as in an opera' but to offer a contrast to the music.

The set's levels lent an extra dimension to the production in that the court was present on stage and thus an observer of the proceedings throughout. As an on-stage audience, the court viewed the action before it, which assumed the status of a play-within-a-play. The King and Queen watched the events unfold without tension or concern. The villagers' torment at the hands of the Commander, their growing organization and their collective act of political violence did not trouble the rulers at all. The action was little more than a provincial drama in which the villagers thought they had power, whilst control apparently remained in Madrid. The twist came at the end of the play when the indolent court failed to realize that the 'drama' they were watching had a reality of its own. The material squalor and brutalization of the villagers led to a real revolution in this production.

There were, however, problems with the première. The layered space proved restricting and one reviewer noted that Raben had been forced to arrange his characters 'in groups which fill the stage and which are often merely "nice"'.[49] Wolf Donner agreed: 'the production got stuck in empty choreographed arrangements', which accentuated its weaknesses.[50] Peter Iden felt that Raben had been inhibited by

---

[48] Carstensen, who played Laurentia, told me that Raben was more interested in the actors delivering the text neutrally than colouring the production with any particular concept or interpretation.

[49] gr, 'Das Theater als Melange', *Frankfurter Allgemeine Zeitung*, 9 November 1970.

[50] Wolf Donner, 'Barocker Faltenwurf statt Agitation', *Die Zeit*, 13 November 1970.

the *Stadttheater*, and had not been as daring as he was in Munich.[51] The compromises made towards the system were best articulated by Wilhelm Herrmann, who wrote, 'the play lives from its action, the production from its images. The production seems to say: that's not such a bad thing. It makes the action consumable, a reproach often levelled at the "bourgeois" theatre.'[52] Only occasionally did the critics find glimpses of an alternative theatre, which, all the same, required more thorough development.

While Raben was directing in Bremen, Fassbinder was down in Bavaria filming *Pioniere in Ingolstadt*, the second return in a year to his days with the *action-theater*. The filming allowed him to prepare a production of the play in its wake, which was premièred in Bremen on 26 January 1971. The play unofficially opened a new theatre space, the Concordia, which was the Bremen theatre's third venue. The Concordia had no fixed seating and was designed to accommodate a range of experimental productions. The studio theatre was supposed to open with Minks' production of *Yvonne, Princess of Burgundy* by Witold Gombrowicz on 6 February, but Fassbinder was able to sneak in first with his quickly directed piece.

The venue was originally a rehearsal space for the theatre but, as noted earlier, the theatre system was keen and financially able to identify alternative performance styles and adapt itself to become the primary provider of such theatre in competition with the *Kellertheater*. Bremen's development of the Concordia was just another example of the *Stadttheater*'s ability to place itself at the forefront of innovation by updating its physical resources to expand its repertoire. A flyer that preceded the opening set out the aesthetic parameters of the venue: 'our concept: every play begins in an empty space. The director and set designer build the space according to the play. Directing, consequently, doesn't just mean considering where every actor is situated but also every spectator.'[53] The bareness of the flexible

---

[51] Cf. Peter Iden, 'Revolution als Orgasmus', *Theater heute*, 12 (1970), pp. 33–5, here p. 34.

[52] Herrmann, 'Amoklauf der Dörfler'.

[53] Flyer, reprinted in *Bremen*, p. 417.

Fig. 15. Irm Hermann reprises her role as Alma in Fassbinder's Bremen version of *Pioniere in Ingolstadt* (*Military Engineers in Ingolstadt*) as two soldiers turn to admire her. The geometrical arrangement of scenes was a feature of Fassbinder's direction from his earliest theatre productions. © Rainer Werner Fassbinder Foundation

studio offered Fassbinder a return to the sort of spaces he had known in Munich.

Annette Sabelus has studied the three different versions of Fassbinder's *Pioniere* text, from its inception at the *action-theater* via its further transformation for the film to the *Stadttheater* incarnation at Bremen. She notes that the Bremen version cut two scenes from the *action-theater* adaptation. Fassbinder then took a further five scenes from Fleisser's new version of the play (which was premièred in March 1970 in Munich) and added ten short dialogues of his own.[54] The changes mark the difference between the forty-five-minute version in Munich and the production in Bremen, which lasted almost an hour and a half.

Although the new production had reverted to Fleisser's original title, *Pioniere in Ingolstadt*, the playing style and the emphasis on situations and relationships rather than characters and psychology meant that it retained the exemplary quality of the *action-theater* production (see fig. 15). Sabelus finds that Fassbinder accentuated violent incidents in the text and pared down the dialogues to their fundaments in order to concentrate on social mechanisms and not local colour. The result of the process was a text which was 'more radical and more drastic'.[55]

The production itself tried to generalize the experience of the town of Ingolstadt by making certain modernizations to the text and by dressing the soldiers in NATO-style fatigues. The decision not to regionalize the accents was criticized by one reviewer,[56] and was almost certainly predicated upon the inability of several of the North German actors to master the Bavarian of the original in such a short space of time. All the same, the drive to generalize in this case sacrificed the link between syntax and a regionally specific mindset. Yet Fassbinder's sparseness did gain plaudits in a way that was noticeably

---

[54] Cf. Sabelus, '*Mir persönlich*', p. 46. In a rough reckoning Sabelus estimates that the ratio of Fleisser's work to Fassbinder's was 4:1. Fassbinder was thus far more present in the text than at the *action-theater*.

[55] Ibid., p. 50.

[56] HH, 'Kleinbürgermief', no further details supplied.

absent in Munich: 'the quotidian is drawn out in a Fassbinderly phleg-
matic style, which actually concentrates the dramatic into a handful of
pregnant poses and configurations of actors'.[57] Fassbinder explicated
the importance of the creation of the individual from his or her experience of the social in an interview he gave during rehearsals by referring
to a basic element of a character's movement: 'one's gait must never
be private. It always has to have something to do with the character
[i.e. with its social construction].'[58]

The space in the Concordia resembled something between 'an
air raid shelter and an aeroplane hangar'.[59] Jost Nolte enjoyed the
simplicity of the choreography, although there was something about
the modernization which did not sit quite right.[60] Other critics considered the show not quite finished or rushed. Fassbinder's decision
to push the première date ahead of the official opening almost certainly contributed to this, and his role as the male lead, Karl, did not
have the same degree of precision as the rest of the ensemble, because
Fassbinder sacked the original actor during the rehearsal period. His
decision to cast *antiteater* actors with those from Bremen, too, created
stylistic inconsistencies, similar to those seen in the discrepancies
between the two productions of *Das Kaffeehaus*.

A break from Bremen, or two possibilities: *Blut am Hals der Katze* and *Die bitteren Tränen der Petra von Kant*

A brief notice in the July 1970 number of *Theater heute* announced
that Fassbinder would be 'enriching' the celebrations in Nuremberg
in honour of Albrecht Dürer's fifth centenary in 1971 with a play
called *Blut am Hals der Katze* (*Blood on the Cat's Neck*).[61] It was
confirmed that Fassbinder would not be working with the ensemble in

---

[57] Jürgen Schmidt, 'Kälter als der Tod', *Deutsche Zeitung/Christ und Welt*,
5 February 1971.

[58] Fassbinder quoted in Henning Harmssen and Karsten Peters, 'So geht es
nicht', *Abendzeitung*, no date supplied.

[59] HH, 'Kleinbürgermief'.

[60] Cf. Jost Nolte, 'Die Verhältnisse, sie sind nicht mehr so . . .', *Die Welt*, 8
February 1971.

[61] Anon., 'Notizen', *Theater heute*, 7 (1970), p. 57.

Nuremberg but would be engaging the *antiteater*. By 20 March 1971, the première of the play, it was difficult to assert that the name 'antiteater' could have meaning any more.

Despite the various short tours in the first half of 1970, the *antiteater* had effectively ceased to exist after *Werwolf* in December 1969. The production in Essen for the Deutscher Bühnenverein was a commission; Fassbinder assembled a cast and redirected an earlier production. Actors from the group certainly continued to appear in Fassbinder's films, some of which were still being at least co-produced under the 'antiteater-X-Film' banner, and some of them had roles in *Das brennende Dorf* and *Pioniere*. Yet the *antiteater* as a theatre ensemble was a phantom. Of the ten-person cast performing under the auspices of the '*antiteater* munich [sic]' on the programme of *Blut* in Nuremberg, only five had appeared in *antiteater* productions in Munich. Four of the remaining actors had never performed in a Fassbinder production on stage at all.

Blut developed the form of *Katzelmacher* and *Preparadise*, a montage of mostly unrelated scenes. Yet this time, Fassbinder's arrangement had a definite structure which carefully realized in the text what he was trying to achieve elsewhere in performance. The play is about language. Phoebe Zeitgeist, a quotation of a comic-book character of the time, is an alien who has come to Earth to learn about democracy. Yet, as the opening stage direction puts it: 'Phoebe has difficulties, however: she doesn't understand human language, although she has learnt the words' (*Stücke*, p. 498). Fassbinder dramatizes a tension between Saussure's *langue* and *parole*, where *langue* is the totality of words in a given language and *parole* their articulation into meaningful discourse. He suggests that the society Phoebe encounters is flawed at the level of communication, that the *parole* is false.

In her research Phoebe encounters nine figures who have generalized titles such as the Model, the Policeman or the Dead Soldier's Wife. The first eighteen scenes contain two monologues from each character, one alone and one with Phoebe as observer. The monologues are mainly biographical and tell of suffering, oppression or sometimes both. They are arranged symmetrically so that the first character with a monologue with Phoebe is the last one to have a monologue alone.

The pattern is interrupted only in the middle, where, to follow the apparent pattern, the female Lover should have had a monologue with Phoebe and a monologue of her own next to each other. The male Lover has an extra scene here, and one assumes this is because the female Lover would have gained undue emphasis by such strict adherence to the symmetry.

The second phase of scenes involves a further thirty-six short scenes in which each member of the cast encounters each of the others in a duologue in an order from which no pattern can be said to emerge. Phoebe is present for each scene and extracts certain lines from the brief exchanges which she then repeats at the end of the scene to form new sentences, a new and challenging *parole*. While the first phase of the play presented the audience with monologues consistent with the given character's biography, the situations in the second destroy any sense of uniform identity. The scenes are versions of the 'contres' from *Preparadise*, in which everyday conflicts are presented as a series of glimpses. The only difference here is that the conflicts feature one oppressor and one victim rather than the two-against-one format of *Preparadise*. The shifting roles played by the nine figures explode the idea of a discrete identity, as the actors have to assume a range of personae defined by the relationship. Because of their brevity, the scenes as a whole suggest, rather than present, situations, and it is here that the audience's role in the staging as active spectators becomes evident. As I have discussed elsewhere: 'in this sort of whirl, the spectator has to work quickly to make sense of the vignettes . . . The spectator is forced to realize that meaning is being generated by his or her recognition of linguistic and kinetic signs.'[62] In other words, the spectator is complicit in the generation of meaning by being able to identify the unpleasant situations through a short set of clues. The ease of recognition is then called into question when Phoebe reprocesses the very language used to make the scenes comprehensible. Phoebe suggests an alternative to the familiar through her naivety.

[62] David Barnett, 'Dramaturgies of *Sprachkritik*. Rainer Werner Fassbinder's *Blut am Hals der Katze* and Peter Handke's *Kaspar*', *Modern Language Review*, 95 (2000), no. 4, pp. 1053–63, here pp. 1056–7.

The third phase of the play takes place at a party during which, at various points in the single long scene, Phoebe deploys the blocks of language she has assembled throughout the second phase. Her remarks elicit curiosity but ultimately indifference and a refusal to engage with the alien. By the end of the party, she sinks her teeth into each guest. Once all have crumpled to the floor, the vampire recites a dense passage from Hegel's *The Science of Logic*.[63] The philosophical extract discusses the contingency of knowledge, something the social role-plays of the second phase had been pointing to all along. In a text inspired by the rehearsal process, Fassbinder commented that: 'to chop everything up into its component parts and then put them back together anew, that's a wonderful thing'.[64] Fassbinder was busy reordering the clichés by which his characters lived so as to recontextualize and defamiliarize the language, with the aim of opening up critical attitudes in the audience.

The original production carried the subtitle 'Marilyn Monroe contre les vampires', something which shows how Phoebe, the naive Monroe figure, is at first witness to the social vampirism which is explicitly portrayed in the second phase, before succumbing to it, or learning from it herself at the play's conclusion. Yet the play's title has always remained something of a mystery. There is neither hide nor hair of a cat in the whole piece. The title actually started its life with a very different project. A fragment in the Fassbinder Foundation with the title *Blut am Hals der Katze* accompanies an incomplete treatment and script for a film. An outsider, Marie, comes to the city from the country, takes a place at an evening school and has a short series of supernatural encounters. One is with a clairvoyant who predicts that she will soon die. In her desperate solitude, Marie swings a cat around the room and bites its neck. The clairvoyant calls the

---

[63] The passage in question is the first paragraph of the first chapter of the section entitled 'Subjectivity' from the second part of the work. Cf. Georg Wilhelm Friedrich Hegel, *Die Wissenschaft der Logik*, second part (Leipzig: Felix Meiner, 1934), p. 239.

[64] *Programme for Rainer Werner Fassbinder's 'Blut am Hals der Katze'*, Städtische Bühnen, Nuremberg, première 20 March 1971. Each member of the team submitted a short text for the programme.

Fig. 16. Margit Carstensen as the alien Phoebe Zeitgeist, who fails to find comfort in the indifference of her human companions. The relaxed bar-room set is deliberately at odds with the tales of oppression and suffering that pervade *Blut am Hals der Katze* (*Blood on the Cat's Neck*). © Gerhild Lehnert

police, Marie is then interviewed and she proceeds to bite the neck of a woman. As is evident, there is little to link the two works, except for the fact that a female outsider, ground down by her environment, becomes a vampire.

The play is alive with quotation, from the figure of Phoebe to the social types themselves and the language they use. The text features many sententious remarks, some of which derive from a host of well-known figures, including Dürer, Brecht and Einstein. Their easy deployment as universal wisdom in the second phase and their repetition by Phoebe in the third are at odds with the specificity of the scenes which generated them. Fassbinder's most explicit foray into the politics of language exposes as lazy, clichéd shorthands the 'simple truths' with which the characters process the conflicts they encounter and create. As the situations in the second phase assume a standard pattern of oppressor and victim, so does the nature of the language deployed. Fassbinder combats a universalized reading of conflict as 'natural' or 'human' by means of the sparseness and specificity of the scenes themselves. In order for the scenes to have meaning, the relationship between the two speakers must be defined.[65] The determination of the characters' roles, away from individual psychology, points back to the social mechanisms at work and not to unchanging pictures of human misery (as obliquely expressed in the final passage from Hegel).

Fassbinder and Raben directed the première together.[66] The stage was little more than a bar from which drinks could be taken, and some furniture (see fig. 16). The relaxed atmosphere of the party

---

[65] Hirschmüller, who played the Soldier, told me that Fassbinder was still very much concentrating on the articulation of 'attitudes' in order to depict the relationships with clarity. It was not a question of 'the Soldier would do this', as if the Soldier lived independently of the situations, but rather the character might be defined by a relationship: 'how would a pimp behave to a whore?'.

[66] Raben told me that they used a similar technique to *Preparadise* and *Das Kaffeehaus* in a bid to suspend surface realism whilst maintaining relational tensions. Yet, in contrast to those productions, the cast entered and exited rather than staying on stage all the time.

pervaded all three phases, not just the last. Thus the conflicts of the second phase became more artificial, demonstrations of conflicts rather than naturalist 'slices of life'. The typologized figures went through their social rituals while Phoebe, played by Margit Carstensen, tried to 'imitate their attitudes', not their characters, as she told me. Phoebe followed the scenes 'like a child'. Come the conclusion, she was told by Fassbinder to deliver the complex Hegel text 'as lightly as possible', holding a glass of champagne. This direction did not attach too much weight to the text and allowed the audience an uninterpreted version so that they could approach it in their own ways. Another production detail was that a soprano, Hanna Köhler, was engaged. She delivered the opening stage direction, quoted above, and it was she and not Phoebe who sang the lines Phoebe picked up from the scenes of the second phase (although Phoebe, as per the script, delivered those lines at the party). The mock gravity of the operatic tone again helped to banish a realist reception of the action.

The widely reviewed première was met by a barrage of criticism, which seems largely to have been the result of laziness or prejudice on the part of the critics. The most frequent comparison made to the play was one with the language-centred works of Peter Handke. Hermann Hofer called the play a 'modish' tapping into Handke's seam.[67] Slighting comparisons with Handke's *Kaspar, The Ride across Lake Constance* and *Quodlibet* were to be found in many of the reviews. One critic praised Handke as an analyst of language, whereas Fassbinder was only concerned with presenting it.[68] Benjamin Henrichs, one of the few positive voices, countered that the strength of the play lay precisely in that naivety.[69] By leaving the scenes open Fassbinder was far more able to allow the audience space to reflect on its own implication in the action.

There were also criticisms of the political worthlessness of the production. Ernst Wendt wrote that, 'using a critique of the

---

[67] Hermann Hofer, 'Brutalität der Sprache', *Donau-Kurier*, 22 March 1971.

[68] halef, 'Märchen vom antiteater', *Nürnberger Zeitung*, 22 March 1971.

[69] Cf. Benjamin Henrichs, 'Wohl doch ein guter Mensch', *Süddeutsche Zeitung*, 23 March 1971.

system as an alibi, the trendies from the underground are only presenting their good selves; enlightenment has been reduced to theatrical
gesture'.[70] Peter Iden accused the production of being 'static and without a [political] perspective' and 'consistently ahistorical', a Marxist
critique that failed to grasp the play of ahistorical universalizing language and socially defined attitudes.[71] He was, all the same, able to
admire 'a beautiful, gentle sense of calm' and acknowledged that the
actors' skills were of a high quality. Dietmar N. Schmidt was one of
the few reviewers to embrace the aesthetic and the play, recognizing
the continual and kaleidoscopic 'patterns of utterance and behaviour'
and concluded: 'the evening drifts into total defeat, an endgame, similar to Beckett's'.[72] The characters may not have been able to learn
anything, but that was not to say that the audience could not.

The production was taken on tour in April and travelled to
Frankfurt, Bremen and Zurich. Reviewers, however, were pleasantly
surprised to find that a play that had been torn apart in Nuremberg had
something to offer them after all. One critic in Zurich enjoyed the fact
that the actors 'don't invent but rather reproduce' the situations, con-
fronting the audience with uncannily recognizable attitudes.[73] Erich
Emigholz in Bremen praised the tightness of the play's construction
and a more human approach to linguistic examination, and Thomas
Kirn in Frankfurt observed how Fassbinder was searching for meaning in the everyday and found little.[74] Fassbinder and Raben certainly
would have been able to tighten up on some of the scenes as the production ran, but the surprisingly contrastive reviews suggest that the

---

[70] Ernst Wendt, 'Fassbinder sinkt in den Bodensee', *Die Zeit*, 26 March
1971.

[71] Peter Iden, 'Es ist schade um die Menschen', *Frankfurter Rundschau*,
24 March 1971.

[72] Dietmar N. Schmidt, 'Fassbinders Stück fürs Dürer-Jahr', *Die Welt*,
22 March 1971.

[73] msch, 'Fassbinder in Zürich', *Die Weltwoche*, 23 April 1971.

[74] Erich Emigholz, 'Gesellschaft mit Echo', *Bremer Nachrichten*, 5 April
1971; cf. Thomas Kirn, 'Lauter miese kleine Schweine', *Frankfurter
Neue Presse*, 3 April 1971.

critics at the première might have had their minds too tightly closed to engage with the play on its own and not Handke's terms.

The extreme formalism of *Blut* is almost impossible to compare with the dramaturgy of Fassbinder's next drama to be staged, *Die bitteren Tränen der Petra von Kant* (*The Bitter Tears of Petra von Kant*). The melodramatic aesthetic that Fassbinder had embraced had its roots in a new inspiration for the writer. At the end of 1970, the Film Museum in Munich ran a six-film retrospective dedicated to the work of the German émigré Douglas Sirk.[75] The films profoundly influenced Fassbinder and primarily expanded his cinematic palette, but also touched the theatre work. The impact of Sirk is visible in one of Fassbinder's few essays, 'Imitation of Life. On the Films of Douglas Sirk'.[76] The essay lauds Sirk's ability to engage with people *and* their emotions without ignoring social context and political implication. The marriage of superficial and accessible characters with carefully enacted analysis allowed Sirk the freedom to have his cake, in his mainstream appeal, and eat it, in the films' critical depths. If we understand Sirk's concept of melodrama thus, a link between Fassbinder's reception of Sirk and *Blut* becomes apparent. The situations in *Blut* are all eminently recognizable while the constructed form of the play provides Fassbinder with the means to analyse them. *Petra*, on the other hand, moves away from form as a counterpoint to content and enacts its critique through the qualities Fassbinder praised in the less overt mechanisms of Sirk's Hollywood fare.

Petra is a five-act play that depicts four episodes in the life of a successful fashion designer, Petra von Kant. In the expository first act, we learn about Petra's two failed marriages through dialogues with her

[75] Michael Töteberg puts the record straight by showing Sirk to be a German and not a Dane, as Sirk had often maintained (cf. Töteberg, *Rainer Werner Fassbinder*, pp. 73 and 143). One assumes Sirk preferred to present himself as a non-German, having worked in the Third Reich until his emigration in 1937.

[76] Cf. Rainer Werner Fassbinder, 'Imitation of Life. Über die Filme von Douglas Sirk', in Fassbinder, *Filme befreien den Kopf. Essays und Arbeitsnotizen*, ed. Michael Töteberg (Frankfurt/Main: Fischer, 1984), pp. 11–24.

aristocratic friend, Sidonie, who introduces Petra to a friend of hers, the lower-class Karin Thimm.[77] In the second act, Petra gets to know Karin better over dinner at Petra's flat and their lesbian relationship begins. By the third act, the relationship is on the rocks. Karin leaves at the act's conclusion, a move which leads to misery in the fourth, Petra's birthday party, which her daughter, her mother and Sidonie attend. The short final act takes place in the wake of the disastrous celebration and suggests that Petra has learned something from it, although this, as we shall see, is questionable.

While the relationship with Karin is the most visible, the most fascinating is the one with Marlene, who is little short of a slave to Petra. The completely silent role is the most problematic in that it resists the conventions of melodrama. To appreciate this dramaturgical strategy, we need first to understand the dynamics of Petra's relationships with the other characters and how they expose her own characteristics. Fassbinder, as always, is fascinated by the worlds created by his characters through language. Petra is set up from the outset of the play as a liar. In a phonecall to her mother in the opening monologue, Petra tells her she is listening while she is giving instructions to Marlene. Later in the act Petra criticizes Sidonie's belief that one should construct a relationship in mutual 'humility' (*Stücke*, p. 561). This does not prevent her from advocating the quality in her persona of the caring potential lover to Karin in the next act. Throughout the play, Petra is portrayed as both a slippery linguistic operator and as someone whose life has become so confused by such fictions that a feeling of cautious compassion might be evinced from a spectator. Petra's self-deception is so pronounced that her blindness may elicit sympathy. Fassbinder betrays his debt to Sirk in that he cannot treat Petra with contempt. Her suffering and her self-deception are recognizable human weaknesses, and even though Petra lures Karin with a show of constructed compassion, her world of lies becomes nothing but a pitiful sham rather than a web woven by a master manipulator.

---

[77] Quite what the relationship is between this character and Karin Thimm, a reviewer of Fassbinder's early theatre work, defies obvious interpretation.

In the third act, when Karin tells Petra that she has been out the previous night and slept with a man, Petra is visibly shaken, despite her dubious claims to have no problems with an open relationship. Karin surmises:

> KARIN: . . . You want to be lied to.
> PETRA: Yes, lie to me. Please lie to me.
> KARIN: Right then, it wasn't like that. I spent the whole night alone, walking and thinking about us.
> PETRA: Really? *Full of hope.* That's not true?
> KARIN: Of course not. I slept with a man . . .
>
> (*Stücke*, p. 581)

The knowledge that Petra lives in an imaginary world relativizes her words and actions. The closing passage of the play, in which she offers Marlene her freedom and a relationship as equals, is thus just as suspect as any other positive moment in the play. Her desire 'to love without making demands' (*Stücke*, p. 601) is noble but might just suggest that she has acquired a new line in self-deception. To believe that Petra has actually learned something in so short a period of time (between her breakdown at the party and its aftermath where she is lying in bed) is open to speculation.

Petra, the central figure, presents the spectator with a carefully constructed example of Fassbinder's melodramatic aesthetic: although the character is unpleasant, unable to control herself, her feelings or her lies, there is still a shred of attachment one feels for her pitiful, deluded state. Her use of language has marked her as a character to be wary of, a character not worthy of trust, yet her inability to control events, and the way in which this manifests itself in her pain, salvages her, however slightly, for the audience.

Marlene cannot work on the same level, the spectator is never allowed an insight into the psychology, not to mention the emotions, of someone who seems to be a willing, silent victim. Indeed, one of the few stage directions attributed to her tells her to go down on one knee, a mark of servility, when Petra offers her equality and says, 'you should be happy' (*Stücke*, p. 602). Petra is met with Marlene's most overt show of submission. Marlene offers nothing but question marks to a spectator. She allows herself to be exploited, both domestically with the chores she performs without complaint and in the business sphere. In the first act, Petra instructs her to work on a design Petra has put in a drawer. At the end of the act, Petra notices that Marlene has changed the cut of the sleeve. Petra's initial anger gives way to the approving acknowledgement of the modification. Marlene is universally exploitable but we know so little about her. Marlene simply does not conform to the melodramatic aesthetic because she is not portrayed as a woman of flesh and blood and human flaws. She is not Brecht's dumb Katrin, who evokes sympathy and anger at her murder when walking the city of Halle in *Mother Courage and her Children*. The relationship between Marlene and Petra is an enigma and poses questions that go beyond the exaggerated realism of the rest of the play. As Ann and John White note, with reference to the film version, the inexplicable has the effect of 'making uncanny' and not 'making strange', the latter being a reference to the use of the Brechtian aesthetic of *Verfremdung*.[78] Because Marlene works on a different semiotic level from the other characters in *Petra*, it may be that the Brechtian play of familiar/unfamiliar in the construction of Petra is called into question without being wholly rejected by the ambivalence of Marlene. Karl-Heinz Assenmacher argues that the play links the sexual and the emotional with the commodification of feelings and the role of private property in the broader social context.[79] Petra's treatment of Karin and Marlene as objects and her financial superiority help to support this argument, but the mysteries of human

---

[78] Ann and John White, 'Marlene's Pistol and Brady's Rule. Elements of Mystification and Indeterminacy in Rainer Werner Fassbinder's Film *Die bitteren Tränen der Petra von Kant*', *German Life and Letters*, 53 (2000), no. 3, pp. 409–25, here p. 415.

[79] Karl-Heinz Assenmacher, 'Das engagierte Theater Rainer Werner Fassbinders', in Gerhard Charles Rump (ed.), *Sprachnetze. Studien zur literarischen Sprachverwendung* (Hildesheim and New York: Olms, 1976), pp. 1–86, here pp. 53–4.

agency as dramatized in Marlene frustrate a purely political, dialectical exegesis.[80]

One interpretive trap that we should be wary of is the allegorical relationship between *Petra* and Fassbinder's biography. Fassbinder had told Wolfgang Limmer in 1980 that the impulse for *Petra* was his homosexual relationship with one of his actors, Günther Kaufmann, but that elements of his platonic relationships with Irm Hermann, Peer Raben and Ursula Strätz also informed the play.[81] Kurt Raab's and Harry Baer's separate decoding of the allegorical mappings of fictional characters onto real people reveals discrepancies from associates who very much formed Fassbinder's 'inner circle'.[82] There is no agreed 'key' to the cast. All the same, biographical readings by various commentators, aimed at telling the reader about Fassbinder's life, obscure and ignore the artistry of the play.[83] The failure to agree on 'who was who' and the reduction of art to biography both contradict Fassbinder's own comments that the play was based on several relationships and simplify the complexity generated on stage.

Petra is one of Fassbinder's most produced plays (and one of his most popular films). The reception of its première on 5 June 1971 would never have led one to have believed it. The play was commissioned by the Landestheater Darmstadt and shown at the Experimenta, one of West Germany's leading experimental drama festivals. Raben directed, and imported Carstensen as Petra and Irm Hermann as Marlene (roles they would retain for the film) as guests into the Darmstadt ensemble. He chose to use mirrors and dummies in a bid to add *Verfremdung* to the action on stage (used so effectively by Fassbinder in the film version) but failed to engage the reviewers with his decisions (see fig. 17). Raben told me that he 'hadn't done anything

---

[80] Marlene's determination to subjugate herself is made even more evident in the conclusion to the film version. On being offered her freedom she packs her bags and leaves Petra.

[81] Cf. Limmer, *Rainer Werner Fassbinder, Filmemacher*, p. 74.

[82] Cf. Raab and Peters, *Sehnsucht*, p. 163; and Baer, *Schlafen kann ich, wenn ich tot bin*, p. 98.

[83] Cf. Berling, *Die 13 Jahre*, p. 182; Thomsen, *Fassbinder*, p. 110; or Hayman, *Fassbinder: Film Maker*, p. 61.

Fig. 17. Carstensen again, this time starring in the title role of *Die bitteren Tränen der Petra von Kant* (*The Bitter Tears of Petra von Kant*). The original production, directed by Peer Raben, was mainly dismissed as 'trivial' by the critics. Fassbinder's film of the play reignited interest in the text. © Pit Ludwig

special' with the production by trying to stage it as closely as possible to the text as it stood on the page. He worked intensively with his leading lady on the language, but this quality did not rescue the production.[84]

The critics could not see past the play's veneer. This may have come from the disappointment that the subtly unconventional play had been shown at the avant-garde Experimenta. All the same, the dismissal of *Petra* revealed very little effort to engage with anything but

[84] Carstensen concurred that the première was 'nothing special' and 'more modest' than the film. She commented that Fassbinder changed little fundamentally from Raben's production, but worked on the constellations of the actors' bodies. He took over Raben's carefully crafted use of language but directed the actresses to concentrate on 'speaking past each other rather than speaking to each other'.

the play's surface. The German critics' favourite withering epithets, that the play was 'kitsch' and 'trivial', were deployed with unflinching regularity. The tone was perhaps best set by Botho Strauss: 'the method is no longer "critical" quotation, rather complete imitation, including the emotional reactions such a story triggers'.[85] Even those trying to salvage something from the show found it difficult. Klaus Coberg wrote that the kitschy production did damage to 'the very well-observed tale of people's inability to love'.[86]

It was not long, however, before the film version redeemed the play, and the text was reconsidered as a far more complex document than its original reception suggested. The film, subtitled 'a case study', points to the qualities an actress must bring to the role of Petra. Petra is an object of inquiry and not an easy vehicle for stars in their middle age. Raben's emphasis on the way Petra used language, developed and accentuated by Fassbinder in the film, provides the point of entry for a considered approach to the character. The ambiguities and ironies have to be brought out if Fassbinder's critical melodrama is to be presented in all its contradictions. And this is precisely what Fassbinder, aided by Kurt Raab, did for a Swiss touring production of the play in 1975. The reviews show a much more favourable reception that understands the many counter-currents of the play. Fassbinder was also able to assemble a very tight cast, including Lida Baarova. Baarova was one of Joseph Goebbels' lovers when she was a starlet in the 1930s. Her role as Petra's mother on tour may have added a certain biographical spice when she offered her opinions on relationships.

A farewell to Bremen, but not quite to Hübner

Fassbinder returned to Bremen for his last production there in December 1971. The play he wrote was another commission, just like *Das Kaffeehaus* and *Das brennende Dorf*, but this time the dramaturge Burkhard Mauer presented him with documentary materials rather

---

[85] Botho Strauss, 'Über Rührung und Emphase', *Theater heute*, 7 (1971), pp. 46–7, here p. 46.

[86] Klaus Coberg, 'Fassbinder bei der Modeschöpferin', *Münchner Merkur*, 7 June 1971.

than a classic play. The documents concerned the life and very public death of a local Bremen woman, Geesche Gottfried, who systematically poisoned fifteen people, including her parents, her three children, her twin brother, two husbands and a fiancé. Mauer wrote that the theatre was interested in how 'Enlightenment and bourgeois moderation' had been forgotten so quickly for the last public execution in the town in 1831.[87] The resulting play was polemically titled *Bremer Freiheit* (*Bremen Freedom*) because Fassbinder read the events as Geesche's 'craving for freedom and self-realization'.[88] The murders were thus Geesche's attempt to liberate herself from the oppressive conditions under which she lived. In the belief that the documents he was using may have been unreliable, that the confessions may have been coerced, Fassbinder opined, 'the story could have taken place exactly as I've written it'.[89] According to a note in the Foundation archive, the play was written between September and December 1970 in Munich and Paris.

The drama collapses the fifteen years of murder (from the first, of her husband, Johann Miltenberg, in 1813 until her arrest in 1828) into a succession of scenes divided only by blackouts, which last roughly an hour-and-a-half in total. The play shows incidents from Geesche's life and mainly imply the murder of the various characters after Geesche offers them poisoned coffee. Geesche actually killed her victims with arsenic-laden butter, but it seems that Fassbinder preferred to opt for a more refined, bourgeois medium. He chose to ignore the detail given in one of the historical documents that Geesche was

---

[87] Burkhard Mauer, 'Oberhäuptling Fassbinder', *konkret*, 1 (1977), pp. 30–1, here p. 30. Some of the documents provided by the Bremen theatre are still preserved in the Fassbinder collection at the Kinemathek in Berlin, which includes a slew of obituaries as they appeared in the newspapers of the time and a photocopied article on Geesche. Another historical piece giving important biographical details is to be found in the Fassbinder Foundation.

[88] Rainer Werner Fassbinder, transcript of a radio interview given to Radio Bremen, no further details supplied, held in the Fassbinder Foundation archive.

[89] Fassbinder, ibid.

a part-time actress, and a good one at that, yet her ability to deceive in *Bremer Freiheit* might owe something to that fact.

The plotting of the play emphasizes Geesche's social milieu and the contradictions within it, such as Geesche's obvious intelligence and her continued frustrations in the face of men who will not bend to her aspirations and women happy in their servitude. The compression of time has the effect of sidelining the tensions of the murder plot and concentrating attention on Geesche's situation. The play's conclusion, the historically accurate reappearance of the character Rumpf, who has had capsules he had found in his coffee analysed by the police, is completely unprompted. The play is not a 'thriller' and there is no crafted build-up of suspense as to when or whether Geesche will be caught. Rumpf's revelation is the penultimate speech of the play. Fassbinder is far keener to present the action as a series of episodes for the audience, to emphasize the process of murder rather than the denouement, which is little more than a postscript.

Fassbinder subtitled the play 'Ein bürgerliches Trauerspiel', a genre originating in the eighteenth century which roughly translates as 'a middle-class, or bourgeois tragedy'. The genre did not originally refer to the middle class in a negative way as such but explored its problems as an emerging social formation. For Fassbinder, *Bremer Freiheit* was a tragedy of middle-class values and the pernicious effects they had on their victims. Patriarchy and the church permeate the social morality of the play. Geesche's will to emancipation always comes at a price. The oppressive nature of her relationship with her first husband, renamed Miltenberger in the play, is clear when he humiliates her in front of his male friends, but there is also a sexual dimension. Geesche's opening line in the printed version is 'I want to sleep with you' (*Stücke*, p. 605). Geesche's sexual initiative is just as unacceptable as her shrewd business ability that is challenged by both her father and her brother later in the play. The only man with sense enough to avoid her power is Bohm, a none-too-bright relative, who, after an exchange with his potential wife, recognizes that he would never be the man of the house if he married her.

Religion is also used as a weapon against Geesche, most prevalently through her mother, who tries to fill Geesche with the same guilt and shame she feels for Geesche because she is living in sin with Miltenberger's successor, Gottfried. Yet Geesche cannot distance herself from the church, just as she is unable to live without men. To mark every murder she sings a hymn, or the tune of the hymn is played. In addition, having witnessed the death of Gottfried straight after her marriage to him, she confesses her crimes to the priest who married her and carried out the last rites almost in the same breath. Yet religion does not merely inhabit its own spiritual realm. The meeting of religion and commerce is signalled most explicitly in an authentic obituary that Fassbinder inserts into the text almost word for word. Geesche's father dictates the text in which Geesche's feelings of loss are supposed to be expressed, but its hollow nature is exposed when her father adds a codicil to the effect that the family saddlers firm will still honour its contracts so as not to undermine business confidence.

Peter Iden calls the play a sequel to Friedrich Hebbel's 'bürgerliches Trauerspiel' *Maria Magdalene* (1844) in which the female lead, Klara, takes her own life when middle-class values and a domineering father lead to disaster. Iden considered *Bremer Freiheit* a play 'which continues Hebbel's *bürgerliches Trauerspiel* as a drama of liberation'.[90] Two non-theatre specialists take issue with this claim, believing there was no evidence to suggest that Fassbinder had known the play.[91] They forget that Hebbel's play was a classic of the German canon and that Fassbinder had read a great deal of such literature in his youth. *Maria Magdalene* is also famous for the final line delivered by Meister Anton, Klara's father, after catastrophe has struck his house: 'I do not understand the world any more.'[92] The same line is slipped into the middle of *Bremer Freiheit* as Geesche expresses her incomprehension at why Gottfried will not marry her (*Stücke*, p. 622). That

---

[90] Peter Iden, 'Der Eindruck-Macher. Rainer Werner Fassbinder und das Theater', in Peter W. Jansen and Wolfram Schütte (eds.), *Rainer Werner Fassbinder*, fifth expanded edition (Frankfurt/Main: Fischer, 1985), pp. 17–28, here p. 27.

[91] Cf. Thomsen, *Fassbinder*, p. 316; and Watson, *Understanding Rainer Werner Fassbinder*, p. 152.

[92] Friedrich Hebbel, *Maria Magdalene*, in Hebbel, *Gedichte und Dramen*, vol. II (Hamburg: Hoffmann und Campe, n.d.), pp. 211–63, here p. 263.

Geesche is now tarred with Meister Anton's patriarchal brush tells the spectator something about Fassbinder's ambivalent relationship to his heroine.[93]

Murder as self-realization is, of course, a highly questionable means of liberation, yet Fassbinder is happy to entertain the idea and to undermine its validity at the same time. The Meister Anton intertext is one such moment, as is the murder of the children. Their crime is an unknowing one; they are putting off Gottfried from marrying the recent widow. The frequency of Geesche's murderous rhythm also smacks of a pathological condition and suggests that once she started, her bid for freedom made her an unreflecting slave to a murderous impulse. The final poisoning, that of Geesche's friend Luise, is particularly problematic. Geesche gives as her motive to the dying woman: 'I wanted to protect you from leading the life you're currently living' (*Stücke*, p. 642). In a deleted passage from an earlier handwritten version held in the Kinemathek, Geesche expands: 'You say you're content, but . . . actually you're not. You can't be, because . . . contentedness, that's to do with reason and reason's something women aren't allowed to have.' Fassbinder may have felt he was spelling things out just a little too clearly in this additional text and preferred to leave the audience with the cold paternalism Geesche displays, something she rebelled against at the beginning of the play.

Geesche's journey into becoming that which she despised makes her relationship with the audience something of a reversal of Petra von Kant's. Whereas Petra had to suffer and expose her weaknesses to elicit sympathy, Geesche becomes gradually less palatable, someone that the audience has to come to terms with rather than learn to accept. This transformation is also evident in a tiny change made by Fassbinder to Geesche's first line. Originally, Geesche said: 'And what about me? I want to sleep with you.' The egocentric opening question was cut to allow for the development of a sense of self during the play, which later assumes such brutal dimensions. The once-desired quality becomes highly questionable.

[93] As we shall see in chapter 4, Fassbinder also planned to direct *Maria Magdalene* at the Theater am Turm.

The première of the play took place on 10 December 1971 in Bremen's still new studio theatre. Minks was again the set designer and his stage and treatment of space were hailed almost universally by the press (see fig. 18). The flexible Concordia had two grandstands set up in a traverse. In between them was a mouldy-green cross-shaped stage surrounded by a sea of red. The bloody waves were solid and awash with the detritus of the age. Furniture on the rotting cross was skewed to suggest disharmony. European flags on bunting adorned the ceiling. This may have been a play set in Bremen, but its implications went far further into a Western manifestation of individuality. The non-representational set took up central themes of the text and offered itself as a contrast to the predominantly realistic language of the piece.[94]

Fassbinder the director also offered resistance to the realism of the language by deploying attitudinal rather than psychological characterization. Social relationships defined the characters on stage. Hirschmüller, who played Miltenberger, told me that he had started the first speech of the play barking orders to Geesche. Fassbinder urged the very opposite. By delivering his text in a soft, gentle voice, Hirschmüller revealed more about the social context. He did not have to bellow for Geesche to do his bidding. Her gratification of his wishes without force suggested either years of a process that had led to her submission or even more insidiously, a state in which a master-and-servant relationship was merely expected.

The reviewers were broadly positive, the first time Fassbinder had experienced such positive unanimity that year. Praise was lavished upon the set and the skills of Carstensen. Hans Fröhlich rated her 'degree of artificiality' which was so well honed that it appeared 'natural' and unforced.[95] He further noted that Fassbinder

---

[94] Carstensen, who played Geesche, told me that Fassbinder was instantly inspired by the set. Once he had seen the stage as crucifix, he set about mapping movements and formations to exploit the novelty of the playing area.

[95] Hans Fröhlich, 'Ein bürgerliches Trauerspiel', *Stuttgarter Nachrichten*, 13 December 1971.

Fig. 18. Wilfried Minks' set for *Bremer Freiheit* (*Bremen Freedom*) was acclaimed for its strength as a visual contrast to the action. The assemblage of European detritus, mixed with the centrality of the crucifix was an inspiration to Fassbinder during the rehearsal process. © Andreas Buttmann

had managed to drain the performance of psychology and had thus left motivational questions open. Hellmuth Karasek also viewed the performance style as one that was at odds with the style of the writing: 'the production predominantly formulates itself here beside and outside language, in gesturally and optically visible dependencies, in a "language" in which the body knows more than the mouth'.[96] He also found that the position of the audience looking down onto the action was reminiscent of 'an operating table'. The spectators were invited to partake in social dissection. The main criticism was, as Jürgen Schmidt put it, that 'everything is playing for Margit Carstensen'.[97] Other critics also noted her centrality and her mobility when compared with the more static arrangements of the other characters. Although this was pleasing, Schmidt felt that Fassbinder had undermined his own dramatic impulse because Geesche should have been the object of her environment for a good part of the play.

The production was successful and was invited to the Berliner Theatertreffen, one of the most important festivals for professional productions in the FRG. This was Fassbinder's only trip there. Fassbinder was enthused enough to film the production for television in 1972, with Carstensen in the lead role again. First broadcast almost a year after its theatrical première on 27 December 1972, the set for the film version consisted of a white stage with a few pieces of period furniture set against a backdrop of projected coastal images. Although the film gives a taste of the relational acting style, it is a very different creature from the original, especially in the way it uses space.

Bremer Freiheit and *Petra* are two of Fassbinder's most frequently staged plays, but one feels that both works' naturalistic speech patterns leave them open to undynamic productions. Unimaginative companies may only see the recognizable surface and find little formally to prompt a more considered examination of the more critical

---

[96] Hellmuth Karasek, 'Mörderin, Vorläuferin', *Theater heute*, 1 (1972), pp. 14–15, here p. 14.

[97] Jürgen Schmidt, 'Trauerspiel mit Luft', *Stuttgarter Zeitung*, 15 December 1971.

elements of the dramaturgies. While the awkward form of *Preparadise* or *Blut* demands creative approaches, the subtleties of *Bremer* and *Petra* require a concerted excavation of the lead characters' contradictions, which is not a formal prerequisite.

Bremer Freiheit was Fassbinder's final commission for Bremen. His next work in the theatre took him to Bochum in the following year, as we shall see in the next chapter. But Fassbinder worked for Hübner one last time in 1973. By then, the *Intendant* had been ousted from Bremen by the SPD, the equivalent of the British Labour Party or the American Democrats. Hübner's unceremonious dismissal led him to the Theater der freien Volksbühne in West Berlin for a stay that was hardly marked by the triumphs he had celebrated in Bremen. An article in *Theater heute* at the end of Hübner's first season, subtitled 'The Misery of the Freie Volksbühne', took stock of his first year and compared the statistics for his season with those of the previous one. While only 61 per cent of the seats were taken in the year 1971/2, a sign that all was not well before Hübner came, he himself was only able to fill 51 per cent.[98]

Fassbinder directed Ibsen's *Hedda Gabler*, the first performance of which was given on 21 December 1973. Carstensen again took the lead and Karlheinz Böhm played Tesman (see fig. 19). Böhm was an actor of an older generation whose first period of stardom came from a string of films in the 1950s.[99] Fassbinder had effectively rediscovered him and cast the actor against Carstensen in the critical melodrama *Martha* (1973). Böhm suggested *Hedda Gabler* (as he was to suggest *Uncle Vanya* a year later in Frankfurt), and Fassbinder was happy to agree.[100]

Rehearsals, as always, were swift, yet the production diary that is reprinted in the brutally frank programme reveals many difficulties. Kurt Raab, who played Brack, reported, 'we're working cheerlessly,

---

[98] Rolf Michaelis, 'Ein Theater, das nicht sterben kann?', *Theater heute*, 7 (1974), pp. 23–4, here p. 24.

[99] English-speaking audiences might know him best for his lead role in Michael Powell's *Peeping Tom* (1960).

[100] Karlheinz Böhm in Lorenz (ed.), *Das ganz normale Chaos*, p. 317.

Fig. 19. One of the few examples of Fassbinder's film work influencing his theatrical direction: the obsession with mirrors and reflections makes its presence felt on stage. Carstensen is again in the lead role, as Hedda Gabler at the Theater der freien Volksbühne, West Berlin. © Ilse Buhs

miserably and it isn't fun', and Fassbinder complained that he 'simply didn't have enough imagination to think out everything for six people and still be able to direct the play in such a radical style'.[101] Such open wounds, despite their candour, were not going to inspire an audience.

Rolf Michaelis called the production an 'anti-Ibsen'.[102] Tight plotting and clearly defined characters were rejected along with the naturalism of the play, which instead offered 'a mosaic of scenic miniatures'. Friedrich Luft called the production, 'a morgue of the feelings' and Günther Rühle felt it was more like 'Strindberg's painful tableaux

[101] Cf. *Programme for Henrik Ibsen's 'Hedda Gabler'*, Theater der freien Volksbühne, West Berlin, première 21 December 1973.
[102] Rolf Michaelis, 'Bestien im Käfig', *Die Zeit*, 28 December 1973.

than Ibsen's plunging dramatic cataracts'.[103] Michaelis found so little communication in the performance that he likened it to 'a quintet of monologues', which he believed grossly misinterpreted Ibsen's ideas on isolation. The production did not help Hübner's fortunes, although he did tell me that the production was 'not exactly a flop' either.

Fassbinder offered Hübner another play. In a letter of 29 September 1972 in which Fassbinder confirmed his commitment to direct *Hedda*, he also said he was prepared to dramatize the film *Warnung vor einer heiligen Nutte (Beware the Holy Whore)*, which had been filmed in September 1970, 'or to write any other new play for you . . . My most basic condition for this, however, is my desire to direct *Othello* at the end of the [1973/4] season'.[104] The *Othello* project was never realized, but the Verlag der Autoren, Fassbinder's publisher, holds an unpublished copy of the *Warnung* version for the theatre.

The text of *Warnung* follows the film script fairly closely in that it depicts the problems facing a libidinous cast and crew on a foreign set as they wait for the director and the cash needed to continue the shoot. There are slight deviations from the film, especially in the scenes written around the relationship between the director Kosinski and Perrudja, described in the *dramatis personae* as a 'fascist'. There is more intensity and concentration on single locations in the theatre version, and it ends with a twist. One of the crew finds the possible reason for Kosinski's late arrival. A Munich paper reports the arrest of one Jeremias K. for flashing. The Munich detail also ties in with references to the *antiteater*. At one point, Kosinski asks about the availability of other actors. All those he lists were regulars in the plays and films of the early 1970s.

Harry Baer, one of Fassbinder's closest film associates, has reproached critics who called the film version painful and desperate, a mark of artistic crisis for Fassbinder.[105] Baer found its excesses both

---

[103] Friedrich Luft, 'Ibsen auf der Untertreppe', *Die Welt*, 24 December 1973; and Günther Rühle, 'Die schöne Tochter des Generals', *Frankfurter Allgemeine Zeitung*, 24 December 1973.

[104] Rainer Werner Fassbinder, unpublished letter to Kurt Hübner, 29 September 1972, Fassbinder Foundation archive.

[105] Baer, *Schlafen kann ich, wenn ich tot bin*, pp. 60–1.

ironic and funny. The theatre script seems to push the in-jokes and hysteria even further. The Fassbinder figure, the director Kosinski, is far more wilful and manipulative here. Yet while the film made after Fassbinder's death, *Ein Mann wie EVA*, was a tasteless swipe at Fassbinder's memory barely a year after his death, *Warnung* in its theatrical version is more playful in its extreme view of Fassbinder on set because it is written in a spirit of self-mockery. Indeed, Fassbinder's success in the cinema may have inspired him to pull out further stops in his reworking for the stage.

The production was never seen. Although it was announced in the 1973 special issue of *Theater heute*, in which all major theatres and publishing houses advertise their offerings for the coming season, the play was never staged.[106] Peter Berling maintains that Hübner did not think the play was of a high enough quality, but Berling is an unreliable biographer who fails to substantiate or reference many of his more fanciful claims (such as the sauna incident mentioned in chapter 2).[107] The play remains unperformed, despite the efforts of the head of the Fassbinder Foundation, Juliane Lorenz. On the advice of Heiner Müller, the 'postmodern Brecht', Lorenz offered the script to Frank Castorf, one of the most important and experimental *Intendanten* of the 1990s, shortly after the fall of the Berlin Wall. Castorf did not pursue the project.

Fassbinder was to go on to Frankfurt to take up the position of Artistic Director after *Hedda Gabler*, but before we follow his journey, we should briefly take stock of his achievements as a dramatist in the post-*antiteater* period. The breadth of his output confirms Fassbinder as a writer whose driving force was the challenge of the new. He rewrote classic texts, reconsidered melodrama, returned to the

---

[106] Advert for Verlag der Autoren, *Theater heute*, Sonderheft 1973, p. 58. The director is slated as Charles Lang. The publisher also promoted Fassbinder's *Die schönen Tangos der Faschisten* (*The Fascists' Beautiful Tangos*) at the Schauspiel Frankfurt under the direction of Peter Palitzsch. There is, to my knowledge, no evidence that this play was ever written.

[107] Cf. Peter Berling, *Die 13 Jahre*, p. 244. Hübner, in an interview with me, did not remember Berling's version of events.

experimental play and modernized the *bürgerliches Trauerspiel*. In each case he imbued the chosen genre with modifications that enhanced its ability to ask questions of its audience. Yet among all the differences of approach in the writing as a whole, there remains an ambivalence towards the characters and the subject matter that typifies Fassbinder's dramatic oeuvre as a whole. The categories of good and evil are forced to concede their mutual debt to one another as Fassbinder reveals sets of social mechanisms that are too complex to be limited to simple shorthands. Fassbinder's non-judgemental dramaturgies, in which victims and oppressors trade roles without opprobrium, frees up the spectrum of moral responses for spectators and makes them the active creators of meaning. Fassbinder's directorial practice, concerned with the presentation rather than the interpretation of the material on stage, reflects his dramatic ethics and offers the audience the requisite space to consider the subject matter treated on stage. The confluence of feeling and thinking marks Fassbinder as a post-Brechtian in that he was happy to offer empathy as long as the audience was prepared to reflect on their allegiances within the theatre.

Fassbinder's assimilation into the mainstream of the West German *Stadttheater* offered him the opportunity both to work within a financially stable and well-resourced theatre and to benefit from professional wages, which made the business of writing plays less a necessity and more an enjoyable creative activity. His appointment in Frankfurt, however, would introduce Fassbinder to the irksome tribulations of running a poorly funded theatre and would thus reapply the pressures he thought he had put behind him in Munich.

4   The big time

Reforming the *Stadttheater*: the concept of *Mitbestimmung*
The malaise in the West German *Stadttheater* in the 1960s was, as
we have seen, mainly attributable to its inability to redefine itself
against a backdrop of political and social change. Minor challenges to
its dominance were apparent in the growing *Kellertheater* scene, but
this short-lived rivalry was quickly dealt with by the superior financial
position of the *Stadttheater*. Yet all was not well within the system
itself. The question of how to confront the autocracy of the *Intendant*
and the unwieldy hierarchies that supported and deferred to this figure
was raised within the *Stadttheater* in the pivotal year of 1968 and was
discussed most prominently in the magazine *Theater heute*.

A first stirring of dissent came in an article in the February
number, when Gidy Sinter pleaded for a change of emphasis in the
theatre by putting dramatists at the helm.[1] This suggestion, which
merely replaced one type of *Intendant* with another, was not taken
up in later issues, whereas a polemic published in the April issue
was to unleash a debate which would make its presence felt in the
very heart of the system. Barbara Sichtermann and Jens Johler asked
the question whether the state of affairs could be improved by better
Intendanten or rather by the introduction of new structures. Their
article pointed to the near-feudal organization of the *Stadttheater*
and the need not for reform but structural revolution in the form of

---

[1] Cf. Gidy Sinter, 'Wie soll ein Intendant beschaffen sein?', *Theater heute*,
2 (1968), pp. 2–3, here pp. 2–3. The position of the article is noteworthy
in that the magazine was keen to publish polemics in its opening pages.
Much of what followed was also found in this position.

Mitbestimmung.[2] *Mitbestimmung* literally means 'co-determination' but is perhaps more helpfully translated as 'collective decision-making'. The two actors' central question was how the theatre could be considered 'a partner for discussion with society' if there was no possibility for discussion within its own ranks.[3] The proposal was countered in the next month's issue by Hans Lietzau and Ernst Wendt, both prominent left-wing members of the creative staff of a major *Stadttheater* in Munich. Their arguments mainly criticized Sichtermann and Johler for naivety and revolutionary romanticism.[4] Lietzau and Wendt's response to the crisis in the theatre was to demand a new aesthetic, not a change in structures, although they stated a need for the latter to be clarified. Sichtermann and Johler hit back a month later, joined by a further four colleagues, to repudiate Lietzau and Wendt. Proposals for collective management and the observation that there was more democratization within the system since the rise of the APO were tinged with a slightly more critical view from two of the group's new members. Hansjörg Utzenrath and Martin Wiebel wondered whether *Mitbestimmung*-based reforms could play any meaningful role in the theatre if the rest of the economy and society was still based on hierarchy and authority.[5] This point would be of vital importance in the years to come, as we shall see when Fassbinder took charge of the Theater am Turm (TAT) in Frankfurt in 1974. The *Theater heute* yearbook of 1968 acknowledged that *Mitbestimmung* was 'undoubtedly *the* topic of the year in the theatre'.[6] What is interesting is that the magazine named Beckett's absurdist, apolitical *Endgame* its production of the year at the same time. Clearly the political debate

---

[2] Cf. Barbara Sichtermann and Jens Johler, 'Über den autoritären Geist des deutschen Theaters', *Theater heute*, 4 (1968), pp. 2–4.

[3] Ibid., p. 2.

[4] Cf. Hans Lietzau and Ernst Wendt, 'Wie autoritär ist das deutsche Theater?', *Theater heute*, 5 (1968), pp. 1–3.

[5] Cf. Barbara Sichtermann, Jens Johler, Claus Bremer, Horst Klaussnitzer, Hansjörg Utzerath and Martin Wiebel, 'Wie autoritär ist das deutsche Theater?', *Theater heute*, 6 (1968), pp. 1–3, here p. 2.

[6] Anon., 'Theater und Revolte', *Theater heute*, yearbook 1968, pp. 25–37, here p. 25.

within its own pages had not yet translated into action in the *Stadtthe-ater* itself.

Sichtermann, Johler and two other actors announced in the February number of 1969 that they had left the *Stadttheater* and now worked 'in [West] Berlin in a free workers' commune on pedagogies for actors'.[7] Their view that theatre collectives were the only way to intro-duce revolutionary working methods was, however, untenable within the highly subsidized and developed structures of the *Stadttheater*. Although the authors never graced the pages of the magazine again in the following months, their articulation of a perceived need was re-echoed within the *Stadttheater* for several years. In a series of articles entitled 'Material on Collectivity in the Theatre' published in the fol-lowing month's edition, *Theater heute* collected impressions of work in the theatre system, reporting on productions in Kassel, West Berlin and Bremen.[8] The events discussed in the Bremen section crystallize the contradictions endemic to the system.

Kurt Hübner, was, as we have seen, a radical reformer who brought about an innovative and provocative approach to the stag-ing of plays through his unrelenting search of new talent. Hübner, for all his vision and élan, still held the position of *Intendant* and an attempt to introduce collective practices to a production of Aristo-phanes' *Women in the Assembly* proved an innovation too far. Yet the process itself also revealed the potential problems of *Mitbestimmung* within a highly subsidized structure. The director Rolf Becker wanted to stage an adaptation of the play and planned to use collective direc-tion as well as more democratic structures for the realization of the play. Rehearsals soon became protracted discussions, often about the ways in which the theatre worked rather than the production itself, and it soon became evident that a production was no longer possi-ble. The première was cancelled and replaced with a discussion enti-tled 'Reforming the Theatre'. Hübner, standing symbolically above

---

[7] Klaus Gurreck, Jens Johler, Barbara Sichtermann, and Stefan Stein, 'Zerschlägt das bürgerliche Theater', *Theater heute*, 2 (1969), pp. 29–30, here p. 29.

[8] Cf. Various authors, 'Materialien zur Kollektivarbeit im Theater', *Theater heute*, 3 (1969), pp. 22–5.

the debaters on a lighting gantry, posed questions to the group and heckled. As Peter Iden commented: 'the political discussion on working practices within the theatre had produced a theatrical scene all the same'.[9] The *Intendant* railed against ideological talk-shops that got in the way of the theatre's main purpose, the production of plays. His stance led to the resignation of one of his brightest stars, Peter Stein, who went on to found one of the few successful theatres that adopted a *Mitbestimmung* model, the Theater am Halleschen Ufer in West Berlin.

The question of democracy in the theatre was to continue well into the 1970s as various *Intendanten* experimented with reforms whilst other theatres attempted to introduce sweeping changes that did away with the all-powerful *Intendant* completely. Suffice to say, Der Deutsche Bühnenverein, made up of West German *Intendanten*, initially found it hard to accept such moves. After some hesitation, the association first considered *Mitbestimmung* in 1969. The decision to endorse structural modifications in 1970 led to heated debates at the AGM at which the *antiteater* performed *Die Verbrecher* and led to the resignation of one prominent *Intendant*.[10] The conservative organization was spared its blushes a year later when early *Mitbestimmung* experiments were failing and it broadly withdrew its support for the idea.

Experiments with democracy: Fassbinder and Zadek within the *Stadttheater* system

In 1971, Fassbinder the theatre director was much in demand. He was also able to wield the power that popular freelance directors were increasingly acquiring. In a letter to the Nationaltheater in Mainz, he wrote that he would not be able to direct Verdi's *Sicilian Vespers* because he found the structures at the theatre a constraint on the artistic freedom he required.[11]

---

[9] Iden, *Die Schaubühne*, p. 23.

[10] Cf. Lennartz, *Theater, Künstler und Politik*, pp. 86–7.

[11] Unpublished letter from Rainer Werner Fassbinder to the Department of Dramaturgy, Nationaltheater Mainz, undated but from 1971, Fassbinder Foundation archive.

Before returning to Bremen after a spell of filming to direct *Bremer Freiheit*, Fassbinder was offered a contract as a guest director at the Münchner Kammerspiele, the first *Stadttheater* to have accommodated the *antiteater* two years earlier. A contract for Christian Dietrich Grabbe's *Scherz, Satire, Ironie und tiefere Bedeutung* (*Jokes, Satire, Irony and Deeper Meaning*), a comedy of 1822, was issued on 13 September 1971.[12] Rehearsals were due to start on 15 November and the date for the première was fixed for 29 December at the latest. Fassbinder was to receive the not inconsiderable fee of 10,000 DM. Yet he turned his back on his promise to direct the play in order to show political solidarity. The head dramaturge at the Kammerspiele and a well-established dramatist of the documentary theatre, Heinar Kipphardt, had been sacked by *Intendant* August Everding for controversial texts in a theatre programme for which he had been responsible. No less a figure than Günter Grass had led the campaign to oust him. It was reported that Kipphardt had never really recovered from the blow.[13] The dismissal led to a boycott of the Kammerspiele called by Verlag der Autoren, which allowed Fassbinder to muse publicly about the state of the *Stadttheater*. In an open letter to Everding, Fassbinder wrote that the Kammerspiele were certainly not any worse than theatres anywhere else but that the boycott was

> the opportunity to exemplify how power is wielded within the theatre system. I have nothing against you or your work. But I am on the side of those who want to demonstrate through the boycott that power isn't always on the side of those who exercise it through their office or their property.[14]

Fassbinder's move, which emphasized its symbolic rather than personal motivation, was clearly unlikely to bring down an *Intendant*,

---

[12] The contract and Fassbinder's reply are both held in the Fassbinder Foundation archive.

[13] Jürgen Flimm, quoted in Uwe Naumann and Michael Töteberg (eds.), 'In der Sache Heinar Kipphardt', *Marbacher Magazin*, 60 (1992), p. 49.

[14] Open letter from Rainer Werner Fassbinder to August Everding, 23 September 1971, Fassbinder Foundation archive. The letter was sent to three newspapers and to his publisher, the Verlag der Autoren.

but sought, through its public form, to indicate the small areas of resistance available to workers in the theatre.

More significant and lasting changes could be brought about by the theatres themselves. Peter Zadek, who had been at the forefront of the *Regietheater* since the late 1960s, was appointed *Intendant* of the Schauspielhaus Bochum and he took up his post at the beginning of the 1972/3 season. Bochum was already established as a major theatre, unlike the theatre in Bremen, which was transformed by Hübner's creative flair. Bochum was a theatre steeped in tradition. Saladin Schmitt was renowned for his conventional but highly professional treatment of the classics, and when he retired in 1949, continuity was the all-important issue: Hans Schalla, another devout classicist, was appointed *Intendant* in his place. Schalla developed Schmitt's classicism, but by the late 1960s it was clear that the theatre was isolating itself from the rest of society. The theatre's management decided that a new *Intendant* was required to reinvigorate the Schauspielhaus, and Zadek was appointed in 1970 and thus given good time to assemble an ensemble.

To Zadek nothing was holy, and this attitude was evident when he joined the theatre. As was (and still is) customary practice in the *Stadttheater*, Zadek reviewed everyone's contracts before the start of his tenure. Seventy-three of the ninety creative staff did not have their contracts renewed and only twenty of the fifty-nine-strong acting ensemble were to retain Zadek's confidence.[15] Zadek also wanted to reform the function of the theatre, and put an end to its bourgeois conventionality. He introduced a populist element which nonetheless strove for high artistic values, not cheap entertainment: this was his idea of a 'theatre for the people' ('ein Volkstheater').[16] One of the consequences which followed this decision was the controversial abolition of the subscription system, which existed in almost all *Stadttheater* at the time. Subscription meant that the theatre could guarantee audiences in that spectators paid for a ticket that would give them access to

---

[15] Cf. Uwe K. Ketelsen, *Ein Theater und seine Stadt. Die Geschichte des Bochumer Schauspielhauses* (Cologne: SH, 1999), p. 252.

[16] Ibid., p. 234.

a predetermined number of productions in a particular season. The subscription system was, however, one of polite society's social rituals. The predominantly middle-class clientele purchased the tickets and patronized the arts in time-honoured fashion. Thus one of Zadek's keys to opening up his audience was to make the spectators commit themselves to the productions rather than attend because of a ticket purchased before the work had hit the stage. The move alienated many regular spectators, but Uwe Ketelsen reports that the average age of the audience dropped, helping to fulfil Zadek's aims.[17] Zadek also introduced a partial policy of *Mitbestimmung*, in which some decisions were debated by the theatre whilst others remained solely his. Zadek as *Intendant* was introducing reforms rather than a revolution.

In a bid to enliven the theatre, Zadek engaged Fassbinder as a freelance director and found him to be most enthusiastic in the preparation of the repertoire for Zadek's first year.[18] Although Zadek was initially sceptical, Fassbinder convinced him to allow his closest associates and favourite actors to join him in Bochum and all was set up for what promised to be productive co-operation. Newspapers reported the negotiations between Zadek and Fassbinder in March and April of 1971. Fassbinder was full of praise for Zadek in one article and talked of 'a possible appointment [for himself] as head director'.[19] By the end of the year, agreement had been reached: Fassbinder was to direct two plays but not to assume the high post.[20]

One of West Germany's most important newspapers printed an excerpt from Zadek's publicity brochure for his new theatre in June 1972 in which Fassbinder took pride of place. A large picture of Hanna

---

[17] Ibid., p. 249.

[18] Cf. Peter Zadek, *My Way. Eine Autobiographie 1926–1969* (Cologne: Kiepenheuer und Witsch, 1998), p. 376.

[19] Cf. Joachim Straeten, 'Zadek verhandelt mit Werner Fassbinder', *Westfälische Rundschau*, 26 March 1971; and Dietmar N. Schmidt, 'Fassbinder verhandelt mit Peter Zadek', *Stuttgarter Nachrichten*, 3 April 1971, respectively.

[20] Cf. Anon, 'Zadeks Engagements', *Süddeutsche Zeitung*, 4/5 December 1971.

Schygulla was accompanied by the text 'Fassbinder to direct *Käthchen von Heilbronn*', a classic text by Heinrich von Kleist.[21] The legend 'Zadek to direct *The Merchant of Venice*' with no picture was placed underneath. However, although Fassbinder did indeed direct two productions at Bochum, *Das Käthchen von Heilbronn* was not to be one of them.

The irresistible force and the immovable object: Fassbinder's work in Bochum

The season had not even started in Bochum before a major row blew up. Fassbinder refused to sign a contract with Zadek that did not give him the freedom he and his team required to work elsewhere, particularly in the areas of film and television. Nonetheless, it was agreed that Fassbinder would direct Ferenc Molnár's *Liliom*, the play on which the musical *Carousel* was based, and one other play in the season. Fassbinder also criticized the pressure of having to fill houses following the abolition of the subscription system.[22] Zadek was quick to retort in a manner that was combative and at times condescending. He reproached Fassbinder for wanting 'an enslaved subscription audience that has to come and see his [Fassbinder's] productions'.[23] Zadek also played the old soldier when responding to his cancellation of *Käthchen*. Fassbinder had apparently wanted a budget of 150,000 DM for the set in a production that was to last seven hours including three hours for set changes.[24] Later Zadek said that Fassbinder wanted a fully functioning waterfall for the production.[25] Zadek put Fassbinder's plans down to his inexperience and patronizingly asserted, with respect to producing for the theatre: 'you

[21] Anon, untitled, *Frankfurter Allgemeine Zeitung*, 7 June 1972.
[22] Cf. Zi, 'Bochumer Freiheit', *Die Welt*, 18 August 1972; and ur, 'Bei *Käthchens* Ausstattung griff der Intendant zum Rotstift', *Ruhrnachrichten*, 18 August 1972.
[23] Anon, 'Peter Zadek äussert sich zu Fassbinder-Interview', *Die Welt*, 19 August 1972.
[24] Cf. ur, 'Bei *Käthchens* Ausstattung'.
[25] Cf. Zadek, *My Way*, p. 377.

know, it can be learned'.[26] Zadek's ironic tone precipitated a running quarrel that lasted for the duration of Fassbinder's time in Bochum. Peter Iden, reflecting on the initial skirmish, feared the worst for the still-to-be-realized partnership but ultimately sided with Fassbinder when he surmised that Zadek had come to a rather late understanding that Fassbinder did not have the '*Stadttheater* temperament' because he thrived on his own brand of chaos as a modus operandi.[27]

The very public quarrel boded ill for Fassbinder's work in Bochum. Rudolf Waldemar Brem, a member of Fassbinder's group, gave up a safe acting contract at the Schauspielhaus Hamburg to join the group to find that Zadek was constantly trying to frustrate the work of the Fassbinder team, for example by double-booking rehearsal rooms. The problem for Fassbinder and his associates, though, was the impossibility of deciding whether Zadek meant his ruses to be taken seriously. As far as Brem was concerned, Zadek was 'the English ironist' whose motives could never be discerned. Peer Raben, who had worked with Zadek on the music for the first première of his *Intendanz*, believed that the rivalry was indeed a game, but one which had turned serious before anyone could laugh it off. The view is shared by Margit Carstensen.[28] Hanna Schygulla preferred to understand the conflict as the result of 'two *provocateurs* together' who simply could not cede ground. Whatever the reasons were for the escalating tension, its effects were not at all positive for Fassbinder's work.

Fassbinder's *Liliom* was an attempt to turn the play into something weighty and symbolic. Liliom, a barker at a carousel and an all-round jack-the-lad, finally finds love with Julie and is dismissed by the carousel's owner, Frau Muskat, out of jealousy. A botched robbery to help pay for Liliom and Julie's as yet unborn child ends with Liliom taking his own life to evade capture. After sixteen years in purgatory, Liliom is allowed one day on Earth to visit the daughter, Luise,

[26] Peter Zadek, quoted in Peter Iden, 'Wer dem Wind ins Gesicht bläst', *Frankfurter Rundschau*, 19 August 1972.

[27] Iden, *Die Schaubühne*.

[28] Margit Carstensen told me that it was difficult to take up contact with the Bochum ensemble as factions quickly developed.

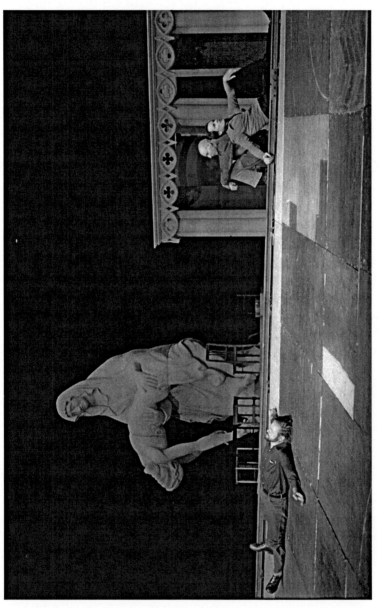

Fig. 20. A portentous set: this rehearsal picture of *Liliom* in Bochum shows the giant *pietà* and altar that served as backdrop to a production that sought weightiness through its design. © Stadt Bochum, Presseamt

whom he has never met. Unfortunately Liliom hits his daughter on the hand and is taken back to the afterlife, but Julie is able to explain to Luise that it was her father who beat her and that the blows were not meant maliciously. Fassbinder's most striking decision was to use a wildly symbolic set, replete with an overlarge *pietà*, a carousel with sheep dangling from its roof and a large altar (see fig. 20). The religious imagery was designed to make as much of the supernatural themes as possible and to present Liliom as a Christ-like figure, a martyr to the exigencies of his world. There was no theatre programme to speak of to offer other perspectives, as at that time Zadek believed that such explanatory literature undermined the integrity of the productions. Fassbinder seems to have been trying to get away from the sentimentality of the play by draining it of representational reference points. One critic noted that several cuts had been made to the text in order to make the symbolic level work more effectively.[29]

The date of the première, which was moved from 29 November to 2 December 1972, betrays the not entirely orderly arrangements at the Schauspielhaus. Volker Canaris picked up on Fassbinder's extensive use of quotation in the production: 'Fassbinder has consistently appropriated the whole story and made it a part of his world: his world of cinematic and theatrical images, his gestural and linguistic codex, his character and acting arsenal'.[30] Although Canaris considered this to be something of a 'Fassbinder by numbers', he was still able to assert that Fassbinder's fascination with quotation was a good thing for the Bochum audience. Critics applauded the acting ability, although one found the casting of the lead wrong and that the male actors presented far less complexity and contradiction than their female counterparts.[31] On the whole, critics were not dismissive of the production, but there was little praise either.

The next production was Heinrich Mann's little-known play *Bibi*, a comic satire written in 1928 on the commodification of human

---

[29] HD, 'Liliom als Ritual', *Hildesheimer Neue Presse*, 14 December 1972.

[30] Volker Canaris, 'Ist in Bochum wirklich alles ganz anders?', *Theater heute*, 1 (1973), pp. 16–20, here p. 18.

[31] Cf. Henning Rischbieter, 'Missverstandenes Melodram', *Die Zeit*, 8 December 1973.

relationships in which the eponymous hero, a gigolo, sleeps his way up the social ladder. It was originally suggested by Zadek as a text, yet there was little to be seen of the play for Fassbinder's desire bitterly to satirize Zadek's theatre instead.

Zadek opened the season with a successful dramatization of Hans Fallada's novel *Kleiner Mann, was nun?* (*What Now, Little Man?*), written in 1932 as a response to the problems of and choices for the working class in 1920s Germany. Tankred Dorst, one of Zadek's long-term collaborators, had dramatized the novel as a revue, and the mixture of catchy numbers and serious content proved a hit. According to Brem, '*Kleiner Mann* had squeezed *Liliom*' and with an increasingly unpleasant atmosphere developing, Fassbinder hit back at Zadek with a 'revenge revue' of his own at the expense of Mann's play.[32] Again the première was put back, from 31 December 1972 to 21 January 1973, and the rehearsal scripts show a production that was continually chopping and changing its direction.[33]

Many, but not all, of Mann's songs were deleted and replaced by either parodies (of Callas, Elvis, Dietrich and a host of others) or two specially penned numbers which included the final 'Bochum song', a number alive with mock affection for the city. Scenes were added, including a brief quotation from Goethe's *Faust*, a turn given by a Zadek look-alike, and a paraphrase of *Kleiner Mann*, although Fassbinder was satirizing Zadek's style: the *Bibi* props list shows that only one small item was taken from the *Kleiner Mann* production itself.[34]

The reception was not particularly warm. Gerd Jäger's review was one of the least critical, arguing that Fassbinder 'distorts Zadek's method, allowing him the possibility of criticizing it' but still concluding that Fassbinder's failure to take his audience seriously was

---

[32] Benjamin Henrichs, 'Warnung vor einer Theaternutte', *Süddeutsche Zeitung*, 24 January 1973.

[33] Both a prompt book and a running order are kept at the Stadtarchiv Bochum.

[34] Props list for *Bibi*, Stadtarchiv Bochum.

a major mistake.[35] Benjamin Henrichs, usually a champion of Fassbinder's work in the face of critical adversity, was not even able to praise the actors: 'never before had Margit Carstensen been so flat and prickly, never before had Hanna Schygulla stood around the stage so amateurishly, so isolated'.[36] Only the lead, Ulli Lommel, seemed to have committed himself to the production. Ulrich Schreiber found Fassbinder guilty of precisely that for which he reproached Zadek, namely 'the self-satisfaction at the detail of his imitation'.[37]

On reflection it would seem that the meeting of the two radical directors manifested itself in ironic games that were indeed a product of feigned antagonism. Fassbinder dedicated his 1978 film *Die Ehe der Maria Braun* to Zadek, and in an interview of 1979, he elaborated that the dedication was given because Zadek, despite his years, was someone who 'had totally changed himself. I find something very positive and hopeful in that.'[38] Fassbinder particularly enjoyed Zadek's *Othello* and *A Winter's Tale* in the previous theatre season and was astounded at Zadek's unwillingness to stage safe productions in the theatre. He also showed his respect for Zadek by employing him as an actor for a cameo role in the film *Die Sehnsucht der Veronika Voss* in 1981.[39] Zadek, in his 1998 autobiography, did not look back in anger either. Although Zadek is rather playful in the book, there is definite admiration for Fassbinder's work.[40] The mutual lack of enmity suggests that the two simply could not work together as directors, but found time and space outside such a relationship for a more open appreciation of each other's work.

---

[35] Gerd Jäger, 'Fassbinders Anti-BO Theater', *Theater heute*, 3 (1973), pp. 22–3, here p. 23.

[36] Henrichs, 'Warnung'.

[37] Ulrich Schreiber, 'Heintjes Stimme dröhnt durch Zadeks Haus', *Frankfurter Rundschau*, 24 January 1973. None of the cast members I have spoken with could redeem much from the rushed production and all were glad to leave Bochum after the run.

[38] Fassbinder, *Die Anarchie der Phantasie*, p. 139.

[39] Zadek played the 'second director', a version of Max Ophüls, in a short, affectionate sequence.

[40] Cf. Zadek, *My Way*, pp. 374–6.

An *antiteater* with (some) state funding: Fassbinder at the Theater am Turm, Frankfurt

Despite the rather uninspiring work at Bochum, Fassbinder was still in the ascendant, due to his film work and the productions in Bremen, and he had certainly not lost his interest in the theatre. As early as October 1973, there were reports that Fassbinder was in negotiations with the Frankfurt Bund für Volksbildung ('League for People's Education', hereafter BfV). This was a private group which, in spite of its forbidding name, was a liberal educational organization which ran, amongst other things, the Theater am Turm (TAT).[41] Hilmar Hoffmann, a senator for culture in Frankfurt at the time, made no bones about being openly in favour of Fassbinder's appointment as artistic director and on 26 November 1973 Fassbinder was unanimously elected a member of the three-person directorate of the theatre by the BfV's executive committee.

The TAT was a peculiar theatre in that it was not a part of the *Stadttheater* system but was partly subsidized by the Frankfurt local council. Its main competitor was the more heavily subsidized Schauspiel Frankfurt, yet it had known golden days of sorts when a young but highly successful director, Claus Peymann, had staged a series of Peter Handke premières to great acclaim.[42] Unfortunately the theatre was always underfunded and never knew how secure its next year's budget was. Regina Friedrich notes that the TAT continually

[41] Cf. Anon, 'Rainer Werner Fassbinder am Theater am Turm?', *Frankfurter Rundschau*, 29 October 1973. Once Fassbinder actually took control, he tried to abolish the 'TAT' abbreviation. 'TAT' means 'deed' or 'action' and the phrase 'die gute Tat', 'a good deed' was certainly something with which Fassbinder did not want to be associated. Fassbinder also wanted to differentiate his work from that which preceded it, and so the new, full 'Theater am Turm' banner provided a new name for theatre-goers in and around Frankfurt. Suffice to say, Fassbinder's group were never wholly successful in their proposed change of name, as newspapers and spectators continued to use the convenient abbreviation.

[42] Rudolf Krämer-Badoni reckoned that the TAT received about a tenth of the subsidy of the Schauspiel Frankfurt: cf. 'Dem Lieblingskind auf die Beine helfen', *Die Welt*, 16 November 1973.

went through a cycle of financial crises and fresh starts.[43] Indeed, such a cycle had led to the vacation of two seats on the directorate, the condition which necessitated the appointment of a new artistic director in 1973.

The TAT was also one of the few theatres that had persevered with a model of *Mitbestimmung* and the directorate was a part of the structure. The three-person team was to include an artistic director, a representative of the BfV (in this case a manager called Roland Petri) and an elected member from the acting ensemble. A '*Vollversammlung*' ('a complete assembly of all employees') also had a large role in discussing almost all matters of the theatre's business. But, despite the best of intentions, since its introduction in 1971, the model had not worked. The introduction of the system itself had verged on the revolutionary, as *Intendant* Felix Müller was removed by the democratic will of the ensemble. But the *Vollversammlung* became a talking shop that processed every minute detail of the theatre, only for the directors to be unable to fund its suggestions. The result was a riven theatre. This was not a great problem for Fassbinder initially. He was keen to bring his people to the theatre and consequently, in time-honoured fashion, he kept only five actors on contract from the ensemble he inherited.[44]

Fassbinder was competing for the post of artistic director against six actors from the TAT and a further three from one of the few other theatres in West Germany that had successfully developed a workable system of *Mitbestimmung*, the Schaubühne am Halleschen Ufer. Although an artist of Fassbinder's calibre had little to fear from the competition, especially since he had the support of the senator

[43] Cf. Regina Friedrich, '"Mündel will Vormund sein". Oder: die TAT-Story', in Katherina Bleibohm and Wolfgang Sprang (eds.), *Neue Szene Frankfurt. Ein Kultur-Lesebuch* (Frankfurt/Main: Waldemar Kramer, 1976), pp. 22–7, here. p. 22.

[44] Cf. Dietmar N. Schmidt, 'Ob das wohl gut geht?', *Stuttgarter Nachrichten*, 28 November 1973. Raben told me that he thought Fassbinder had taken up the challenge of *Mitbestimmung* at the TAT to show the culture industry precisely how to run such a system, and it seemed that he was doing so with the best of intentions.

for culture, he still had to submit a viable proposal. His concept's title owed more than a passing nod to Zadek: 'a theatre for the people [*Volkstheater*] in the broadest sense'.[45] The document set out a series of points designed to benefit not only the audience but the ensemble as well in a symbiotic process. Under the season's theme of 'group psychology', Fassbinder wanted to stage *Measure for Measure*, a dramatization of Zola's *Germinal*, Gorky's *The Lower Depths*, a Feydeau comedy and two plays on Frankfurt itself. He also hoped to reform the current *Mitbestimmung* model by defining the decision-making process more clearly. In addition, the TAT was to tour local towns which did not have their own theatres and the Frankfurt base for the TAT was to become 'a forum for encounter'.[46] Fassbinder planned to reopen the theatre's café and to introduce matinees, film shows and exhibitions to turn the theatre into a cultural centre. He also promised to honour the TAT's traditional contribution to youth theatre and to theatre for children. The scope of the document meant that Fassbinder and his team intended to stay for at least three years in order to achieve their objectives.

The plans were ambitious and writers on theatre were sceptical. Rudolf Krämer-Badoni feared the TAT would become a 'Fassbinder theatre' but acknowledged that Fassbinder's renown would benefit the theatre and offer competition for the Schauspiel Frankfurt, the main theatre in the city.[47] Others wondered whether someone with such a strong will could deal with a *Mitbestimmung* structure.[48] Fassbinder hoped to prove them wrong by firming up plans at a meeting in late January 1974 at the Appartmenthotel, West Berlin, with the ensemble he would be bringing to Frankfurt.

The minutes of the meeting show a considered review of the *Mitbestimmung* structure and an attempt to resolve the decisions of the *Vollversammlung* with the needs of a given production's

[45] Cf. Rainer Werner Fassbinder, 'Volkstheater im weitesten Sinn', *Frankfurter Rundschau*, 28 November 1968.

[46] Ibid.

[47] Krämer-Badoni, 'Dem Lieblingskind'.

[48] Cf. Dietmar N. Schmidt, 'Ob das'; or Günther Rühle, 'Fassbinder erhält ein Theater', *Frankfurter Allgemeine Zeitung*, 28 November 1973.

director.[49] It was agreed that each production would have a 'production team' made up of various elements from the creative personnel
which would follow the process of realization and offer advice. There
would also be an elected 'Theatre Council' which would be placed
between the directorate and the *Vollversammlung*. The repertoire for
the year was also refined. Shakespeare was voted down by the ensemble and Gorky was replaced by *Die Verbrecher* because of the poor
translation proffered; Strindberg's *Miss Julie*, Chekhov's *Uncle Vanya*
and Hebbel's *Maria Magdalene* joined the list in their place. Fassbinder made an important change to the way in which the productions were to be offered to the audience, too. The *Stadttheater* in the
FRG predominantly performs plays in repertoire; a month's shows will
present almost all the plays a given theatre has ready at any one time.
In order to attract guest actors, Fassbinder wanted to show plays in
fixed blocks rather than have them stay in the repertoire for a whole
season. To add to the quality of the productions and the profile of
the theatre, the group also discussed inviting guest directors of high
standing. These included Douglas Sirk and Volker Schlöndorff. Fassbinder had also tried to recruit a group dedicated exclusively to theatre
for children. Fassbinder's first choice, Hoffman's Comic Theatre, had,
however, disbanded, but two of its members were to take responsibility for the provision at the TAT. Kurt Raab, a Fassbinder stalwart,
was elected the ensemble's member on the directorate, a move ratified
by a *Vollversammlung* in August when the team arrived in Frankfurt
en masse. A monthly newsletter was also proposed, but perhaps the
most peculiar decision was to engage a psychologist, who would help
the development of the group and initiate sessions to work through
problems. The model was based on R. D. Laing's psychiatric practices
and the proposal called for an analyst or more curiously 'a student in
his or her final semesters'. The student Jörg Albrecht was appointed
for the start of the season.

---

[49] Unpublished minutes of the *Vollversammlung* of the TAT's artistic
  ensemble for the season 1974/5, 27 January 1974. I am exceptionally
  grateful to Heide Simon and Eberhard Wagner for the provision of this
  and all the other documents from the TAT, taken from their private
  archive.

Although this initial meeting in West Berlin may have been tinged at times with post-hippie, post-APO hopes for a healthy, creative group, the intentions were sincere for many of the ensemble. Even during a crisis meeting in November 1974, Fassbinder referred back to the minutes of the gathering earlier in January and pointed out that they had hoped to make the TAT an autonomous theatre from whose ranks talent would be developed and nurtured.[50] The plans made in West Berlin were ambitious and were feeding off sentiments and aspirations that had driven the disaffected in 1968. By 1974 few theatres were still committed to *Mitbestimmung* at all. The move to run the TAT presented Fassbinder with the chance to recreate the spirit of the *antiteater* with a more solid, less chaotic base. That, at least, was the theory.

Working for the enemy: Fassbinder directs Handke at the Schauspiel Frankfurt

Before the team actually made the move to the TAT, Fassbinder directed a play at the TAT's main rival, the Schauspiel Frankfurt, in May 1974. Peter Handke's *Die Unvernünftigen sterben aus* (translated as *They Are Dying Out* but literally *The Irrational Are Dying Out*) was one of the big premières of the season. Fassbinder was one of six directors who had been offered a production of the new play in the space of two months. What helped cause a stir was that Handke had moved into what was, for him, a new type of dramaturgy, one with characters. His earlier 'speaking plays' either refused to attribute character to text or played with such abstract ideas that reference to character made little sense. In *Die Unvernünftigen*, Handke chronicles the downfall of an industrialist, Hermann Quitt. Quitt is fed up with his life at the top of the social scale and feels that the ruthless business logic that has got him there has not made him any happier. He believes that modern individualism is but the repetition of older models and that he is merely a living copy. Having betrayed three business rivals, he secures his position at the top of the heap but is confronted by a need for irrationality. The play ends with his suicide when he rams

---

[50] Cf. Unpublished minutes of the ensemble meeting, 11 November 1974.

his head against a rock. Despite the representational plot, the text is still quite distant from naturalism. Extended monologues and lengthy exchanges confer an elegiac, meditative quality on the piece. Time is slowed down and the play exploits the means of the theatre to share the experience of events as opposed to the events themselves.

According to Irm Hermann, who played Quitt's wife, Fassbinder accentuated the monological form to present the whole piece as Quitt's 'brainchild', his 'inner world', which was 'however, translated into the sensual'. The solipsistic approach meant that the production became the landscape of Quitt's consciousness. In this context, the set played an important role. Unlike the bombastic symbolism of *Liliom*, the *Unvernünftigen* set was more dreamlike and suggestive. Quitt's home with its opulent splendour and white piano was encroached upon by dunes, made of real sand, from stage right. The dunes had already moved past a giant Statue of Liberty, whose torch was obscured by the ceiling of the almost box-set apartment. The actors walked over and lay upon the dunes as if they were a normal part of the environment. More metaphorical than symbolic, the set, designed by A. Christian Steiof, served as an appropriate correlative to the obviously stylized language. The set also helped to stifle ideas of character development by presenting the whole play as a single mood and a variation on it. As Peter Iden noted, it is not that Quitt's life becomes increasingly unreal, it is unreal from the very outset.[51]

The production also introduced Fassbinder to a collective approach to staging within the conditions of the *Stadttheater*. The programme lists under 'dramaturgy' the dramaturge Horst Laube together with the complete cast, the set designer, the director and his assistant. The style of the production was marked by an engagement with the theatre at a fundamental level. Matthias Fuchs, the actor who played Quitt, told a newspaper that his performance was contextualized by a theatricality which stemmed from the text itself. He asked himself: 'so where does this Quitt actually come from? His father was

---

[51] Cf. Peter Iden, 'Verweigerte Wirklichkeit und verweigertes Theater', *Frankfurter Rundschau*, 27 May 1974.

an actor, his mother made puppets she couldn't sell.'[52] Artifice was predetermined and a concentration on an alternative reality meant that the plot would never take the tension away from the performances. Indeed, just like the denouement to *Bremer Freiheit*, the conclusion was underplayed: Quitt's suicide was 'short and without pathos'.[53]

Fassbinder was praised for playing *Die Unvernünftigen* neither unimaginatively, as it had been at its world première in Zurich, nor in the absurdist style, as Peter Stein had in West Berlin.[54] Rainer Hartmann enjoyed the way in which Quitt had been 'shattered into moods and attitudes' while the other industrialists offered 'only sham deeds, self-presentation and masks of language'.[55] Some critics mentioned the few boos from the audience at the curtain that were then swamped by cheers and applause. One reviewer, having overheard dissatisfied comments during the interval, believed that the audience was far less well disposed to the play than to the production, and that that was why the applause dominated.[56] The run turned out to be so well received that it was scheduled to open the next season at the Schauspiel Frankfurt.[57] Günther Rühle believed that the production marked a new high point for Fassbinder:

> Fassbinder has rarely worked better, more complexly, more
> ambitiously on stage than here. If one compares this Handke
> production with his best up till now in the theatre, Goldoni's
> *Kaffeehaus*, one can appreciate what he has gained in

[52] Matthias Fuchs in Gerd Jäger, 'Erinnerung an das Weltgefühl des Herrn Quitt', *Theater heute*, 7 (1974), pp. 25–34, here p. 32.

[53] us, 'Ein Hamlet der Geschäfte', *Wiesbadener Kurier*, 27 May 1974.

[54] Cf. Ruprecht Skasa-Weiss, 'Ein Salonstück in den Sand gesetzt', *Stuttgarter Zeitung*, 12 June 1974.

[55] Rainer Hartmann, 'Kulturschutt in der endzeitlichen Szene', *Nürnberger Zeitung*, 29 May 1974.

[56] Cf. Stefanie Zweig, 'Die Vernunft hat Sand im Getriebe', *Abendpost*, 27 May 1974.

[57] Cf. Anon, untitled, *Frankfurter Allgemeine Zeitung*, 24 August 1974.

differentiation, mood and colour, emotional shift, clarity and illumination of a milieu, and also visionary imagistic power.[58]

The production marked a triumph in Fassbinder's development as a director, not least because of his ability to work productively within the well-resourced *Stadttheater*. The large stage at the Schauspiel Frankfurt had been magisterially controlled and the well-trained cast was able to engage with Fassbinder's ideas and realize them with sensitivity and enthusiasm. Fuchs commented on the pleasure of acting in the production when he said that after the fourth performance the audience began to find the play amusing rather than weighty, something he enjoyed.[59] The actors were open to a less dictatorial directing style and rose to the challenge. How different things would be at the TAT.

Promise and problems: The 1974/5 season opens at the TAT
Fassbinder's arrival at the TAT in August 1974 was accompanied by high expectations for both the productions and the profile of theatre itself (see fig. 21). An advert published in Frankfurt's theatre magazine *Akt* in March 1974 proclaimed: 'Achtung! Fassbinder. From September he'll be here / be directing / want to be seen'.[60] The Carl Hanser publishing house was so interested in the experiment that it planned to bring out a documentation of the first year's work and members of the ensemble were asked to keep production diaries and other material for possible inclusion.[61] The mood was buoyant and the ensemble was keen to work hard. The relative penury of the theatre meant that almost everyone was additionally involved in a host of subcommittees and groups such as publicity, compiling the theatre newspaper

---

[58] Günther Rühle, 'Die *Unvernünftigen* verlaufen sich sehr schön im Sand', *Frankfurter Allgemeine Zeitung*, 27 May 1974.

[59] Fuchs in Jäger, 'Erinnerung'.

[60] Advert reprinted in Kai Gniffke, *Volksbildung in Frankfurt am Main 1890–1990. Festschrift zum hundertjährigen Jubiläum* (Frankfurt/Main: Waldemar Kramer, 1990), p. 74.

[61] Unpublished, anonymous notice to the ensemble of the TAT, 9 August 1974.

Fig. 21. Fassbinder's office in the TAT in happier days. The spirit of *Mitbestimmung* and the interpersonal support required to make it work were both in short supply after Christmas 1974. © Rainer Werner Fassbinder Foundation

or programmes. That areas like these were not covered by departments of their own indicates not only the financial position of the theatre but also the absolute reliance on the good will of the troupe that was needed. At the beginning of the season, the latter was not in too short supply. Elsewhere, the tone of Kurt Raab's letter of welcome to the ensemble was upbeat, although it acknowledged that a lot of hard work stood before them.[62] Similarly, the minutes of the directorate's meeting in mid-August were businesslike but positive, and a *Vollversammlung* was spent productively discussing future plans for the theatre's repertoire.[63] Amongst other things, the group decided

---

[62] Unpublished letter from Kurt Raab to the ensemble of the TAT, 20 August 1974.

[63] Unpublished minutes of the meeting of the Directorate of the TAT, 14 August 1974; and unpublished minutes of the *Vollversammlung* of the TAT, 17 August 1974.

to stage a production of Fassbinder's *Iphigenie* to commemorate the 225th anniversary of Goethe's birth in the city. The importance of maintaining the *Mitbestimmung* model was underlined, while plans to reopen the café in time for the première of *Germinal* were approved. All the same, Roland Petri, the representative of the BfV on the directorate, made it clear to a newspaper that *Mitbestimmung* had not been legally ratified as yet and so the directorate still had the last say.[64] This unresolved point would return to haunt the theatre in the coming months.

But in the present all was running well. Rehearsals began for *Germinal* on 5 August. Yaak Karsunke, the left-wing critic who had accompanied Fassbinder through his days at the *action-theater* and the *antiteater*, had written the dramatization. Zola's novel of 1884–5 charts the progress of a strike at a French coal mine. Karsunke took the central incident and developed the political options open to the miners through three representative figures. Etienne Lautier organizes the strike under a socialist banner, Rasseneur, a local pub landlord argues a more reformist line, and Souvarine is the nihilist anarchist whose only goal is destruction. There were a further twenty-one characters, whittled down from the many, many more in the novel, so that almost the whole ensemble was involved in the opening production.

The theatre had contacted Karsunke in early August with reservations about his negative ending in which Souvarine blows up the mine to put an end to its insatiable appetite for human toil. Souvarine then leaves the community in search of more dynamite to bomb more people and more cities. The request for a different ending was made in the spirit of collective understanding and negotiation, and was not the response of a group of fussy actors. Karsunke's reply was similarly collegial. He was against a positive ending because it would be contrary to his aim of activating the audience and wrote epigrammatically, 'no one learns how to bite on food that's been pre-chewed'.[65] His point

---

[64] Roland Petri in Constanze Meyer-Bretschneider, 'Fassbinders Team sucht das Kollektiv', *Frankfurter Rundschau*, 16 August 1974.

[65] Unpublished letter from Yaak Karsunke to Rainer Werner Fassbinder, 7 August 1974.

Fig. 22. Fassbinder's production of Zola's *Germinal* attempted to apprehend the complexity of society by simultaneously portraying the varieties of social strata visually. While critics were impressed by the set design, Yaak Karsunke's adaptation of Zola's novel found little favour. © Manjit Jari

was that the negative ending made it open to critical engagement, and he quoted Brecht on the conclusion to *Mother Courage and her Children* to support his case. That Souvarine learned as little as Mother Courage did not preclude learning in the auditorium. Either way, he wrote that he would come to the theatre to discuss the passage with the production team. At a meeting later in the month, one of Karsunke's additions, the line beginning 'and when the bourgeoisie, on its last legs . . .', was cut as a compromise by mutual consent, and the author was on hand to explain some of his decisions.[66]

Germinal opened on 15 September 1974 under Fassbinder's direction. The set was divided up into several rooms and spaces on a dressed scaffold (see fig. 22). At its base was the mine. As one looked upwards one saw the rising social hierarchy. Workers' hovels and a bar were at the bottom, the mine-owner's residence at the top. And always in the background, the noise of coal production. The huge cast meant that Fassbinder was working in a way with which he was unfamiliar. Not only did he have twenty-four actors to organize, but he was also dealing with realistic, unstylized language for the most part. His choreographic skills were pushed to the limit, and the result was pleasing if not awe-inspiring.

Jutta W. Thomasius commented that little had been left to chance in the production, which also meant that there was little room for strokes of genius. She wrote that Fassbinder had shown, 'how a heavy lump of text can be made almost sylphlike when one approaches it with the eye of an artist'.[67] Reinhard Baumgart found that the sheer number of characters obscured individual definition and left 'a societal atmosphere, no more, no less'.[68] Another reviewer found that staging Zola's novel, 'withered through over-exertion, but this still shows the lofty ambition with which a new troupe of actors has shown itself for

---

[66] Unpublished notes from the *Germinal* production team, 19 August 1974.
[67] Jutta W. Thomasius, 'Drei Stunden in der Hölle der vom Leben Geschundenen', *Abendpost*, 17 September 1974.
[68] Reinhard Baumgart, 'Erst bunter Seelenmüll, dann rote Idylle', *Süddeutsche Zeitung*, 18 September 1974.

the first time'.[69] All the same, he felt that Fassbinder's milieu was not realism and that his directorial strengths in *Germinal* were to be found in the contrastive relationships between the bourgeoisie and the proletariat. Peter Iden, too, surmised that the production betrayed much promise although the lack of edge in the opening offering was a little disappointing.[70]

Yet while Fassbinder and the actors received mainly positive reviews, Karsunke was almost universally attacked for his treatment of Zola. In the programme, Karsunke pre-emptively wrote an article called 'Correcting without Falsifying' in which he defended the change of emphasis his dramatization had given.[71] He wrote that Zola was a bourgeois writer and that his 'class-specific system of prejudice' needed to be reviewed.[72] According to his article, Karsunke offered a more Marxist approach, which included, for example, a report on the First International. Karsunke was certainly upbraided for his political interference by some critics.[73] Others appreciated the dramaturgical problems of turning a large novel into a play, but Karsunke's aesthetic generated as many problems as his politics. One reviewer wrote, 'his [Karsunke's] arrangement of the tiny scenes inevitably leads to the terrible flatness, and the ahistorical superficiality of Fassbinder's production'.[74] Benjamin Henrichs believed that 'this preoccupation with reality and realism makes nothing possible, because he [Karsunke] revives a long-time anachronistic pseudo-realism, that of the merry picture book'.[75] Henrichs developed the idea by positing that the language of

---

[69] gr, 'Die Last des Anfangs', *Frankfurter Allgemeine Zeitung*, 17 September 1974.

[70] Peter Iden, 'Freundlich und rührend', *Frankfurter Rundschau*, 17 September 1974.

[71] Yaak Karsunke, 'Korrigieren ohne zu verfälschen', *Programme of Yaak Karsunke's 'Germinal'*, TAT, première 15 September 1974, pp. 63–6.

[72] Ibid., p. 65.

[73] Cf. Gerburg Treusch-Dieter, 'Was hat Karsunke von Zola verstanden?', *Theater heute*, 10 (1974), pp. 12–16.

[74] Henning Rischbieter, 'Arbeit auf dem Theater', *Theater heute*, 10 (1974), pp. 6–11, here p. 11.

[75] Benjamin Henrichs, 'Zeit der Kunstlosen', *Die Zeit*, 20 September 1974.

the piece was so concerned with moving the plot forward that there was little attention to character and its context.

While superficially the production had worked quite well, there were problems. The collective approach of casting almost every actor made plain the differences between the groups of actors, namely Fassbinder loyalists, the old TAT employees and the members of the children's theatre.[76] What had been achieved in the production was all the more impressive, but divisions were not going to disappear without concerted effort. And this was something that was almost impossible to afford, given the huge pressure on the ensemble to act in plays and to help run a theatre.

Deterioration and a glimmer of hope: *Miss Julie* and the return of *Die Verbrecher*

Trouble was brewing in the area of theatre for children at the TAT. Dietmar Roberg, one of the two specialists in that area, had written the play *Martha, die letzte Wandertaube* (*Martha, the Last Wandering Dove*), and this was to be the first work of the season for children. Yet in a letter to the ensemble, Fassbinder pointed out both the weaknesses of the text and of Peter Möbius' direction.[77] Möbius was the other specialist, yet his directorial inexperience led Fassbinder to suggest Kurt Raab as 'directorial assistance', responsible for the actors, while Möbius looked after the technical and artistic matters. Fassbinder mentioned rumours he had heard that Möbius had threatened to go to the press if he was ousted as director and opined that he would rather part company than continue with someone he could not work with. However, Möbius was kept on. Fassbinder praised the efforts of Raab and TAT actor Volker Spengler who were supporting the project 'out of pure discipline' and concluded the letter with the almost untranslatable word 'Tja' (approximately: 'oh well').

More worrying was the progress of *Miss Julie*, which was due to première on 8 October 1974. Fassbinder was not formally directing but

---

[76] Both Heide Simon and Irm Hermann told me that factionalism was present as early as *Germinal*.

[77] Unpublished letter from Rainer Werner Fassbinder to the ensemble of the TAT, 2 September 1974.

playing the only male role, Jean, in the three-handed drama of class and sexuality. Originally, Corinna Brocher was to direct the play but, when she decided not to make the move to Frankfurt, she was replaced by Ula Stöckl, a film-maker. The story of the fraught rehearsal process is partly documented in a surprisingly candid set of contributions published a little over a month after the opening night in the supplement to the programme of *Die Verbrecher*.

Stöckl presented her version of events as a production diary. Rehearsals started in mid-August with Margit Carstensen as Julie and Irm Hermann as the cook, Christine. Stöckl's vision seems to hark back to Romanticism in that she saw Julie's suicide as 'death as the one true proof of love'.[78] By mid-September, Fassbinder was threatening to leave the production, a move which provoked the same threat from Stöckl. The director also found it difficult to direct Carstensen as she felt the actress was too suffused by Fassbinder's stylization and instead wanted her to achieve 'a tangible vitality'.[79] By the start of October, a more collective direction was introduced, and Stöckl felt that the production had been taken out of her hands. Gottfried John, another TAT actor, took over direction but he only lasted a further week before being excluded from rehearsals on 9 October. The première was put back almost a week to 13 October.

The other two contributors to the debate, the stage manager Achim Geisler and Carstensen, offer different perspectives. Geisler felt that Stöckl was blocking the production too quickly and that her introduction of a Strindberg academic into the process as an advisor merely masked her own difficulties with the text. He noted Fassbinder's nervousness at Stöckl's indecision but also reproached Fassbinder for using *Mitbestimmung* as a means of ousting John. Carstensen was critical of Stöckl, too, pointing out that her diary showed 'in an exemplary fashion the inability of the single "individual" to come to constructive conclusions on common

[78] Ula Stöckl, Achim Geisler and Margit Carstensen, 'Diskussion: *Fräulein Julie*', in *Programme of Ferdinand Bruckner's 'Die Verbrecher'*, TAT, première late November 1974, pp. 19–23, here p. 19.

[79] Ibid., pp. 19–20.

difficulties'.[80] What is refreshing is the openness of the process as documented in the articles. Even though Stöckl's claims are countered by
Geisler and Carstensen, neither Fassbinder nor the theatre are spared.
One critic noted that Fassbinder was conspicuously absent from the
debate, but felt the forum was still a means of injecting 'more honesty, more vitality, more healthiness' into the TAT.[81] Gottfried John
adds another dimension to the story in an interview published over
twenty years after the episode.[82] He points out that Fassbinder wanted
to cancel the production, but a vote by the ensemble democratically
saved it. Once John was taken out of the loop, however, Fassbinder
effectively directed the drama himself.

The original plan to emphasize the kitchen, the site of all the
action, was to be supported by a larger-than-life vase of lilacs centre
stage to mark it as a place that would be appealing to the masters of
the house as well.[83] A flight of stairs leading upwards was to connect
the kitchen with the rest of the estate, which is never seen on stage.
By the time of the première, the lilacs had gone, but the staircase had
become the central feature (see fig. 23). Julie and Jean's inability to
escape was made clear at one point when they started to make the
climb but had to turn back. The set was also brilliant white, daz-
zling the audience with an air of unreality. The acting was typically
cool. The only person permitted an emotional outburst was Christine, while the other two underplayed the pressures and tensions of
their characters. Carstensen told me she considered the play to be 'the
double Julie', as Jean was just as refined and as delicate as his mistress.

The acting received both plaudits and more negative comment.
One reviewer found in Jean 'the submissive and simultaneously defi-
ant mentality of a slave', while another considered him too gentle,

---

[80] Ibid., p. 23. Carstensen contended in an interview with me that Stöckl
also had a feminist agenda of sorts which restricted the possibilities
available to the actors.

[81] sd, 'Die schönen glitzenden Ziele', *Frankfurter Neue Presse*, 27
November 1974.

[82] Cf. Gottfried John in Lorenz (ed.), *Das ganz normale Chaos*, pp. 216–19.

[83] Unpublished meeting of the production team of *Miss Julie*, 11 June 1974.

Fig. 23. Fassbinder and Carstensen anchored at the foot of the giant white staircase by the master's boots in *Miss Julie*. A difficult rehearsal period generated a production of sensitivity that split the audience and the critics. © Rainer Werner Fassbinder Foundation

'without Strindberg's force'.[84] The bright lights of the set led Friedrich Abendroth to feel that he was more in a dissecting room, watching the interaction of human subjects and noted: 'all the gestures were carefully steered'.[85] The element of time also made an important contribution to the production. Just as in *Die Unvernünftigen*, a sense of development through structured time was undermined. Peter Iden felt: 'this Julie has already been destroyed, Jean only brings her to a conclusion' when he orders her suicide.[86] Again Fassbinder had tried to concentrate on the elements of the characters away from the plot to offer the full breadth of their consciousnesses rather than the movement of a chain of events. The response in the press was largely welcoming, and the audience was certainly appreciative. Even the customary cluster of boos was absent. Yet the production had come at a price, and the discord and unease during the preparations for the show pointed to further rifts within the theatre, which did not only make their presence felt in the productions.

At the end of September an anonymous memorandum from the dramaturgy department pointed to funding problems that would drastically curtail its ability to put out programmes and the TAT newspaper.[87] Due to a low budget and administrative errors, the programme for *Miss Julie* would cost more for sixty pages than *Germinal* had for 195, yet the price the TAT charged would have to be lower. This is just one indication of the overstretching of both financial and human resources which would gradually put paid to the good will of the ensemble which was so evident just a month beforehand.

A ray of hope was provided, however, by Kurt Raab's production of *Die Verbrecher* (*The Criminals*), a text with which he was

---

[84] Anon, 'Empfindsames Kammerspiel', *Hanauer Anzeiger*, 16 October 1974; and Wilhelm Ringelband, 'Strindbergs *Julie* wurde Courths-Mahler Schnulze', *Rhein Zeitung*, 19 October 1974.

[85] Friedrich Abendroth, 'Eine Julien-Parabel', *Stuttgarter Zeitung*, 2/3 November 1974.

[86] Peter Iden, 'Ein mähliches Trauerspiel', *Frankfurter Rundschau*, 15 October 1974.

[87] Cf. anonymous unpublished memorandum, 'Problems from the Dramaturgy Department and Other Matters', 29 September 1974.

Fig. 24. Peforming *Die Verbrecher* in the ruins of a bygone age. Kurt Raab's production was one of the few successes of Fassbinder's term at the TAT and featured Irm Hermann (centre). © Manjit Jari

already familiar after the performance at the AGM of Der Deutsche Bühnenverein in 1970. Raab made some interesting directorial choices, including a deindividuation of the court scene at the heart of the play: he did not use separate actors for the judges and lawyers and instead had the accused and witnesses play the court officials to point to the arbitrariness of the justice in the play. His set, too, was fitting without being pompous. The ruins of a tenement building provided the backdrop to a play from the past whose content persisted in 1974 (see fig. 24). The rubbish was still there, as critics were keen to observe. One reviewer noted Raab's debt to Fassbinder in his banishment of a realistic milieu, his treatment of character as quotation, and his having all the actors on stage throughout.[88] But while Raab drew on Fassbinder's principles, the production was clearly his own work. What was most exceptional was that Raab was predominantly using the TAT's 'b-list' of actors. None of Fassbinder's 'stars' was involved and, with the exception of Irm Hermann, Ursula Strätz and Ingrid Caven, the cast were not that well disposed to Fassbinder either. Peter Iden believed that the production showed 'how a group of actors can grow together and that *Mitbestimmung* doesn't have to end in bickering and negativity, but can actually show its benefits on stage'.[89]

But this was just one instance of tranquillity and productivity. The rushed production of *Iphigenie*, directed by Raben and based on the *antiteater* version of 1968, cut very little ice with the critics. It was deemed outdated and pubertal.[90] Only one reviewer wondered whether the whole production was a parody in which Fassbinder not only targeted himself but the audience as well.[91] The show was rushed

[88] gr, 'Das schöne Bild der Verbrecher', *Frankfurter Allgemeine Zeitung*, 23 November 1974.

[89] Peter Iden, 'Nur veraltete Fragen?', *Frankfurter Rundschau*, 23 November 1974.

[90] Cf. Peter Iden, 'Frechheit, gealtert', *Frankfurter Rundschau*, 30 October 1974; and F. K. Müller, 'Der grosse Fassbinder und der kleine Goethe', *Abendpost*, 30 October 1974.

[91] Dietmar N. Schmidt, 'Fassbinder – Goethe, uns und sich selbst verspottend?', *Recklinghauser Zeitung*, 8 November 1974.

and remained trapped in the subcultural aesthetics of 1968; its only virtue was that it provided a conveniently irreverent contribution to the celebrations of Goethe's 225th birthday. Such laziness was not tolerated by either the audience or the press. What appeared a perfect antidote to the festivities in Frankfurt was executed without verve or freshness; the opportunity to re-evaluate the play had been squandered.

Ever deeper: the growing crisis at the TAT

The various crises at the TAT came to a head at a series of meetings two and a half months into the season. The ensemble met for three sessions from 22 to 24 November 1974 and discussed plans for the organization of the theatre.[92] The attempt to maintain the open nature of the TAT was supported by the invitation of guests to the meetings. The most important was Dieter Reible, who had had extensive experience of *Mitbestimmung* at the *Stadttheater* in Kiel.

One of the problems facing the theatre was the repertoire for the rest of the season. Fassbinder had suggested Arthur Schnitzler's grotesque revolutionary miniature *Der grüne Kakadu* (*The Green Cockatoo*) but was having trouble casting the play. Despite a vote in favour of pursuing the project, Fassbinder withdrew his willingness to direct on 23 November and the production was effectively dead thereafter. He felt that he could not work collectively with the actors required to fill the parts.

Reible felt that Fassbinder's centrality to work at the TAT was not helping matters. The ensemble, even those not well disposed to him, acknowledged the quality and stature of his work, but this did not make for an emancipated ensemble. Reible had seen the same thing happen in Kiel and found that the fixation on a single figure did not help the development of a democratic unit. A vote taken on the final day, however, supported a proposal that Fassbinder should continue to run the TAT with a raft of guest directors instead of a triumvirate of three permanent directors. The feeling was that guests would allow

---

[92] All information is taken from the three unpublished sets of minutes.

for variety without there being any commitment to integrate them into what was becoming an increasingly factional ensemble.

The problem of the provision of theatre for children was also raised and it was pointed out that the ensemble, although in favour of such work, was not keen to perform to such an audience. The financial pressure of producing theatre for children was constant because the TAT received subsidies to serve this purpose. Fassbinder asked Möbius why he had not been able to enthuse the ensemble for children's theatre, Möbius asked Fassbinder why he could not get *Mitbestimmung* to work. Meaningful debate was hard to generate in such conditions.

The final major point on the meeting's agenda was the construction of a plan for the season 1975/6. Fassbinder believed that regional elections in Bavaria and Hesse, the administrative region that included Frankfurt, would lead to a rise in fascism, and so he proposed that the political context should provide the theme for the theatre. After much discussion of the nature of fascism and a theatre's possible responses, a group was appointed to look into the possibilities. This seemingly agreeable solution would, however, create a further schism when a proposal supported by Fassbinder was made in February 1975.

The meetings exposed rifts that were becoming increasingly personalized and resulted from deficits throughout the TAT's organization. The very ideals which had begun the process were proving difficult to manage and were not solving the problems within the theatre. In the programme which carried the debate surrounding *Miss Julie*, two further articles were published which directly engaged with the TAT's holy cow, *Mitbestimmung*. Eberhard Wagner, the chief administrator of the TAT office, posed the question: 'Is *Mitbestimmung* nothing more than a diabolical invention of capitalism?' and used economic arguments to suggest that *Mitbestimmung* actually enhances the bosses' interests rather than reduces them.[93] Philippe Nahoun, a dramaturge at the theatre, continued the critique by positing that

---

[93] Eberhard Wagner, 'Ist die Mitbestimmung eine teuflische Idee des Kapitalismus?', in *Programme of Ferdinand Bruckner's 'Die Verbrecher'*, TAT, première late November 1974, pp. 24–5, here p. 24.

the TAT model of *Mitbestimmung* had done little to overcome a cleft between the ensemble and the directorate, so that contradictions seemed to disappear, whereas in fact they had only been cloaked.[94] A cartoon of a cleaning lady happily dancing on stage with Wagner's question in a thought bubble and the complex model under which the TAT was working also appeared in the programme. Although, just as with *Miss Julie*, the public debate was a good sign, it was difficult to deny the very concrete problems, which were admirably brought to light but which showed little sign of going away.

In the wake of the three days of meetings held in November, members of the ensemble composed a resolution to the theatre council of the TAT to allow a meeting of the ensemble at which the directorate was not present. The thrust of the motion was that the theatre should not be founded by the ensemble 'solely on the love for Rainer . . . but far more on the aim of emancipating themselves at the theatre by means of collective work'.[95] The paper was signed by nine actors. A supplementary handwritten piece found the proposal 'imprecise' but agreed with its overall thrust and was signed by a further six actors. Fassbinder and Raab responded soon after to tell the ensemble that the decisions taken in their meetings in November had no foundation in the *Mitbestimmung* regulations, and that only the *Vollversammlung*, which included technical and administrative staff, could make suggestions that were to be ratified by the directorate.[96] The letter accused the ensemble of wasting an important opportunity, although it mentioned that healthier working relationships could lead to the more productive return of the *Vollversammlung* in future.

Matters were not helped by the TAT's next production, *Uncle Vanya*, under the direction of Fassbinder. While Fassbinder had underplayed moments of dramatic tension in the past as a way of opening up the language of the characters and presenting their qualities to an audience without colouring them, Chekhov presented a play where

[94] Philippe Nahoun, untitled article, in *Programme of Ferdinand Bruckner's 'Die Verbrecher'*, p. 28.

[95] Cf. unpublished resolution to the theatre council of the TAT, undated.

[96] Cf. unpublished letter from Rainer Werner Fassbinder and Kurt Raab to the ensemble of the TAT, 1 December 1974.

understatement and submerged character traits were central to the dramaturgy. Fassbinder slowed the play down even further; the result was not a new insight into a classic text but widespread boredom. To add to the communication difficulties, the set included a great glass wall that virtually separated the audience from the stage for the whole of the first act (see fig. 25). The response from the press to the play as a whole was almost universal rejection, and one critic noted that about a third of the audience of the opening night left at the interval.[97] Eberhard Seybold found one positive comment in that the observer, Dr Astrov, was placed at the centre of the drama, as a counterpoint to Vanya, a move which lent the interpretation a certain originality. Yet the 'monotony of self importance' that pervaded the production roundly undermined the occasional good performance.[98] That Vanya himself was played by a man too young for the part and that the text itself had been altered to reduce his age to thirty-seven drew accusations of miscasting, and, as we have seen, especially at the *antiteater*, one of Fassbinder's gifts was to cast well, based on the strengths he had identified in his actors.[99] The production, unlike previous ones, was not accompanied by a thick programme. The opportunity to continue the discussion on *Mitbestimmung* was gone; the ensemble's public organ had lost its voice. Money and patience were running out.

Towards dissolution: Fassbinder's final months at the TAT
Fassbinder, Raab and Fassbinder's lover, Armin Meier, headed off to the Bahamas in the wake of the *Vanya*. They sent back a postcard to the ensemble depicting a local policeman and wrote: 'take this . . . figure of order and authority and get yourselves off on him'.[100] The barbed satire on the ensemble was typical of relations at the time.

---

[97] Dietmar N. Schmidt, 'Tschechow, wie wir ihn lieben?', *Main-Echo*, 11 December 1974.

[98] Eberhard Seybold, 'Auf der Suche nach neuen Heilmitteln', *Frankfurter Neue Presse*, 10 December 1974.

[99] Cf. Wilhelm Ringelband, 'Fehlbesetzter Tschechow am TAT', *Trierischer Volksfreund*, 22 December 1974. Seybold also agreed.

[100] Unpublished postcard from Rainer Werner Fassbinder, Kurt Raab and Armin Meier to the ensemble of the TAT, 16 December 1974.

Fig. 25. The closed glass doors of this set acted as a partition that separated the actors from the audience in the first act of *Uncle Vanya*. That the doors opened in the second act was one of the few moments of relief for an audience exposed to a most peculiar approach to distancing in the theatre. This picture shows a rather young Vanya, played by Gottfried John. © Manjit Jari

The open bitterness led to a fraught 1975 in which the TAT became more prominent through its appearances in the press than for any of its work on stage. Fassbinder did not direct another production for the rest of his time at the theatre.

January saw the airing of a popular cultural magazine on West Germany's second national television channel, ZDF. One of the items on *Aspekte* was a fifteen-minute reportage on *Mitbestimmung* at the TAT. Fassbinder criticized the actors for 'not being emancipated enough' for collective work, although the journalist Rainer Hartmann questioned whether this was just a cliché excuse.[101] The announcement in the press that Möbius, Roberg and other actors would not be renewing their contracts at the end of the year pointed to more serious trouble.[102] The month ended with what seemed to be an ultimatum from Fassbinder. He demanded an extra 145,000 DM for the coming season or else he would resign. The money was to pay for four new actors, an increase for lower-waged actors and the extension of some temporary contracts. Fassbinder may well have been involved in a war of nerves with the city authorities, but his call drew attention to the shortcomings he perceived in the quality of the acting ensemble. The press conference at which the ultimatum was announced also exposed the rift between Fassbinder (together with Raab) and the BfV's administrator, Roland Petri. Fassbinder believed that Petri's managerial position meant he should not be a part of the directorate. Günther Rühle wondered whether Fassbinder still had the power to make such demands, seeing as the problems at the TAT had made him a less attractive proposition than he was at the start of his tenure in Frankfurt.[103] Rühle did not have to wait long for his answer. At the beginning of February, the city authorities agreed to give the TAT the extra money, which would partially be financed by the selling of Fassbinder's TV rights.

---

[101] Rainer Hartmann, 'Aspekte im TAT', *Frankfurter Neue Presse*, 17 January 1975.

[102] Cf. hd, 'Keine Lust zum Kindertheater?', *Frankfurter Allgemeine Zeitung*, 21 January 1975.

[103] Günther Rühle, 'Die letzte Chance', *Frankfurter Allgemeine Zeitung*, 29 January 1975.

In mid-February the theatre announced its plans for the coming season. The theme of fascism was present, as suggested back in November, but Fassbinder and his faction had triumphed over the more orthodox left wing of the ensemble. Rather than staging antifascist plays of the 1920s, Fassbinder preferred to engage with the roots and the manifestations of fascism by looking at dramas from the beginnings of modern German nationalism, the 1890s. Plays that were forerunners of Nazism would be staged to investigate the impulses that led to the phenomenon. Brecht's *Trommeln in der Nacht* (*Drums in the Night*) would also be produced, in which the main character, Kragler, turns his back on the Spartacist uprising of 1918–19 in favour of satisfying his own desires. Wedekind's *Lulu* plays were also on the roster as an example of woman as commodity.[104] The programme was certainly challenging, and the two proto-fascist plays were unlikely to please ensemble members looking for positive heroes. However, Fassbinder's intention here to confront issues head-on differs little from his treatment of *Gastarbeiter* in *Katzelmacher* or insurgence in *The Burning Village*. One other plan for the coming season was Fassbinder's own *Frankenstein am Main* (*Frankenstein on the Main*, a pun on Frankfurt's river) which was to be based on the life of the 'celebrity prostitute' Rosemarie Nitribitt. Mentioned in this announcement as just a detail of the forthcoming season's attractions, the play would make Fassbinder the most notorious playwright in post-war West Germany, as we shall see in the next chapter.

Fassbinder's Frankfurt play was a response to the ensemble's inability to devise a Frankfurt play for themselves. The group charged with the task were not 'Fassbinder actors' and when he cancelled the production due to the low quality of the work, they set up an evening that would showcase elements of their work. On 22 March seven actors took to the stage for a show called *Ich will nichts als leben wie ein starker Baum* (*I Only Want to Live Strong Like a Tree*). Günther Rühle considered it self-indulgent and Peter Iden could understand why the directorate had cancelled the production on the basis of the

---

[104] HS, 'Am deutschen Wesen will das TAT genesen', *Frankfurter Rundschau*, 14 February 1975.

scraps presented.[105] The evening of carping and obvious satires on Fassbinder came a week after an anonymous letter, written presumably by the protesting actors and typed on TAT-headed paper, had been sent to the press. The letter complained about Fassbinder's whims, divisiveness and favouritism, but seems never to have been printed.[106]

By this time the ensemble was thoroughly demoralized. Raab had resigned as a member of the directorate in early March. The enthusiasm which had marked his letter to the ensemble at the start of the season was nowhere to be found in his letter of resignation, which was tinged with the weary recognition that he was no longer able to represent every member of the ensemble. In the theatre as a whole, work had become a chore and indiscipline had led to actors appearing late for rehearsals, often in various states of inebriation. The replacement for *Der grüne Kakadu* was Goldoni's *The Flatterer*, but the guest director Dieter Reible, for all his experience of *Mitbestimmung* in Kiel, could not work with the cast and its slovenly attitudes. He left the production days before its première in April.

Falling quality meant less income from the box office. The TAT's financial cycle had once again moved into crisis. A plea from Petri to the ensemble to maintain its professionalism, but more directly to Fassbinder to make the theatre work, had little effect.[107] Fassbinder brought a new model for *Mitbestimmung* to the *Vollversammlung* held on 25 April but it was criticized by the new member of the directorate, Heide Simon, for being too 'complicated and lacking in transparency'.[108] The vote on the new model produced the following snapshot of the indifference at the theatre: eighteen members voted for it, seven against, and a staggering seventeen abstained. Fassbinder

---

[105] Cf. Günther Rühle, 'Un-TAT', *Frankfurter Allgemeine Zeitung*, 24 March 1975; and Peter Iden, 'Der Sache nur geschadet', *Frankfurter Rundschau*, 24 March 1975.

[106] Cf. (unpublished) anonymous statement to the press, 'Warum im TAT niemand Direktor werden will', 14 March 1975.

[107] Cf. unpublished letter from Roland Petri to the ensemble of the TAT, 22 April 1975.

[108] Simon quoted in the unpublished minutes of the TAT *Vollversammlung*, 25 April 1975.

also announced that he would step down from the directorate for the new season but remain a stage director. He proposed as his successor his old collaborator Peer Raben.

High noon for Fassbinder and the TAT came at the beginning of June. An embarrassingly poor production of Pavel Kohout's *Around the World in Eighty Days* for the children's Experimenta festival cemented the belief that the TAT no longer cared about itself or its work.[109] Meanwhile Fassbinder was pushing for extra money so as to be able to employ a dwarf for his Frankfurt play. In a letter to Petri, he said he would pay the dwarf's fee as long as he could go on unpaid leave from the end of August until the end of the year to finance such a move via work in other media.[110] Petri had spoken to the executive committee of the BfV and was able to report to Fassbinder the following: leave was impossible as the TAT had to be made to work, especially in the light of figures that showed only 38.5 per cent of the theatre's seating capacity had been taken in the season 1974/5; the conservative CDU had already called for a lowering of the TAT's subsidies and so full effort would be required from all; finally, the committee could not introduce a new *Mitbestimmung* model in the current climate as time and effort would be required to implement it.[111]

Petri's understandable reply sealed Fassbinder's future at the TAT. On the same day that Petri's letter was written and received, Fassbinder tendered his resignation. A twenty-strong petition, made up of Fassbinder's faction, was then submitted to the committee, demanding the acceptance of the new model, as ratified by the ensemble, and the replacement of Fassbinder by Raben as a member of the

---

[109] Cf. Rainer Hartmann, 'TAT-Ensemble fühlt sich genasführt', *Frankfurter Neue Presse*, 6 June 1975; or Rudolf Krämer-Badoni, 'Es war nichts mehr zu retten', *Die Welt*, 6 June 1975.

[110] Unpublished letter from Rainer Werner Fassbinder to Roland Petri, 22 May 1975.

[111] Cf. unpublished letter from Roland Petri to Rainer Werner Fassbinder, 3 June 1975.

directorate.[112] What followed was a round of recriminations and the almost wholesale resignation of Fassbinder's faction from the theatre. Within days, the city of Frankfurt initiated plans to make the TAT a municipal theatre.

Fassbinder's year at the TAT exposed the weaknesses of both the *Mitbestimmung* practices of the theatre and the fact that good will can only go so far in the face of chronic underfunding. Fassbinder's temperament was certainly not well suited to the permanent duties of a quasi-*Intendant*, but there is evidence that he invested considerable effort in the venture before it started to turn sour towards the end of 1974. One is reminded of Hansjörg Utzenrath and Martin Wiebel's observation, discussed earlier in the chapter, as to whether *Mitbestimmung* was actually possible in a society in which it was not being practised at all levels. The group meetings became sites for the application of political leverage and, ultimately, a disunited ensemble simply could not reconcile its own differences under the banner of greater democracy.

Fassbinder was to return to the German theatre for one final time in the wake of the year at the TAT. He certainly had other plans for plays and directing projects, as the following chapter shows, although none of them came to fruition. His own Frankfurt play was also yet to be staged, and the eventual realization of the production would seal his place in post-war West German theatre history – but for all the wrong reasons.

---

[112] Cf. unpublished letter from Rainer Werner Fassbinder to the executive committee of the Bund für Volksbildung, 3 June 1975; and petition to the executive committee of the Bund für Volksbildung, 3 June 1975.

5 Post Frankfurt, post mortem

New York in Hamburg: Fassbinder directs for the theatre for the last time

Fassbinder's experiences at the TAT in Frankfurt were to have a major impact on his relationship with the theatre. In the years leading up to his appointment as artistic director, Fassbinder had regularly written and directed plays despite his growing fame as a film-maker. After Frankfurt he directed for just one more time, and then not on his own initiative, but to help out a colleague. The Schauspielhaus in Hamburg was mounting a production of Clare Luce Boothe's *The Women* under the title *Frauen in New York* (*Women in New York*) as part of a season to mark the USA's bicentenary in 1976. The play was Boothe's only major success on Broadway, but its run, from 1936 until 1938, made her almost $1 million. *The Women* has been filmed twice, most famously by George Cukor in 1939 in a version starring Joan Crawford and Norma Shearer. The comedy is a satire on the higher echelons of New York society, their vanity and their pretensions. The plotting is complex, but the basic strand follows Mary as she loses her husband to a young shop-assistant, Crystal, and finally wins him back again. Comic colour is added by the meddling and manipulative Sylvia, whose bitchiness also gets its comeuppance in the final scene.

The cast is interesting in two respects. First, it is large. There are forty-one parts, which dramatize the interaction between the leading ladies and their army of hairdressers, beauticians and assorted underlings. Second, not one of the many roles is written for a man. However, four of the main characters are referred to as appendages to their husbands – for example, Mary is listed as Mrs Stephen Haines. This definition adds to the social critique as the principals are presented as willingly parasitical and subservient to the wealth and standing of their husbands. Back in 1976, the play caused hackles to rise because of the unremittingly beastly behaviour of the majority of the main characters and their inability to show any female camaraderie. Gertie M. Schönfeld criticized the play for being 'so absolutely lacking in solidarity, so harsh and cynical, so devoid of any trace of the possibility for change or development'.[1] One might be forgiven for imagining that the review emanated from the other Germany, reproaching a writer for not offering a positive hero. Indeed, Donata Höffner, an actress in the cast, pulled out of the production two weeks before the première on 17 September 1976 because she could not reconcile herself with the comedy's perceived politics. Yet Boothe's own biography shows that through her own efforts, as opposed to the parasitism exhibited by her leading ladies, she became the first female US ambassador to a major country (Italy) in 1953. The author was condemning a certain type of woman, but certainly not women in general.

The director in Hamburg, Ulrich Heising, had left the production after only a few days of rehearsals, fearing that he would only be able to deal with the text by staying 'on its surface' rather than probing its depths for a more resistant reading.[2] Ivan Nagel, the *Intendant* of the theatre, invited Fassbinder to take over as director, and a newspaper confirmed his appointment on 18 August 1976.[3] Fassbinder directed Margit Carstensen, who was by then a member of the Schauspielhaus's ensemble, Eva Mattes, with whom he had already worked on film, and Irm Hermann, who was drafted in at the last minute to replace Höffner, as well as a host of well-trained and talented actresses.

Fassbinder changed little in the text. Hermann's copy of the script in the Fassbinder Foundation archive shows minor cuts and alternative formulations but the text was ultimately a version of the original rather than one of Fassbinder's more elaborate adaptations.

[1] Gertie M. Schönfeld, 'Eine Art Herrenabend', *Deutsches Allgemeines Sonntagsblatt*, 26 September 1976.

[2] Cf. ibid.

[3] Cf. JSch, 'Fassbinder inszeniert in Hamburg', *Stuttgarter Zeitung*, 18 August 1976.

Unlike the more melancholic rewrite of Goldoni in Bremen, this play remained a comedy. Fassbinder, like many German directors, had little experience of directing comedy – he had only directed one, his film *Satansbraten* (*Satan's Brew*), earlier that year. The film was not well received in Germany, but to an English-speaking audience its bitter irony and quirky misanthropy tapped into a comic tradition that was eminently recognizable. Indeed, Ronald Hayman compared the film to the dark farces of Joe Orton.[4] The film's hysterical style was to influence the direction of *Frauen* and banish any sense of naturalism from the production.

The sets and the costumes were stylish, theatrical recreations of 1930s fashion. Art Deco designs and extravagant dresses were matched by precise and geometrical hairstyles. A circular motif pervaded the set design, a visual correlative to the unending cycles of apparently changing fortunes which in fact modified little. Unlike his recent experiments with slowness and deceleration of tempo in the theatre, Fassbinder chose to have his actresses deliver their speeches with great pace, implying that there was a code of sorts that underpinned the exchanges. No one paused for thought, although occasional shifts into a lower gear indicated unexpected twists in the dialogues before normal service was resumed. The hysteria that tinged many of the main characters was not pushed to caricature but rather suggested that this was the usual mode of communication. The production progressed as if moving from pose to pose, which led one critic to surmise: 'Fassbinder . . . offers the artificiality of a Park-Avenue world . . . and creates a hothouse into which not even a breath of fresh air is blown'.[5] Fassbinder's attention to the physical arrangement of the eighteen-strong cast also had the effect of heightening the comedy. The shifting allegiances within single scenes were communicated through the careful arrangement of the actresses and exposed the ephemeral nature of friendship and loyalty in the play. The manoeuvring of the finale that finally puts paid to Crystal's plans was constructed so tightly

[4] Cf. Hayman, *Fassbinder: Film Maker*, pp. 89–90.
[5] Werner Burkhardt, 'Dreimal Broadway-Melodie . . . von 1936 bis 1941', *Süddeutsche Zeitung*, 7 October 1976.

that Kurt Lothar Tank found that 'Fassbinder has brought out with precision the disturbing nastiness of the happy ending'.[6]

The production also had its gainsayers. Gerd Jäger believed he had identified 'Fassbinder's attitude to the play: kitsch as kitsch can'.[7] He considered that Fassbinder did not probe the play for contemporary meanings, a charge echoed by Mechthild Lange as well, who regretted the production's inability to be 'critical from a modern perspective'.[8] Yet Fassbinder's critique was certainly 'modern' and was located in both the acting style and the extensive multi-casting of the minor roles. Lange noted with dismay that the actresses 'show types and avoid the appearance of individuality at every turn'. But to Fassbinder it was not only the lower social strata which were faceless in the production, but the society ladies too, who echoed each other to such a degree that their own identities were replaced by what Klaus Wagner approvingly called 'a theatricality of marionettes'.[9] Fassbinder's critique of individual autonomy was indeed a relevant contemporary theme and questioned the power of the individuals to carve out a path for themselves in such a moneyed and privileged world.

In spite of the criticism levelled by those who wished for a more overtly intellectual production or one that offered positive role models (as if Fassbinder would ever engage with such thoughts), the show was a great success and helped a major West German theatre to boost its flagging audience numbers. Fassbinder was pleased enough with the production to film it with almost the same cast in March 1977. As usual, slight changes were made to the production for television, and these included the use of contrastive camera angles to heighten the ironies of the scenes. At the end of Wagner's review of the

---

[6] Kurt Lothar Tank, 'Sieg mit einer Broadway-Satire', *Der Tagesspiegel*, 3 October 1976.

[7] Gerd Jäger, 'Hin zu Hollywood', *Theater heute*, 11 (1976), pp. 26–9, here p. 28.

[8] Mechthild Lange, 'Die absesenden Männer spielen die Hauptrolle', *Frankfurter Rundschau*, 22 September 1976.

[9] Klaus Wagner, '*Die Frauen in New York*, wie Fassbinder sie sieht', *Frankfurter Allgemeine Zeitung*, 20 September 1976.

stage version, he hoped that the success of the production would woo a resigned director back to the theatre. Although Fassbinder had not completely given up on the institution, he would never direct in the theatre again.

Non-fictional subjectivity: *Theater in Trance*

Fassbinder gave his most public show of interest in, or maybe fascination with, the theatre in the only documentary he ever made. *Theater in Trance* (*Theatre in a Trance*), commissioned by the ZDF television channel, was shot over the fourteen days of the 'Theatre of the World' festival held in Cologne, 1981. The documentary is peculiar in that it managed to signal its own subjective aesthetic without being clouded by whimsy or discomforting contrivance. Dedicated to Ivan Nagel, the festival's initiator, the film opens at the event's first-night reception. While Nagel's welcome speech is heard in which he discusses the need for art and life to move closer together, the camera follows a waiter around the large hall as he serves drinks to the well-dressed guests. Social division is signalled early. During this sequence, the titles of the following thirteen scenes are flashed across the screen and are not repeated later. Barbara Büscher argues that by getting rid of such formalities at an early stage, 'the montage of the thirteen sequences from the individual performances appears as an ordering of found objects, whose specific styles become the focus'.[10] Fassbinder dispenses with the norms of the documentary genre to offer a series of impressions of the thirteen groups and performers that drew him most. These included Magazzini Criminali from Florence, the Squat Theatre of New York, Sombrad Blancas from Mexico and West Germany's own Pina Bausch.

In between the various scenes and sometimes over their sound-tracks, Fassbinder reads from Antonin Artaud's *The Theatre and its*

---

[10] Barbara Büscher, 'Liebesmomente und Grausamkeiten: W. Schroeters und R. W. Fassbinders Filmessays über Theater – und andere Zustände um 1980', in Inga Lemke (ed.) with Sandra Nuy, *Theaterbühne – Fernsehbilder. Sprech-, Musik- und Tanztheater im und für das Fernsehen* (Anif/Salzburg: Müller-Speiser, 1998), pp. 119–35, here pp. 128–9.

Double in a neutral yet remarkably engaged tone. Fassbinder was presenting text to the viewer without interpretation, but not without interest. Wolfram Schütte linked Artaud to the nature of the festival's performers, a very different line-up from that normally encountered by West German theatre-goers. He found a 'reconsideration of the Dionysian origins of theatrical action, of the non-verbal gestures and movements'.[11] Fassbinder was quoting from a theatrical manifesto that was being realized in more physical and more visceral styles of theatre than the festival's audience was used to. Brigitte Jeremias noted: 'the cocktails offered to the elegant guests . . . provided the ironically soft frame for apocalyptic theatre'.[12] Artaud's agenda of a theatre beyond reason and order was also evident in the form of the film: Schütte enjoyed the way that Fassbinder avoided the trap of merely presenting a series of highlights 'in that the montage itself took on the style of a trance, of dreamlike reminiscence'. This very quality was criticized elsewhere, however, when Thomas Thieringer was disconcerted by the 'lack of engagement, the lack of fascination or curious interest'.[13] One man's meat was evidently another man's poison.

The hard cutting between the different performances from around the world threw the various elements into relief and accentuated cultural difference. The apparent lack of logical order meant that the film gained a dreamlike quality in which the deliberate arrangement of subject matter deferred to the associative rationales of the unconscious. That said, Büscher was still able to identify a broad thematic coherence of 'violence, loneliness and emptiness, rigidity and unfulfilled desire'.[14] Christian Braad Thomsen considered the film, 'a theoretical experiment that went wrong' because he felt, 'in most cases there's no sense of any real tension between theory and practice',

[11] Wolfram Schütte, 'Doppel-Dokument', *Frankfurter Rundschau*, 10 October 1981.
[12] Brigitte Jeremias, 'Der Kölner Dom in grünen Wiesen', *Frankfurter Allgemeine Zeitung*, 13 November 1981.
[13] Thomas Thieringer, 'Fassbinder kam gar nicht vor', *Süddeutsche Zeitung*, 13 November 1981.
[14] Büscher, 'Liebesmomente', p. 129.

but he failed to pick up on the brooding associativity of the form.[15] It is true that we might not share Fassbinder's choice of performers all the time, but the film is not founded upon tension, rather it offers vistas which the spectator may share or reject. The seamless presentation of contradiction, a central quality of any dream, was the guiding structural principle.

The performances themselves offer the viewer a snapshot of international theatrical diversity. It would be difficult to identify Fassbinder's interest in each example he chooses. It may be that the director was deliberately selecting extremes, from the physical discipline of a group of whirling dervishes to the frantically critical anticolonialism of Jérôme Savary, which might not have been shared by any one viewer. The confrontation with the other seems to have been Fassbinder's main interest, one which, by its very definition, would never please all the people all the time. This combative approach again tells us more about Fassbinder's understanding of the relationship between a work of art and its audience than it does about Fassbinder's tastes in theatre.

Keeping an oar in: Fassbinder's plans for the theatre after 1976

While *Frauen in New York* and *Theater in Trance* mark Fassbinder's final visible contact with the theatre, a raft of unrealized plans betray his ongoing interest in the medium. The only evidence of further sustained work as a dramatist is the fragment based on the Hippolytus myth, *Faedra*. Margit Carstensen told me that she had been asking Fassbinder to write her a version of the myth for some time. Fassbinder was only able to send her an incomplete first act, written, according to the cover sheet, between January 1979 and December 1980 in Berlin, Munich, Miami, Paris, Tangiers and Athens.[16] The draft was apparently a commission from the Staatstheater Stuttgart and Carstensen was to play the lead. Fassbinder outlined his ideas for the myth to Wolfgang Limmer in 1980: the plot revolved around a father and a son

---

[15] Thomsen, *Fassbinder*, pp. 309 and 297.
[16] Fragment provided from Carstensen's private archive.

(called Rainer) who cannot communicate with each other.[17] Both fall in love with Faedra and all three try to maintain a *ménage à trois*. Faedra is unable to bear the arrangement, because neither man wants to fight for her, and so she kills herself. Fassbinder also considered an alternative ending in which the father and son fall in love with each other. For all its melodrama, Fassbinder's version ironically taps into the very same issues as the Greeks, namely insoluble human problems. He offers no answers but allows the plot to follow the passions of his characters. An alternative and probably earlier draft of the play is kept at the Fassbinder Foundation archive. It retains many of Euripides' original characters with Fassbinder's new ones added in brackets. Although this fragment is closer to the original myth in its structure, it is still a long way removed from either the ancient Greeks or Racine.

In an interview in 1978, Fassbinder mentioned that he was working on a new play called *Ende endlos (An End without an End)*.[18] The piece was to be a meditation on death and the way in which it impinges on living human beings as a concept. Fassbinder also looked to drama for inspiration for his work in other media and rewrote Jean Cocteau's *La Voix humaine* as *Anormal Human Ugly Voice* (the title is written in English in the typescript) for the television. Another unrealized plan was the oddly titled *Dolci Canti di Cancor (Sweet Songs of Cancer)*, an opera, which was to be directed by Fassbinder and his old colleague Peer Raben in June 1980 in Essen.[19] The work may have been a new approach to *Ende endlos* in that the themes of death and mortality recur. Fassbinder had expressed an interest in the opera back in 1976, when he told an interviewer: 'my theory on opera is that I think opera can only start when people don't have an opportunity to speak, when feelings become so overwhelming that all they can do

---

[17] Cf. Limmer, *Rainer Werner Fassbinder, Filmemacher*, p. 60.

[18] Fassbinder in Horst Laube, 'Die Kuller des Systems zerstören', in Laube (ed.) with Brigitte Landes, *Theaterbuch*, vol. 1 (Munich: Carl Hanser, 1978), pp. 324–6, here p. 326.

[19] Cf. unpublished (and unsigned) contract between the Städtische Bühnen Essen and Rainer Werner Fassbinder, 4 January 1979, Kinemathek, Berlin.

is sing'.[20] In the same interview, Fassbinder also talked of a different plan to give Raben a libretto based on a story by Gerhard Zwerenz.[21] One newspaper reported that the opera in Essen was to deal with the sick son of an industrialist who was suffering from cancer.[22] The plan was postponed indefinitely, however, when Fassbinder started filming his thirteen-part masterpiece, *Berlin Alexanderplatz*.

Other projects included a possible return to the TAT in the early 1980s as a guest director. A letter from Peter Hahn, the director there at the time, told Fassbinder that the theatre existed in a new form without its own ensemble. He mentioned that Karlheinz Braun, Fassbinder's publisher, had 'told me about your two-handed project, a love story'.[23] Nothing became of that either, but it is difficult to say whether this was because Fassbinder was too busy or simply could not entertain the idea of returning to the TAT. Volker Spengler, an actor Fassbinder kept on at the TAT in 1974 and with whom he worked closely in the late 1970s, told me of a plan to direct Heiner Müller's experimental and, at that time, unperformed *Die Hamletmaschine* (*The Hamletmachine*). Fassbinder and Spengler had seen another Müller play in Frankfurt in January 1979 and had hated the production. They wanted to stage *Die Hamletmaschine* to show the city how it should be done properly. According to Spengler, Müller was happy with the idea, as was Karlheinz Braun, who at the time was heavily involved with Frankfurt's main theatre, the Schauspiel.

---

[20] Fassbinder, *Anarchie der Phantasie*, p. 81.

[21] Wallace Steadman Watson erroneously conflates the plans to adapt the Zwerenz story and to write an opera in Essen in *Understanding Rainer Werner Fassbinder*, p. 183. Zwerenz's story was 'Nedine oder die fünfzehnte Rose' ('Nedine or the Fifteenth Rose'), which appeared in the book *Nicht alles gefallen lassen. Schulbuchgeschichten* (Frankfurt/Main: Fischer, 1972), pp. 83–95. According to Zwerenz the story was to be renamed 'The Love of my Father'.

[22] Anon., 'Keine Krebs-Oper', *Frankfurter Allgemeine Zeitung*, 13 August 1979.

[23] Unpublished letter from Peter Hahn to Rainer Werner Fassbinder, 17 January 1980, Kinemathek, Berlin. The letter does not make clear whether the 'project' is a new Fassbinder play or one written by another dramatist. In an interview with me Braun did not remember the plans.

The pair were ultimately refused the rights, however, which had been given to the theatre in Essen, where the German première of the play took place in April 1979.

Fassbinder had also planned two further productions for the theatre shortly before his death in 1982. He wanted to tour Tennessee Williams' *A Streetcar Named Desire* and had already signed contracts with two actresses. There was also a plan, according to Juliane Lorenz, to stage Frank Wedekind's *Musik*. While the Wedekind may have been just another idea that would have fallen by the wayside, it was likely that the Williams play would have been realized (because of the contracts) and would have thus marked Fassbinder's return to the theatre.

It might have been expected that Fassbinder's death would have allowed him a respectable afterlife in the theatre, with his plays enjoying productions both in Germany and the rest of the world. However, lurking in Fassbinder's portfolio was a text that had never been produced during his lifetime and which would cause the greatest scandal in post-war West German theatre.

Drama as social dynamite: *Der Müll, die Stadt und der Tod*

In the introduction, I argued that Fassbinder's work in and for the theatre had been under-researched and largely ignored. The claim holds true for all his dramas bar one, *Der Müll, die Stadt und der Tod* (*Rubbish, the City and Death*, hereafter *MST*). Although the dramaturgy of the play is central to an understanding of its reception, the controversy it sparked concerned far more the social and political climate of a post-Auschwitz West Germany. *MST* was Fassbinder's Frankfurt play, which was scheduled to open the 1975/6 season at the TAT and which was a part of the plans for the coming season that had been announced in February 1975.[24] Fassbinder had offered to write a play about Frankfurt at a *Vollversammlung* in September 1974. While he preferred that a collective should research and devise the piece, he said that he would write his own drama later in the season, asserting that it would not be written for the Experimenta festival, 'because he

---

[24] Cf. HS, 'Am deutschen Wesen will das TAT genesen'.

didn't write experimental plays'.[25] Nonetheless, it is difficult to view the fruit of his labours as anything but one.

Fassbinder stood true to his intention of writing a play about Rosemarie Nitribitt, the Frankfurt prostitute who rose to prominence in 1957 when she was found murdered in mysterious circumstances at the age of twenty-four. It transpired that her clients included wealthy doctors, lawyers and captains of industry. In *MST* Rosemarie becomes Roma B.[26] At the beginning of the play she takes her place alongside a host of other prostitutes touting for business. Having been sent back onto the street by her pimp and lover Franz B., she is left alone and she meets a character known only as the Rich Jew, the source of the public furore caused by the play in the FRG. As the play progresses, Roma achieves high status through her association with her wealthy benefactor. As the introductory comments to the first published edition put it: 'she gains insights, which finally become so overpowering that they destroy her'.[27] The 'insights' concern the soullessness of a life that only seeks its own advantage in a world driven by capital. Searching for someone to kill her, Roma finally turns to the Rich Jew who agrees to murder her out of love. When the body is found, the Little Prince, one of the Rich Jew's henchmen, denounces his boss to the police. The police commissioner, Müller II, has the Little Prince thrown out of the window and Rosa's former pimp, Franz, is framed for the crime.

The Rich Jew is not a major character in the play; it is about Roma, her rise, her experiences at the top end of society and her death. The Rich Jew is, however, an important representative of the forces at work in the anonymous city. He is a Rachmanist landlord who buys houses cheaply, evicts the tenants and then sells the redeveloped

---

[25] Fassbinder reported in the unpublished minutes of the *Vollversammlung* of the TAT, 17 September 1974. This document, like those in chapter 4, was supplied by Heide Simon and Eberhard Wagner.

[26] In early versions of the manuscript, she is called Roma Bahn, the actress who, amongst other things, played Polly in the world première of *Die Dreigroschenoper* (*The Threepenny Opera*) in Berlin, 1928.

[27] Anonymous introductory copy in Rainer Werner Fassbinder, *Stücke*, vol. III, p. 2.

property on to large companies at a profit. The practice was prevalent in the Frankfurt of the early 1970s and Jewish businessmen made up some, but by no means all, of the speculators. Yet as the text clearly states, the Rich Jew is only given this licence by his superiors: 'the city protects me, it has to. And then I'm a Jew. The police commissioner is my friend, if you can call that friendship, the mayor likes to invite me round, I can count on the city councillors' (*Stücke*, p. 681). The character's ethnicity is central to his function in the play, as the quotation illustrates. The Rich Jew exploits the philo-Semitism that defined the official attitude towards Jewish citizens in post-Auschwitz West Germany. I shall return to this point later.

The Rich Jew's position in the socio-economic system makes him a large profit, but this is only guaranteed by his special status within the city. There are those who resent this, and they are represented by the transvestite cabaret singer Herr Müller, who is also Roma's father, and Hans von Gluck, one of the Rich Jew's business rivals. Müller believes that the Rich Jew blames him for the death of his parents in the death camps. Müller is not certain that he was responsible, because he killed so many, but adds: 'I would have been happy to [have murdered them]' (*Stücke*, p. 704). Hans von Gluck presents a different anti-Semitism. In similarly repugnant terms, he states: 'he sucks us dry, the Jew' (*Stücke*, p. 696), and wishes that the Rich Jew had met his end in the gas ovens. The line is followed by the reflection, 'so denkt es in mir' (ibid.), which does not easily translate into English. Literally he says: 'that's how it thinks in me' – it is an impersonal construction that defers agency. He claims his anti-Semitism is beyond his control, yet the envy at the loss of profit to his main competitor suggests that his feelings have a more material and less mysterious basis.

An analysis of Fassbinder's drafts of the play reveals a very deliberate strategy in the construction of one of the racists. There are at least three versions of the text, two drafts and the printed version.[28]

---

[28] The earliest draft is held in the Fassbinder Foundation. Two copies, presumably of the second draft, are also extant. One is likewise held in the Foundation and includes a dedication to Klaus Löwitsch, who

An examination of the first draft reveals two subtle changes Fassbinder was later to make in which Müller refers to his actions and beliefs. In the printed version Müller says: 'I didn't worry about the individuals I killed [in the death camps]' (Stücke, p. 703), whereas in the first draft he talks of 'the individuals I had to kill'. The shift in meaning is extended into a change of tense a few lines later. The printed version reads: 'it isn't a burden to be the murderer of Jews when you have the convictions I have' (Stücke, p. 704), whereas the first draft refers to 'the convictions I had'. The changes are not major but they indicate Fassbinder's obligation to an unrelativized and conscious commitment to Nazism in the characterization of Müller. In the revised versions, Müller is given back his agency and retains his beliefs despite the distance in time.[29] Fassbinder presents an unrepentant Nazi as a challenge to the audience.

Although it is difficult, if not impossible, to determine an author's intentions, especially after Barthes' 'Death of the Author' essay, one may surmise that Fassbinder's treatment of a Jewish character and his anti-Semitic antagonists was deliberately provocative. The crass title 'the Rich Jew' and the directness of the anti-Semitism seemed designed to unsettle an audience in as shocking and unmitigated a way as was possible in a Germany that was extremely sensitive to such provocation. Fassbinder's characterizations are extreme and fierce in a way that was hitherto unheard of in post-war West German theatre. Whether he was holding up a mirror of brutal frankness to his society, trading on the shock value of such harsh depictions to raise his own profile, or indulging in a mixture of the two is impossible to

played the Rich Jew in the film version of the play, Schatten der Engel (The Angels' Shadows), which was directed by Fassbinder's friend Daniel Schmid. The other copy, which is identical but does not include the dedication, is in the possession of Gerhard Zwerenz. Although the drafts are undated, small deviations from the printed text indicate a definite chronology.

[29] The second draft, which already includes the corrections to Müller's speeches, proves that Fassbinder made the changes and not his publisher, who, as we shall see, took liberties with Fassbinder's public statement on MST in 1976.

divine. The lack of moderation is the only undeniable factor and this fed the scandal that was to surround *MST*.[30]

The play is mainly set in the twilight world of red-light districts, slum housing and nightclubs. There are songs and a variety of un-naturalistic devices that confer an unreal atmosphere on the events on stage. The opening stage direction, for example, says that the scene is set *'on the moon, because it is as uninhabitable as the earth, especially the cities'* (*Stücke*, p. 667).[31] Only two of the nineteen characters have real names, the rest are symbolic or representative, thus emphasizing the artifice of the play and its unwillingness to engage in individual psychologizing. Fassbinder is concerned with types. Herr Müller is a part of this scheme, too, as Fassbinder uses one of the most common surnames in German to generalize Müller's anti-Semitism. The police commissioner, Müller II, is Müller's philo-Semitic double, suggesting that the special treatment of the Jewish character is problematic in both its negative and positive manifestations. By supporting philo-Semitism, Müller II helps to create the Rich Jew as a bogeyman, a destroyer of homes, who is nonetheless beyond reproach because of his extraordinary status in the FRG. The plotting also frustrates linear, naturalist chronology. A flashback to Roma's family life occurs in scene 6 and, just as in other plays by Fassbinder, long-term plot tension is underplayed in favour of the processes on display within the scenes themselves.

Fritz Wefelmeyer offers a reading of the play as an analysis of society as a closed system that permits no flouting of its rules. Either one accepts its logic or is destroyed by it. He calls the characters 'mere

---

[30] Moderation was also lacking in Peter Zadek's production of *The Merchant of Venice* in 1972. Zadek deliberately provoked his audience with a characterization of Shylock constructed in the most repulsive and aggressive of terms. Zadek, however, avoided censure because he himself was a Jew and there could thus be no suggestion of anti-Semitism on his part.

[31] This stage direction makes direct reference to one of the play's major influences, Gerhard Zwerenz's novel of 1973, *Die Erde ist unwohnbar wie der Mond* (*The Earth is Uninhabitable, Like the Moon*).

symbols of social relations' and argues, 'allegories do not stand alone, only the system explicates their value and meaning'.[32] Wefelmeyer stresses the contingency of meaning in the play and thus identifies the meaning of the Rich Jew as a function of the interpretive frame through which we choose to view him, a point we should bear in mind when considering the play's reception in the FRG. Within the 'closed system' of *MST*, the Rich Jew offers resistance to the status quo in two ways. He is the only figure both to show love and to question the language that supports the socio-economic structures. Fassbinder, as has previously been noted, was fascinated by the relationships between language, the individual and society. In one speech the Rich Jew goes to the heart of the capitalist matter when he muses on 'the profit that I need to be able to afford the things that I need. That I need? Need, need – funny, if you use a word often enough, it loses the meaning that it only had by chance anyway' (*Stücke*, p. 681). The Rich Jew is the only character to meditate on such constructed logic which everyone else, apart from Roma, considers natural. Wefelmeyer sees these qualities as positive – they distinguish the Rich Jew from those around him. On the other hand, one might add that the character is dependent on a range of anti-Semitic clichés drawn from centuries of European hatred. The ambivalence, typical of Fassbinder's character construction throughout his career as a dramatist, was so difficult to resolve that it almost inevitably left the character, and Fassbinder, open to criticism. In a society that was particularly sensitive to such a problematic representation of a Jewish character, arbiters of public morality accused Fassbinder of anti-Semitism.

The contradictions of philo-Semitism: two early reactions to *MST*

West German society faced an unprecedented task in the wake of the Holocaust. How a populace reconciles itself with such atrocity and how it treats the survivors cannot be prescribed. However, the

---

[32] Fritz Wefelmeyer, 'Die Ästhetik sich schliessender Systeme. Judendarstellung bei Rainer Werner Fassbinder', in Pol O'Dochartaigh (ed.), *Jews in German Literature since 1945: German-Jewish Literature?* (Amsterdam: Rodopi, 2000), pp. 549–65, here p. 556.

post-war years were more concerned with the *Wirtschaftswunder* ('economic miracle') than with serious political or psychological engagement with anti-Semitism or fascism. Alexander and Margarete Mitscherlich's famous study of 1967, *Die Unfähigkeit zu trauern. Grundlagen kollektiven Verhaltens* (*The Inability to Mourn. Basics of Collective Behaviour*), underlines the degree of repression that was required to blot out this unthinkable past. In addition, the 1950s witnessed former Nazis seamlessly reintegrated into politics, the judiciary, medicine and other public offices, yet the official face of German-Jewish relations was marked by philo-Semitism. It was not that West Germany had perpetuated fascism after the Second World War but that it had not dealt with its legacy in a concerted or adequate fashion. Frank Stern characterizes the dominant German attitude towards Jews after 1945 as involving a tension between 'the garb of philo-Semitism and the latency of anti-Semitism'.[33] Werner Bergmann confirms this assertion through his analysis of opinion polls on the issue, in which the discrepancy between private anti-Semitism and official 'anti-anti-Semitism' indicates the problem of such a public policy.[34] The official response to Jewish suffering was to continue to give Jewish citizens special treatment but in a positive way this time around. A philo-Semitic taboo arose in which one was not allowed to portray Jewish people in a negative light or treat them badly. Stuart Taberner points out its two faces: 'the rejection of racialist prejudice, naturally, has been as much about the stabilisation of political culture in the FRG as about sparing the feelings of Jews'.[35]

[33] Frank Stern, *Im Anfang war Auschwitz. Antisemitismus und Philosemitismus im deutschen Nachkrieg* (Gerlingen: Bleicher, 1991), p. 341.

[34] Werner Bergmann, 'Sind die Deutschen antisemitisch? Meinungsumfragen von 1946–1987 in der Bundesrepublik Deutschland', in Werner Bergmann and Rainer Erb (eds.), *Antisemitismus in der politischen Kultur* (Opladen: Westdeutscher Verlag, 1990), pp. 108–30, here p. 117.

[35] Stuart Taberner, 'The Final Taboo? Martin Walser's Critique of Philosemitism in *Ohne Einander*', *German Life and Letters*, 37 (2001), no. 2, pp. 154–66, here p. 154.

Although the main scandals surrounding *MST* took place after Fassbinder's death, they were heralded by two important incidents. The first took place while Fassbinder was still at the TAT. In the days before his resignation, he started to rehearse the play with a group of actors.[36] Indeed, his financial wrangle with the BfV over the fee for a midget actor arose because he wanted to cast the actor as one of the Rich Jew's henchmen, 'The Dwarf'. The BfV was also unhappy about the representation of anti-Semitism in the play and asked Fassbinder to make Hans von Gluck wear a Nazi armband when delivering his anti-Semitic monologue.[37] The request tells us much about the climate at the time. Gluck represents an anti-Semitism that is not ideological – Herr Müller is the former Nazi – but which demonstrates racism as both sublimated business envy and unconscious collective guilt felt in the aftermath of Auschwitz. Whereas Müller is a standard figure, Gluck embodies a new kind of anti-Semite. That the BfV wanted to conflate the two and thus neutralize the discrepancy shows just how problematic this character was to a more one-dimensional treatment of anti-Semitism. The presentation of a new kind of anti-Semitism acknowledged the reality of a category that was not supposed to exist in the FRG. Indeed, in 1986, in the wake of the scandal surrounding *MST* in Frankfurt, discussed below, Chancellor Kohl declared that he did not accept a report on anti-Semitism in West Germany and asserted that the majority of citizens were 'immune' to it.[38]

The request made of Fassbinder by the BfV was to provide the prelude to a far more public row the following year when the play

---

[36] A full cast-list is kept in the Fassbinder Foundation archive. Carstensen was to play Roma B., Kurt Raab the Rich Jew.

[37] According to Ingrid Caven, one of the actresses, quoted in Watson, *Understanding Rainer Werner Fassbinder*, p. 182.

[38] Dirk Cornelsen, 'Für Kohl sind die Bundesbürger "immun" gegen Antisemitismus', *Frankfurter Rundschau*, 27 February 1986, also in Intendanz Frankfurt (ed.), *Der Fall Fassbinder. Dokumentation des Streits um 'Der Müll, die Stadt und der Tod' in Frankfurt* (Frankfurt/Main: Stadt Frankfurt, 1987), p. 286; hereafter Doku 2.

was published. The subsequent controversies were bound by a desire to replace the effects of a work of art with pre-fabricated positions which colonized the uncomfortable aspects of *MST* and rendered them harmless.[39] The need for such solutions may be traced back to the replacement of anti-Semitism with philo-Semitism and the failure to engage with the social implications of the Holocaust in the decade that succeeded it. A persistent, if latent anti-Semitism, as discussed above, was presented in a particularly extreme form in the figure of Gluck, but this was an 'anti-Semitism without Jews', as Sigrid Weigel has argued.[40] Although there were still Jewish communities, albeit small ones, after 1945, they had almost no public profile and thus the feelings of antipathy emanated from a persistent guilt which had never been addressed through politics or culture.

MST was published as one of three plays in a third anthology of Fassbinder's drama early in March 1976. Helmut Schmitz wrote a review in which he compared the Rich Jew to Gerhard Zwerenz's Abraham, the Jewish protagonist in the novel that inspired the play, and found that 'only a pale copy remained, which could be fatally ingested into the clichéd anti-Semitic image of the rich, sexually potent and nonetheless sentimental Jewish businessman'.[41] Schmitz warned of misinterpretation, but his subjunctive mood ('could be') did not condemn the play. In contrast, a reviewer at another newspaper, Joachim Fest, was happy to misinterpret and cast Fassbinder in a highly dubious light: 'the concept of "left-wing fascism" has certainly

---

[39] For a full discussion cf. David Barnett, 'The Simulation of a Reception. Or: Rainer Werner Fassbinder's *Der Müll, die Stadt und der Tod* in Germany, Holland, and Israel', *Contemporary Theatre Review*, 14 (2004), no. 2, pp. 29–40.

[40] Cf. Sigrid Weigel, 'Shylocks Wiederkehr. Die Verwandlung von Schuld in Schulden oder: Zum symbolischen Tausch der Wiedergutmachung', *Zeitschrift für deutsche Philologie*, 114: Sonderheft (1995), pp. 3–22.

[41] Helmut Schmitz, 'Müllkutscher Fassbinder', *Frankfurter Rundschau*, 12 March 1976, also in Heiner Lichtenstein (ed.), *Die Fassbinder-Kontroverse oder das Ende der Schonzeit* (Königstein: Athenäum, 1986), pp. 25–8, here p. 26.

long been used in a polemical and ill-defined sense. Here we have a case which the term in question covers exactly.'[42] Fest exemplified conservative philo-Semitism in the FRG. Fassbinder's anti-Semitism was presented as a given and Fest offered the racist passages in Müller's and Gluck's speeches as confirmation of his claim in a section that followed the article. Eliding an author with his characters is obviously an indefensible position in criticism, but that did not stop Fest. The journalist dubbed the play anti-Semitic, a term of such great power in a philo-Semitic society that it has never been fully excised from *MST* in West Germany. Yet Fest's own credentials were far from immaculate. Peter von Becker noted that in the 1983 edition of Fest's biography of Hitler (written 1973), a whole four-and-a-half pages of the 1190-page two-volume set were devoted to the plight of the Jews.[43] Becker was not accusing Fest of anti-Semitism but of hypocrisy.

One ground for the public and vociferous championing of the Jewish cause by conservatives in the FRG is offered by Moishe Postone. He suggests that conservatives opposed anti-Semitism as a way of reducing fascism to racism and thereby ignoring hierarchical and pernicious fascist structures that persisted beyond 1945. Postone argues that the corollary of this approach was to enable conservatives to relegate fascism's status in their own political iconography: 'to accuse him [Fassbinder] of anti-Semitism allows the conservatives to emphasize their distance from National Socialism in a manner that costs them nothing'.[44] CDU Chancellor Konrad Adenauer had, after

---

[42] Cf. Joachim Fest, 'Linksfaschismus', *Frankfurter Allgemeine Zeitung*, 19 March 1976, in Intendanz Frankfurt (ed.), *Fassbinder ohne Ende. Eine Dokumentation anlässlich der Uraufführung von Rainer Werner Fassbinders 'Der Müll, die Stadt und der Tod' im Kammerspiel von Schauspiel Frankfurt am 31. Oktober 1985* (Frankfurt/Main: Stadt Frankfurt, 1985), p. 20; hereafter Doku 1.

[43] Peter von Becker, 'Fast verspielt', *Theater heute*, 12 (1985), pp. 3–9, here p. 9.

[44] Andrei S. Markovits, Seyla Benhabib and Moishe Postone, 'Rainer Werner Fassbinder's *Garbage, the City and Death*: Renewed Antagonisms in the Complex Relationship between Jews and Germans in the Federal Republic of Germany', *New German Critique*, 38 (1986), pp. 3–27, here p. 26.

all, presided over the *Wirtschaftswunder*, the period in which economics took precedence over coming to terms with the past. We shall see further conservative attacks on Fassbinder in the 1980s. Again it should be emphasized that the FRG was not an anti-Semitic state under the conservatives, but that their priorities and unwillingness to open a debate on the past (and thus to repress it) did little to deal with the social or psychological repercussions of the Holocaust. The largely latent feelings of resentment that developed without a palpable Jewish presence in West German society indicate that the repression did not lead to a forgetting but persisting, unconscious guilt.

Fest had provoked a debate which continued in the cultural pages of West German newspapers for a further month. Fassbinder himself issued a statement on the matter, but this was sanitized and censored by his publisher of the time, Suhrkamp.[45] The main changes to the statement eliminate the link between the Rich Jew and the city authorities who permit his actions and Fassbinder's belief that Jews in the FRG had become a taboo subject, something which prevented a serious understanding of their place in society after the Holocaust. But by the time Fassbinder published his thoughts, the damage had been done, and the play was inexorably tarred with the brush of anti-Semitism in West Germany.

To play or not to play: the reception of *MST* in West Germany
The furore at the TAT over the play and Fest's attack on its publication were localized events and did little to affect Fassbinder's reputation in a broader context. Fassbinder continued to make films which were a success both at home and increasingly abroad. The publication of *MST* in 1984, two years after Fassbinder's death, in an edition together with *Petra* failed to generate any controversy at all. Yet a planned production of the play in the summer of that year raised its profile and was the prelude to a far greater scandal in 1985. Both attempts at performance were dependent upon conditions set out in Fassbinder's

---

[45] Both the original and the censored versions of Fassbinder's replies are printed in Doku 1, pp. 36–7.

oral will, which was fully accepted by his publisher and holder of his performing rights, the Verlag der Autoren. Fassbinder had decreed but never committed to paper that *MST* could only have its first public performance in Frankfurt, the city that inspired it, or Paris or New York, cities of cultural significance in which Fassbinder had spent a great deal of time when away from Germany.

Ulrich Schwab, the *Intendant* of the Alte Oper in Frankfurt, wanted to add *MST* to the programme of the 'Frankfurter Feste' in Summer 1984. The festival, a light celebratory occasion, was not the ideal context in which to perform such a difficult play and Schwab may have been trying to achieve all manner of aims by including *MST* on the bill. All the same, it was not for its incongruity that the play was prevented from being staged there. The cancellation of the production was more the triumph of local politicians over the creative process, deploying their power and rhetoric in order to avoid the staging of an uncomfortable text.

Walter Wallmann, the conservative CDU Mayor of Frankfurt, sat on the supervisory board of the Alte Oper and had expressed his concerns about the play before the affair reached the public domain after a meeting of the same board on 29 May 1984. Schwab insisted that the production should go ahead and had enlisted former TAT actor Volker Spengler to direct and one of Germany's most important dramatists, Heiner Müller, to act as dramaturge. Spengler himself had previously directed an all-male *Petra* to critical acclaim and Müller had directed his own plays three times with a great deal of success. Indeed, Müller's main idea for *MST* in Frankfurt was to stage it in the shafts and building site of the then unfinished Alte Oper underground station, a location well suited to the unreal and ruinous landscape of the play. It is thus ironic that Wallmann and his SPD senator for culture, Hilmar Hoffmann, countered that the festival would not be able to guarantee the quality of the production of such a sensitive play. The city councillors' argument, namely to criticize a potential production on aesthetic grounds, almost beggars belief, but the tactic can be explained by the fact that there was no legal justification for the actual censorship of the play. The West German constitutional court had already scrutinized the text back in 1976 during the debate which had followed Fest's article and had found no grounds for any form of prosecution. Furthermore, the FRG's constitution, the *Grundgesetz*, banned censorship, except in the case of protecting minors. The incident was finally resolved when the city authorities recapitulated a decision taken on 19 May 1981 which prevented the Alte Oper from staging its own productions so as to reduce subsidized competition between the Frankfurt theatres. Schwab then responded by announcing that the Renaissance-Theater of Berlin would produce the play for the festival. His manoeuvring only had the effect of raising the stakes. Schwab was forced to quit his position and Frankfurt had once again prevented a production of the play.

Perhaps the most insidious aspect of the affair was the way in which the rehearsal process itself was influenced by the machinations of the politicians outside. Spengler and Müller were reported to have given assurances that there would be nothing positive in the portrayal of the fascists. In the same way as the Nazi armband had been demanded at the TAT, paternalistic public policy colonized the space where text had the potential freedom to be realized as the result of a rehearsal process, not of political pressure. Schwab had also said that if there was applause from neo-Nazi quarters he would interrupt any performance and initiate a discussion.[46]

The Jewish community in Frankfurt had expressed its opposition to Schwab's plan to stage the play, but had remained in the background of the controversy. Events on 5 May 1985 changed its profile and its willingness to be heard. CDU Chancellor Helmut Kohl shook hands with US President Ronald Reagan at Bitburg Cemetery in a ceremony of reconciliation after forty years of peace between the two countries. That members of the *Waffen-SS* were buried there, and that a trip to a concentration camp was added to the programme as an afterthought to ensure parity (!), provoked the first major public Jewish protest in the history of the FRG.[47] Unsupported by the centre-left Social Democrats, who were reportedly worried about losing voters

---

[46] Cf. anon, 'Müll-Abfuhr', *Der Spiegel*, 9 July 1984, in Doku 1, pp. 60–1.

[47] In the light of Bitburg, Kohl's remarks on the cancellation of *MST* later that year are not without irony. He said he was 'delighted' at the news and added: 'I was most surprised at the lack of sensitivity for the

in an impending regional election (which they went on to win), the Jewish community was joined in protest only by the Green Party.[48] The police were used forcibly to sideline the demonstrators, some of whom were wearing their old concentration camp uniforms. Such a public show of opposition would give the Jewish community in Frankfurt the courage to become far more vocal and active later that year.

The decision to stage *MST* in the 1985/6 season was taken by the new *Intendant* of the Schauspiel Frankfurt, Günther Rühle, formerly the more liberal editor of the cultural section of the conservative *Frankfurter Allgemeine Zeitung*, the paper that had published Fest's accusations that Fassbinder was an anti-Semite.[49] Rühle told me that one of the imperatives for staging the play was to restore Frankfurt's reputation as an open, cosmopolitan city, which was not engaged in censorship and which was strong enough to use the theatre to develop its relationship with its Jewish citizens. Even so, the plan was supposed to be kept a secret but was 'leaked' to the rest of the world in an interview with the play's director, Dietrich Hilsdorf.[50]

The debate about staging the play hung, as usual, on whether or not *MST* was anti-Semitic. The question is, of course, absurd. The text, which had been found to break no laws, was raw material for production which could theoretically be anti-Semitic, philo-Semitic or, preferably, a presentation of taboo-breaking texts, offered to the

obligations that [recent] German history has set us', in anon, 'Kanzler: Heilfroh über die Absetzung der Fassbinder-Affäre', *Offenburger Tageblatt*, 14 November 1985, in Doku 2, p. 213.

[48] Cf. Hajo Funke, 'Bitburg, Jews and Germans: A Case Study of Anti-Jewish Sentiment in Germany during May, 1985', *New German Critique*, 38 (1986), pp. 57–72, here p. 70. Funke cites opinion polls carried out in West Germany in which 70 per cent of those questioned considered Bitburg 'a nice gesture of reconciliation' (p. 67).

[49] In an interview with me, Rühle contended that Fest had written and published his article in 1976 while Rühle, the editor, was away from the newspaper's office on a business trip to Berlin.

[50] Cf. anon, 'Auf dem Weg von Ulm nach Frankfurt: Dietrich Hilsdorf. "Vor mir ist der Intendant genauso wenig sicher wie die Putzfrau"', *Theater heute*, 7 (1985), p. 43.

audience for its own judgement. As the discussion of the text and
the arguments surrounding it did not include the possibilities of practical production, I shall consider some of the broader cultural and
political contradictions surrounding the production. Just as Fest's
incongruous position as both champion of anti-anti-Semitism and
Hitler biographer who found little space in his two-tome study for the
plight of the Jews raised questions about the terms of reference for the
debate, a similar tension was to be found in Mayor Wallmann. Critics
were keen to point out Wallmann's anti-Turkish/immigrant stance,
which helped him to secure electoral victory in 1984,[51] and that he
openly supported the award in 1982 of the Goethe Prize, Frankfurt's
highest cultural accolade, to the highly controversial writer and unambiguous anti-Semite of the 1930s Ernst Jünger. Wallmann was not the
only problematic figure who was against *MST*. Josef Abs, a prominent
banker, was in charge of the 'Aryanization' of Jewish property during
the Third Reich. By 1985 he had become an outspoken philo-Semite.
The figure of the returning prodigal son gave further credence to the
righteousness of the opposition to the play. The programme of the production articulated some of the other inconsistencies in both sides of
the argumentation. Heiko Holefleisch, the dramaturge for *MST*, noted
that Hoffmann, the senator for culture, had insisted in 1984 that only a
well-funded high-quality theatre could be responsible enough to perform the play, while critics argued that a subsidized theatre could
not perform such a potentially inflammatory play because of the public funding involved.[52] Holefleisch noted more logical inconsistency,
based on the view of another *MST* opponent, Michel Friedman. Friedman argued that any private theatre could produce the play to avoid
any allegations that anti-Semitism was being publicly funded, but
Holefleisch pointed out that a Frankfurt première would allow such
a state of affairs by satisfying Fassbinder's oral will. The dramaturge
also noted the contradiction running within his own theatre: 'Günther

---

[51] Cf. Rolf Michaelis, 'Deutscher Müll', *Die Zeit*, 13 June 1984, in Doku 1,
p. 62.

[52] Cf. Heiko Holefleisch, 'Frankenstein am Main', in *Programme for
Rainer Werner Fassbinder's 'Der Müll, die Stadt und der Tod'*,
Schauspiel Frankfurt, première 4 November 1985, n.p.

Rühle is producing *MST* to open up a dialogue. He's putting it on in the chamber theatre to keep it hidden.'[53]

Rühle had initiated a series of public discussions in the weeks before the première but found that the open forums merely served to entrench positions further. The two sides were still polarized and a series of public displays of discontent were organized to coincide with the première, which was scheduled for 31 October 1985. Despite public protests from the Jewish community, a tripartite petition that spanned the CDU, the SPD and the liberal FDP parties, an innumerable number of column inches, and a silent march of Protestant and Catholic opponents, the theatre went ahead with the first production of *MST*, only for members of the Jewish community to prevent the performance by occupying the stage and unfurling a long banner which read 'Subsidized Anti-Semitism'. Although there was often heated debate between the protesters and the audience in the auditorium, the performance had to be abandoned and further ones were cancelled for fear of a repetition of the action.

Although the Jewish community played a prominent part in the protest, the appearance created by a great many newspaper articles that it was an agent or driving force of the scandal was challenged only once. Rudolf Krämer-Badoni, theatre critic and vociferous opponent of *MST*, pointed out that only the support of a broad consensus of politicians, in the form of the tripartite petition against the production, gave the Jewish community the confidence to come into the open.[54] When one considers this point, the agency ascribed to the Jews was far more in keeping with the myth of a 'Jewish conspiracy', helping to further an anti-Semitic impression rather than to quash it.[55]

---

[53] Ibid.

[54] Rudolf Krämer-Badoni, 'Ist die Jagd jetzt wieder offen?', *Rheinischer Merkur*, 9 November 1985, also in Lichtenstein (ed.), *Die Fassbinder-Kontroverse*, pp. 141–4, here p. 141.

[55] The most concrete example of this interpretation is Gerd Knabe's anti-Semitic pamphlet that rests on ideas of a 'Jewish conspiracy', *Bubis contra Fassbinder. Ein Theaterkrach in Frankfurt* (Knüllwald: Winkelberg, 1995), which 'retells' the story of the 1985 controversy from this problematic perspective and concludes: 'it is clear for anyone

In tacit support of Krämer-Badoni, Heiner Lichtenstein, who edited a collection of newspaper articles on the production, lamented the fact that the protest owed much of its success to non-Jewish support and had believed that a singularly Jewish protest would have been more effective.[56]

Rühle was not finished yet, however. He believed that the theatre's final argument was the production itself and, with the acquiescence of the Jewish community, set up a *'Wiederholungsprobe'* ('a repeat rehearsal', itself a neologism in German) exclusively for the press. Although this 'rehearsal' featured the trappings of such an occasion, including the director's table in the middle of the auditorium, there were no interjections from director Hilsdorf and the critics were presented with a full performance of the play. The almost univocal response of the critics, overwhelmingly denying any anti-Semitism in the production, showed up how compromised the latter had become by events outside the theatre. Hannes Heer commented that the production was a triumph of the *'Juste Milieu'* and Hellmuth Karasek argued that the opposite of art was not nature but a production which was 'well-intentioned', that art required freedom of expression, not deference to prevailing attitudes.[57] It would be difficult to call the *Wiederholungsprobe* anything but philo-Semitic. The Nazi armband for Gluck at the TAT and the insistence on unproblematic anti-anti-Semitism at the Alte Oper had been replicated at the Schauspiel Frankfurt. Rühle's hope for a dialogue on sensitive issues was replaced by a placatory production which merely seemed to 'prove' Fassbinder was not an anti-Semite.

> to see that Ignatz Bubis [the leader of the Jewish community in Frankfurt in 1985, chair of the Central Council of Jews in 1995] has taken power in Frankfurt. From today's perspective one has to ask: only in Frankfurt?', p. 30.

[56] Heiner Lichtenstein, in Lichtenstein (ed.), *Die Fassbinder-Kontroverse*, p. 12.

[57] Hannes Heer, 'Um des lieben Friedens willen', *die tageszeitung*, 6 November 1985 in Doku 2, p. 162; and Hellmuth Karasek, 'In den Folterkammern des Gutgemeinten', *Der Spiegel*, 11 November 1985, also in Lichtenstein (ed.), *Die Fassbinder-Kontroverse*, pp. 147–51, here p. 147.

Ignatz Bubis, the leader of the Jewish community in Frankfurt at the time, was amazed to learn that the closed performance, which had been renamed a 'repeat rehearsal', was later recognized as the world première by Fassbinder's publishers on 4 December 1985. He commented that he was 'surprised' by the decision, believing that the performance was only a rehearsal.[58] But this response, too, suggests a certain willingness on Bubis's part to play his role in the extra-theatrical spectacle. Having read the myriad reviews of the performance, it would have been difficult to have reached any other conclusion than that it was not a rehearsal. That said, the performance that might have opened the floodgates for productions anywhere else in Germany or the rest of the world in fact had no such effect. West German theatres were afraid of the potential for large-scale protests and a waste of resources arising from a possible cancellation of a production, despite a willingness in certain quarters to organize rehearsed readings. Theatres beyond the FRG's borders did engage with the text, but in very different cultural and political landscapes. The play has been staged without protest and with success in Europe and the USA, where the first production was in New York, a city with the largest concentration of Jewish citizens outside Israel. The only exception was the aborted première of the play in Holland. The country had been the site of some of the largest Jewish deportations to the death camps and was almost as sensitive to the legacy of the Holocaust as Germany. That said, Jules Croiset, a prominent Jewish actor and protester against a Dutch *MST*, feigned his own kidnap by neo-Nazis to demonstrate the alleged wave of anti-Semitism the play had unleashed. The discovery of his desperate antics brought the protest into disrepute, although Holland was only able to stage the play (after the cancellation of its first tour in 1987) on 26 October 2002.

MST has still not been officially staged in Germany; even a production at the Maxim-Gorki-Theater in Berlin was cancelled in 1998. The same arguments as had been used in Frankfurt thirteen years earlier were regurgitated in the newspapers. The play and Fassbinder were

---

[58] Bubis quoted in wp, 'Rühle beharrt auf "Probe"', *Frankfurter Rundschau*, 6 December 1985, in Doku 2, p. 250.

accused of anti-Semitism; the theatre defended its artistic integrity to engage with a problematic text. The positions were just as intransigent as they ever had been, despite lone voices such as former *MST* opponent Micha Brumlik who believed that the Jewish community had found its voice in Frankfurt and had enough 'self-confidence and strength' to tolerate a production.[59] One of the most worrying aspects of this particular debate was that the events had attracted the attention of the far-right Deutsche Volksunion (DVU). Bernd Wilms, the director of the project at the Maxim-Gorki-Theater, reported that he had read a DVU pamphlet pleading for the freedom of expression 'for a German *Intendant*'.[60] Anti-Semitism was being generated by the glut of newspaper coverage that seemingly sought its defeat. Wilms bowed to the pressure and withdrew the production scarcely a month and a half after its announcement. Given all the above controversies, it is ironic that the play was actually staged in West Germany, in a student production at the Ruhr-Universität, Bochum, in 1979, without the knowledge of the Verlag der Autoren. The production ran for six performances and was reviewed in a local paper.[61] This may have been the only time that the text was presented in Germany with the freedom to experiment in rehearsal without the fear of officially sanctioned indignation.

Although, as we have seen, it was never banned, *MST* is the only play in the history of the post-war West German theatre to have been prevented from being performed in public. Fassbinder found himself at the centre of the biggest theatre scandal of recent times by having written about a topic which was officially taboo. The interest generated revealed much about the FRG's political landscape, the legacy of the Holocaust and the relationship between art and the state. It is difficult not to view Fassbinder as an agent provocateur, yet his motives, after the 'death of the author', remain obscure. The archival details discussed earlier show a defiantly uncompromising stance, yet whether

[59] Anon, 'Der Streit um Fassbinder', *Der Tagesspiegel*, 3 September 1998.

[60] Bernd Wilms, 'Die Stadt, das Stück und die Kontroverse', *Süddeutsche Zeitung*, 11 November 1998.

[61] Anon, 'Geschehen auf drei Ebenen abgespielt', *Ruhr-Nachrichten*, 24 January 1979.

this was a bid to generate headlines or to approach a very German taboo with unprecedented directness can only be speculated upon. The infamy the play brought the writer, three years after his death, may have boded ill for his memory as a dramatist, but, as we shall see in the epilogue, Fassbinder has flourished in the theatre ever since.

Lurking in the papers: *Nur eine Scheibe Brot* and *Tropfen auf heisse Steine*

Fassbinder's reply to the allegations of anti-Semitism might have been a recourse to his play *Nur eine Scheibe Brot* (*Only a Slice of Bread*), which he entered for a drama competition in November 1966, but which was not published in his lifetime.[62] No first prize was awarded, and Fassbinder took the third prize together with another author. A version of the text was submitted as a film script when Fassbinder unsuccessfully applied to the Film and Television Academy in Berlin. The play was 'rediscovered' by Michael Töteberg in 1994, who wrote: 'the manuscripts were kept safely in [Fassbinder's] mother's kitchen cupboards' and that was why they took so long to come to light.[63] The Fassbinder Foundation, however, accused Töteberg, who had been the trustee of Fassbinder's literary estate, of deliberately keeping the play out of circulation because he considered it to be of low quality.[64] However it was brought to light, the new text revealed important elements about Fassbinder's thoughts on the Holocaust which were incompatible with the slurs generated by the *MST* controversies. Although critics might argue that Fassbinder could have changed his opinions in the ten years that had separated *Scheibe* and *MST*, the issues of representation explored in both are remarkably similar.

Scheibe is a short play of ten scenes in which a young filmmaker, Fricke, having been commissioned to make a film about Auschwitz, grapples with his conscience and his interpersonal relationships. In the second scene, Fricke's friend, Friedrich von Saalingen,

---

[62] A typescript in the Fassbinder Foundation, which varies only slightly from the published version, is dated 1965, that is, it was written when Fassbinder was only nineteen or twenty.

[63] Michael Töteberg, 'Fassbinders Erstling', *Theater heute*, 5 (1994), p. 29.

[64] Anon, press release from the Fassbinder Foundation, March 1996.

prophesies the awards and renown that will be bestowed on Fricke once he has made the film, but this is precisely what he fears. While he sleeps with his girlfriend Hanna, a projection of documentary films on the death camps is accompanied by Fricke's voice on tape: 'I can't make this film. No one can make this film. All you can do is trivialize events by portraying them.'[65] Fricke is afraid that he will be making a film that comfortably fits into the public perception of the pain and suffering of the Holocaust rather than one which acknowledges the impossibility of representing such unimaginable inhumanity. Over the course of the filming he finds actors who cannot empathize with the script and who confirm Fricke's concerns that the approved repertoire of images of the death camps has already canalized their consciousness. Fricke strives to offer a different kind of film, based in the documentary form and using the popular culture of the time to contextualize the subject matter. The film is finally shot and rushed into the cinemas for Christmas. It wins three Federal film prizes.

Although Fassbinder was still young and inexperienced at the time of writing, the play approaches the subject of the Holocaust from a surprisingly mature perspective and asks the question of how one represents the unrepresentable. He points to the difficulties of opening up highly sensitive subject matter to unorthodox modes of depiction in order to circumvent official standpoints. He also draws our attention to the material problems involved in making a film about Auschwitz in which actors treat the job just as any other. While there are moments in the play that make it very much of its time, such as the generational clash between the idealistic Fricke and his uncle, Herr Baumbach, the aesthetic questions raised by the play remain current.

Scheibe was first produced at the Bregenz Festival on 12 August 1995. Reviewer Gerhard Mack found that although the material would have been explosive in 1966, it had lost its relevance in the

---

[65] Rainer Werner Fassbinder, *Nur eine Scheibe Brot*, in Fassbinder, *Der Müll, die Stadt und der Tod. Nur eine Scheibe Brot* (Frankfurt/Main: Verlag der Autoren, 1998), pp. 7–39, here p. 15.

1990s.[66] This is an almost incredible assertion, as the première followed Steven Spielberg's *Schindler's List* by a mere two years, a film whose sustained realist form raised many issues as to how one was to represent Auschwitz.[67] The theme of representation goes to the very heart of *MST*, a play in which conventional codes were dispensed with in favour of unapproved depictions. With this in mind, it may be the case that *MST* could only be performed in Germany if it were part of a double bill together with *Scheibe*.

Scheibe was the second play to be rediscovered in the reams of papers and notes that Fassbinder left behind after his death in 1982. The first to emerge was *Tropfen auf heisse Steine* (known in English as *Water Drops on Hot Rocks* in the filmed version by François Ozon), a 'comedy with a pseudo-tragic finale' as its subtitle puts it (*Stücke*, p. 7). The four acts follow nineteen-year-old Franz Meister, who is picked up on the street by the older Leopold Bluhm.[68] The first act, which like the others takes place in Bluhm's flat, shows the edgy communication between the two before they get closer. The second act takes place six months later and shows how a certain friction has entered the relationship due to the pair's very different characters. Franz is young and naive, Leopold more worldly-wise but fastidious and orderly. The third and fourth acts introduce Anna, Franz's fiancée, and Vera, Leopold's ex-wife, respectively. Leopold's charisma tempts both Anna and Vera into bed; Franz takes an overdose and dies. This ending is indeed relativized, as promised in the play's subtitle, when

---

[66] Cf. Gerhard Mack, 'Die Sechziger als Zeit kümmerlicher Klischees', *Stuttgarter Zeitung*, 15 August 1995.

[67] Jean-Luc Godard, one of the most vociferous critics of Spielberg's aesthetics and a hero to the young Fassbinder, turned down a major film prize because Spielberg had tried to recreate a death camp realistically.

[68] There is no overt link between Joyce's protagonist Leopold Bloom in *Ulysses* and Fassbinder's. The name 'Franz Meister', however, refers back to Franz Biberkopf, Fassbinder's alter ego from *Berlin Alexanderplatz*, and Wilhelm Meister, the hero of Goethe's *Bildungsroman Wilhelm Meister's Apprenticeship*. The name thus mixes a fundamentally good but flawed character with one who is entering an intense period of learning.

both women return to the bedroom while Leopold takes to the bathroom to brush his teeth.

The play is autobiographical, just like *Petra*, but Fassbinder, as usual, writes a wealth of devices into the text that transcend the personal and turn the relationships into ironic models of social interaction. The opening act deftly introduces the tension between Franz and Leopold in that the latter is already inside the flat while Franz first speaks from without. The play also probes the nature of the dependent relationships. Leopold's vanity and obsession with order undermines a simple reading of him as a successful bisexual lothario and asks what sort of people find themselves attracted to such a man. Joanna Firaza points out that Leopold's regular cleaning rituals already indicate Fassbinder's preoccupation with the compulsive, the routines that undermine human agency, which are seen most clearly in *Katzelmacher* and *Preparadise*.[69] Leopold's proposition in the first act that people only reveal their characters when playing games sets up a less realistic level in a play whose language is not stylized. If one conceives of the characters as game players (with varying degrees of success) then the idea of the emergence of a 'real' person becomes problematic. The text implicitly sees itself as a game of charades. The increasingly burlesque action merely bears out this position. We are not watching real people but their self-presentation. Irony is liberally deployed in the drawing of the characters, seen in their vanity, their personal tics and their delusions.

The play, like *Scheibe* and indeed *Petra*, has suffered from the unreflected use of realism in production. *Tropfen* was first performed only months after its discovery by the Modernes Theater at the Munich Theaterfestival on 27 May 1985. The decision to start with a realistic acting style which then mutated into that of a Whitehall farce was understood by one reviewer as revealing the director's 'uncertainty' as to how to stage the piece.[70] The mixed reception from the press indicated that the play was weak. Yet these responses reveal

---

[69] Cf. Firaza, *Die Ästhetik des Dramenwerks*, p. 154.

[70] Armin Eichholz, 'So früh schon soviel vom ganzen RWF', *Münchner Merkur*, 29 May 1985.

difficulties left unresolved by the director which were generated by the cleft between realistic language and the pervasive irony of the form. Subsequent productions have also been accused of staging a dated drama, whose shock value has been overtaken by events, in that homosexuality is no longer an issue as such on the stage. Fassbinder answered the critics who considered the stage version of *Petra* trivial kitsch with the film, which exposed the realistic dialogues as sites of examination and not necessarily empathy. François Ozon came to the dead author's rescue in 2000 with a film based closely upon the original text of *Tropfen*. The decision to set the film in the 1970s already conferred on it a camp theatricality with regard to décor and costume. The acting acknowledged the artifice of the setting and elegantly transcended a realist reading. The film played with the tensions between role-play and 'the real', and offered a stylized interpretation of the action. Ozon picked up on the importance of the critical dimension in Fassbinder's aesthetics and offered the viewing public a film that analysed the interactions as models of behaviour rather than as naturalist slices of life.

Fassbinder's dramatic legacy is one which draws attention to the gap between text and performance. While some of his plays openly signal their own artfulness through their blatantly experimental forms, others use realistic language as a smokescreen to hide the author's fascination with the mechanisms that underlie human relationships. Fassbinder did not guard these plays against the possibility that they might be played in an unquestioningly conventional manner. Irony is a subtle device that Fassbinder embedded into all his apparently realistic texts. The ignorance shown by certain directors with respect to this aspect of Fassbinder's dramaturgy has limited the potential for a more differentiated performance style. Films like Ozon's at least help to broaden the horizon and encourage more thorough engagements with plays like *Tropfen*. Quite how Fassbinder has fared in the theatre after his death and how authors and directors have responded to his work will be discussed in the epilogue.

Epilogue

Post-Brechtian, postdramatic: Fassbinder as theatre director
Fassbinder directed three productions for the *action-theater* before
he wrote *Katzelmacher* in 1968. Although we know that he had jobs
as an extra at the Münchner Kammerspiele and had been interested
in the theatre before he joined the *action-theater* ensemble, there is
little to suggest that his directing style derived from the orthodoxies of the time. The *Stadttheater* in Munich produced high-quality
work but it was not a motor of the *Regietheater*, and the amount
of *Kellertheater* activity in the city shows that there was certainly a
market for alternatives to the mainstream at that time. As we have
already seen, however, the *Kellertheater* scene in Munich in the late
1960s was far more backward-looking than its counter-cultural context might suggest; it predominantly staged the modernists and the
absurdists and was thus engaging in a competition with the *Stadttheater* that it could never win, rather than offering fare that challenged the values of the institution. Fassbinder the director seems
to have invented his own rules, based on principles of ever-changing
relationships between characters rather than static psychological
portraiture.

But Fassbinder was not operating in a vacuum, coining directorial practices from nowhere. The examination he had to take to
gain entry to the Film and Television Academy in 1966 included the
question 'What, in your opinion, does Brecht have to offer for people
who want to make films?' Fassbinder replied: 'The *Verfremdungsef-
fekt*, which can be used in films in many different ways.'[1] This is

---

[1] Prinzler, 'The Application', p. 79.

Fassbinder's full answer and it is hardly specific, yet its non-prescriptive openness points to the variety of effects Fassbinder generated in his work not only at the *action-theater*, but also at the *antiteater* and in the productions beyond Munich. His practice was rooted in defamiliarization, in making the recognizable strange, but he was not following Brechtian models or practice to the letter. Fassbinder's dialectical directing style followed Brecht insofar as he believed that the individual was a social being and thus, in part, a function of a particular society. The youths of *Katzelmacher* speak a stylized Bavarian which locates them and their attitudes within a distinct, historicized worldview. Geesche is caught in an historical moment in which, initially at least, her only way of emancipating herself is murder. The Rich Jew of *MST* is not inherently a good businessman, as the cliché would have it, but is guaranteed licence through the sanction of the city authorities. The social component in a character's definition, as witnessed in Fassbinder's dramas, was a part of his direction from *Die Verbrecher* onwards. While one may wish to argue that any drama with a social dimension necessarily affects character, we should not forget that if society is an active component in the make-up of the character, the interrelation will become visible in performance. The character will not have innate traits but will change in subtle and complex ways, as does the situation. Fassbinder's decision to drain dialogue of emotional colour in his early work points to a movement away from Brechtian orthodoxy. The focus on interaction over the individual positions Fassbinder in a far more experimental dialectical theatre than that of Brecht.

Fassbinder's approach to directing put the contingency of character at its centre. The character as individual with sovereign agency and autonomous psychology was replaced by the concept of a figure, a less fixable, more pliable interpretation of the status of a human being in an oppressive society. But Fassbinder rejected Brecht's 'Fabel', the term used for the story that would expose the contradictions of both the characters and their social context. Instead, Fassbinder preferred a theatre of situations, in which short scenes which were not necessarily tied to a greater plotline demonstrated the interaction of human subject and environment. Roland Barthes envisaged a theatre after Brecht and offered an insight into Fassbinder's practices both as a writer and a director:

> doubtless there would be no difficulty in finding in post-Brechtian theatre . . . *mises en scène* marked by the dispersion of the tableau, the pulling to pieces of the 'composition', the setting in movement of the 'partial organs' of the human figure, in short the checking of the metaphysical meaning of the work – but then also of its political meaning; or, at least, the carrying over of this meaning towards *another* politics.[2]

Barthes' comments illuminate Fassbinder's work by understanding the attack on the *Fabel* as a way of distancing oneself from the artifice of a fictional plot. By breaking up a linear story into shorter sequences, Fassbinder invites the audience to make its own connections between the language of a situation and its action. Fassbinder's directorial practice often forsook an emphasis on plot in favour of the intricacies of social interaction and the theme of power in interpersonal relationships. The new politics that Barthes identifies is the politics of perception, of challenging received ('metaphysical') meanings by placing the familiar alongside the strange. Brecht was, of course, involved in such an endeavour, in revealing 'the natural' as a construction, but Fassbinder shifts Brecht's focus and accentuates the artificial through the emphasis on communication and the mechanics of language.

In his work as a director, Fassbinder was involved in paring down the elements of communication so that plot deferred to the mechanisms of social interaction. This may be seen in the adaptation of *Zum Beispiel Ingolstadt* in 1967 in which large scenes were reduced to two- and three-person dialogues as a demonstration of different

---

[2] Roland Barthes, 'Diderot, Eisenstein, Brecht', in Roland Barthes, *Image Music Text*, tr. Stephen Heath (London: Fontana, 1977), pp. 69–78, here p. 72.

attitudes among the figures to different social types. Yet the impulse is still evident in Fassbinder's final production, *Frauen in New York*, in 1976. The society ladies deliver the most elaborate speeches to each other at breakneck speed to suggest that the content does not require cognitive assimilation because it has been said time and time again. Fassbinder the theatre director defined character as a social being in constant interaction with a set of changing circumstances and revealed the ever-shifting attitudes in his figures towards those of higher and lower status. The director actively dismantled the unified character and opened the way to a more dynamic understanding of a decentred human condition.

Fassbinder's methods of dealing with actors eschewed psychological or motivational discussion. It was more important to present text than to interpret it. The audio recordings of *Die Bettleroper* in Munich and *Die Verbrecher* in Essen demonstrate the quotation of emotion rather than its naturalistic portrayal. A character's expressive state was thus something to be appreciated *and* evaluated by the spectator. The offer of text to an audience, without colouring or tone, also moves Fassbinder into the realm of postdramatic theatre practice. The postdramatic theatre is, in short, a theatre beyond representation, in which plot as structured time gives way to the a-linear experience of text, and character itself becomes a 'text bearer', the mere deliverer of words.[3] Directorial practice is concerned with a 'dedramatization' which allows a more associative treatment of the theatre-text.[4] While Fassbinder did not banish plot and character completely from his productions, elements of the postdramatic are clearly evident in his work. The production of *Das Kaffeehaus* in Bremen in 1969 exchanged the lively plotting of an Italian comedy for a pervasive melancholia in which communication was undermined by protracted introspection. Fassbinder's treatment of Handke's *Die Unvernünftigen* in Frankfurt

---

[3] Cf. Gerda Poschmann, *Der nicht mehr dramatische Theatertext. Aktuelle Bühnentexte und ihre dramaturgische Analyse* (Tübingen: Niemeyer, 1997), p. 296.

[4] Cf. Lehmann, *Postdramatisches Theater*, p. 124.

six years later similarly dwelt on the lengthy monologues in the play and presented the audience with the dialogues as emanating from the central character's mind. Plot development deferred to an experience of Quitt's consciousness. The same approach was taken to *Miss Julie*, as we also saw in chapter 4.

Peter Iden, who had reviewed most of Fassbinder's productions since the one-day *Showdown* festival in 1969, wrote: 'in the theatre, Fassbinder, with the distinct exception of *Bremer Freiheit* . . . has always made an impact. He produced sensations which had a short shelf-life and which had already disappeared on the evening of their performance.'[5] This view contradicts the majority of productions under discussion in this book and fails to appreciate the aesthetics of a style that was establishing itself well before the postdramatic began to win more mainstream acclaim in the *Stadttheater* of the 1990s. Fassbinder's productions experimented with forms that, if anything, militated against cheap effects. While one can accuse *Liliom* in Bochum of using a puzzling, symbol-laden set as a cheap, portentous device, the more elegiac approaches to the direction of *Blut am Hals der Katze*, *Das Kaffeehaus* and *Katzelmacher* more than counter arguments of theatrical gimmickry or crowd-pleasing.

Before we leave Fassbinder's contribution to direction in the theatre, it is worth considering the relationship between directing for the stage and for the screen. In a much quoted interview of 1974, Fassbinder said: 'in the beginning it was pretty extreme with me. In the theatre I directed as if it were a film, and then I made films as if they were theatre.'[6] Although there is a certain validity to this statement, a more measured consideration arose when Fassbinder was asked to reflect on filming *Pioniere in Ingolstadt* and staging it in quick succession in the early 1970s. He noted: 'I learn more when I'm working in the theatre. Experiences one makes when shooting a film can't be reused in the theatre, but it does work the other way round.'[7]

[5] Iden, 'Der Eindruck-Macher', p. 19.
[6] Fassbinder, *Anarchie der Phantasie*, p. 51.
[7] Fassbinder quoted in Harmssen and Peters, 'So geht es nicht'.

Fassbinder acknowledged that the communication between the two media did not mutually enrich each other. The filmic aspects of Fassbinder's theatre work are primarily located in his writing, in that the techniques of the editing suite are visible in the fascination with short, disjunctive scenes. In terms of directing practice, however, Fassbinder was able to export the staginess of his theatre into the films. The sense that many of his characters are playing roles, trying (and often failing) to conform to norms that exist outside of them, or deriving their identities from images seen elsewhere, is translated into performance styles developed in the theatre work.

Peter Seibert confirms the lack of interchangeability of different genres for Fassbinder in an article on Fassbinder's work for the stage, the cinema and the television: 'media do not only appear as material bearers of aesthetic programmes for Fassbinder, their interferences and differences themselves are clearly understood as salient moments of such programmes'.[8] Seibert recognizes that Fassbinder had a firm grasp of the contrasts between the media he used and so was able to play with their shifting boundaries whilst acknowledging their discrete distinctions. The theatre work was quite apparent in the artifice of the films, yet the work for the cinema was almost impossible to reprocess in the practical business of making theatre. The films themselves took over the theatricality whilst deploying it through a different prism, the camera. The extra effects offered by editing and different types of shot led to further refinements of the theatrical aesthetic, which could never be realized in a theatre. For example, Fassbinder's fascination with identity in the films is often linked to a predilection for shots involving mirrors. The images that arose out of the reflections could only be set up by appropriate camera angles. Mirrors on stage, as in the première of *Petra*, could only have a thematic effect, as a commentary on the action. A comparison between the stage and television versions of *Frauen in New York* shows how even by filming virtually the same cast in the same location (the Schauspielhaus Hamburg) Fassbinder was able to tease out

---

[8] Peter Seibert, 'Rainer Werner Fassbinder', p. 103.

further ironies by the use of juxtaposed camera angles and judicious cutting.

The textual legacy: Fassbinder as dramatist

Fassbinder's career as a dramatist is one which is characterized by the same restlessness that accompanied his other creative endeavours. Never happy to settle into one particular style or format, Fassbinder continually chose to appropriate new genres and even develop some of his own. The radical montage of short scenes was a form he derived from his experience of film and used first in the play version of *Katzelmacher*. The next logical step, as seen in *Preparadise*, was to grant the scenes an autonomy so that they could be arranged in any number of sequences to generate associative links. *Blut* completed the experiment by using fixed patterns to dislocate the subject and to call social oppression into question through the medium of language. Elsewhere, Fassbinder's work as an adaptor led to further developments in his writing. The treatment of *Iphigenie* is unlike that of *Das Kaffeehaus* or *Das brennende Dorf*. Single sallies into different genre areas, such as historical drama (*Bremer Freiheit*), the contemporary problem play (*MST*) or Holocaust drama (*Scheibe*), for example, all reveal distinct dramaturgies which approach their subject matter from a fresh and often controversial perspective. Fassbinder's drama is typified by its refusal to be programmatic or schematic. His creativity did not entail the continued reprocessing and refinement of an aesthetic, but the ceaseless search for new stimuli and new forms.

Fassbinder left seventeen dramas (if one includes the as yet unpublished and unperformed *Warnung vor einer heiligen Nutte*) when he died. The table below lists the number of productions of the plays according to geographical and temporal criteria.[9]

---

[9] The statistics were kindly supplied by Karlheinz Braun, the head of the Verlag der Autoren, which both publishes Fassbinder's plays and administers their performing rights. I have decided to concentrate on productions to assess the interest in Fassbinder among theatre directors.

Name of Play and Year of Première	Productions in German-speaking countries[10]	Productions in the rest of the world	Productions from 1968 to 1979	Productions from 1980 to 1989	Productions from 1990 to 2002	Total productions
Katzelmacher (1968)	43	27	7	18	45	70
Iphigenie (1968)	4	2	2	1	3	6
Ajax (1968)	1	0	1	0	0	1
Der am. Soldat (1968)	3	1	1	1	2	4
Bettleroper (1969)	3	1	3	0	1	4
Preparadise (1969)	35	34	14	16	39	69
Anarchie (1969)	7	3	1	2	7	10
Kaffeehaus (1969)	22	21	9	2	32	43
Werwolf (1969)	2	2	1	0	3	4
Dorf (1970)	5	7	1	3	8	12
Blut (1971)	8	36	2	16	26	44
Petra (1971)	21	54	13	16	46	75
Bremer Freiheit (1971)	67	64	35	41	55	131
MST (1979)	2	12	0	5	9	14
Tropfen (1985)	10	13	–	9	14	23
Scheibe (1995)	4	3	–	–	7	7
Total	237	280	90	130	297	517

[10] I.e. Germany, Austria and Switzerland.

Six of the plays, *Katzelmacher*, *Preparadise*, *Das Kaffeehaus*, *Blut*, *Petra* and *Bremer Freiheit* have been produced over forty times, yet specific statistics for each play vary greatly. *Katzelmacher*, for example, cast off its Bavarian roots in the 1990s and was played in many German-speaking theatres in the face of a rising wave of xenophobia after the fall of the Berlin Wall. *Blut*, which was initially rejected by the West German press, has been performed more than four times as often in translation than in its native language. The variations in the production histories of the different plays is almost impossible to account for. Clearly the quality of the writing is important, and one might speculate that Fassbinder's most filmic plays have all proved most popular. In addition, the strong female roles of Petra von Kant and Geesche Gottfried have proven alluring, yet, as mentioned before, there is a sense in which the lack of obvious demands on a cast may have been attractive, while the qualities of irony and ambivalence may have been missed or avoided. *Das Kaffeehaus* might have endured, and indeed thrived since 1990, for its sharp observations about the mercantile world and universal commodification in the globalized free market.

If we turn to the broader view and consider the plays as an oeuvre, we may discern two major features. First, Fassbinder is truly an international figure in the theatre, as well as in the cinema. He is more performed abroad than he is in the German-speaking countries, although both figures are large enough to indicate a major interest over the years. The playwright has been able to go beyond his own context and connect with other cultures in Europe and further afield. Second, Fassbinder is becoming increasingly popular over time. Although there is a steady increase in productions from the late 1960s to the 1980s, there is an explosion after 1989 with almost three-fifths of the productions taking place in this period. The publication in German of a single fifteen-play volume in 1991 may well have made the dramatist popular at home, but this does not explain the enormous upswing in stagings in the rest of the world. The plethora of productions might indicate that an engagement with the drama began in the wake of Fassbinder's death in 1982 but only reached a critical mass once the biographical fuss had subsided. Whatever complex grounds led to the global fascination, certain of the plays have signalled enduring qualities which mark Fassbinder as a playwright whose work has been undervalued by scholarship for far too long.

The plays themselves have also been open to reappraisal over time. In 1992, a production of *Preparadise* in Dresden retitled the performance 'It is yours to be German:[11] *Preparadise Sorry Now*' and made the link between Brady and Hinley's fascination with the Third Reich and the wave of neo-Nazism making its presence particularly felt in the former German Democratic Republic. A book on Geesche Gottfried published in the mid-1990s, which was based on recently uncovered archival material on her case, informed a production in Zurich in 1996.[12] Other productions have investigated homosexual identity in the 1990s (*Petra* and *Tropfen*) and the role of money in a global economy (*Das Kaffeehaus*).

The continued production of the drama is not, however, the endpoint to Fassbinder's allure as a dramatist. His plays have also stimulated others to refashion them in other media. Both *Bremer Freiheit* and *Petra* have been turned into operas, a move of which Fassbinder may well have approved if we remember his thoughts on opera and his own interest in the form, quoted in chapter 5. Wolfgang Schenck, the actor who appeared in the première of *Bremer Freiheit*, translated the play into Low German, a dialect associated with Bremen, to confer a regional specificity upon the text.[13] *Petra* was used as the source for a ballet when Weimar was the European City of Culture in 1997. Even the scandal surrounding *MST* when it was cancelled in Holland in 1987 has been rewritten as a novella by Dutch author Harry Mulisch

[11] This is a quotation from the second Brady and Hinley scene (*Stücke*, p. 200).

[12] Cf. Peer Meter, *Geesche Gottfried. Ein langes Warten auf den Tod* (Langenbruch: Jürgen, 1995). The production took place at the Theater Kanton Zürich on 28 April 1996 and used the new historical material to re-evaluate Geesche and her crimes.

[13] Premièred at the Niederdeutsche Bühne, Flensburg, in the spring of 1996.

as *The Theatre, the Letter and the Truth*.[14] The Schauspiel Frankfurt, the site of the aborted première in 1985, staged a dramatization of the novella in the 2001/2 season. In addition, theatre versions of Fassbinder's films are becoming ever popular. *Satan's Brew*, *Why Does Herr R. Run Amok?* and *In a Year of Thirteen Moons* are among the new dramas that have graced Germany's stages in the past few years.

Rainer Werner Fassbinder and the (German) theatre

Fassbinder's nine years of active engagement with the theatre, from the early work with the *action-theater* in 1967 to the fêted production of *Frauen in New York* in 1976, chart the rise of a multi-talented artist. Both elements of his achievement, as a director and as a dramatist, betray the same naivety – Fassbinder only trained as an actor, the other skills were learned through practice and his own initiative. Without the constraints imposed by a set of rules, Fassbinder was able to develop his own approaches to the theatre, and the originality of these approaches has been covered throughout the book. Not only did he write plays on topics hitherto uncharted in the German theatre (the *Gastarbeiter* in *Katzelmacher*, the Moors Murderers in *Preparadise* or lesbianism as a way of life, that is, not as a 'problem', in *Petra*) but he also introduced filmic strategies and avant-garde devices into his dramaturgy in a bid to create dramas that challenged received wisdoms. And in the field of direction, his use of abstraction, slowness and blurred characterization presented audiences with unfamiliar perspectives and alternative modes of perception. The treatment of his own work was not typified by a comfortable accommodation of a text within a performance but by the calculated use of production as a provocation to the audience. One could easily imagine a fast-paced version of *Das Kaffeehaus*, but Fassbinder sought to expose the relationships through slow-motion direction. In almost every one of his productions, the spectator was invited to become an active participant

---

[14] Cf. Harry Mulisch, *Das Theater, der Brief und die Wahrheit. Ein Widerspruch*, tr. Gregor Seferens (Munich and Vienna: Carl Hanser, 2000); the Dutch original was also first published in 2000.

in the creation of meaning because Fassbinder refused to decode his productions by offering interpreted plots or characters.

Fassbinder was, like every artist, a child of his time. The spirit of experiment was pivotal to the creative explosion of the late 1960s. Figures of authority were being questioned and Fassbinder provided a loud voice in counter-cultural reply. Yet, as the statistics above show, Fassbinder has not remained a prisoner of 1968; his plays continue to provoke and stimulate theatre-makers all over the world with their portrayals of human weakness and pernicious social structures. His directing styles, discussed for the first time in this study, also offer contemporary theatre a programme that resists conventional inter-pretive practice in the name of the emancipated spectator. The moral ambivalence of Fassbinder's dramas is mirrored in the refusal to demarcate good, evil or many other categories in performance. This stance, which is now common in the German *Stadttheater*, was pio-neering in the late 1960s and early 1970s.

It is unlikely that Fassbinder's dramas will ever eclipse the gar-gantuan edifice of the films. I nonetheless hope that this book will have introduced the reader to the impressive diversity of Fassbinder's not unsubstantial dramatic oeuvre and enthused him or her enough to read the plays either in the original or in translation.[15] Fassbinder's contribution to post-war German drama can be felt not only in the dra-mas but also in the unorthodox directorial styles he employed, which are now far more visible in the *Stadttheater*. Fassbinder nonethe-less remains a marginal figure in the history of the German theatre, because he is viewed as a film-maker who dabbled in theatre before finding his stride as an artist. This book clearly argues against such a position. The amount of time and effort Fassbinder dedicated to the theatre, and his persisting interest after his final production in 1976, reveals a different side that complements rather than contrasts with the common image. Fassbinder not only developed approaches to

---

[15] Denis Calandra has translated *Katzelmacher, Preparadise, Blut, Bremer Freiheit, Petra* and *MST* into English in Rainer Werner Fassbinder, *Plays*, ed. and tr. Calandra (New York: PAJ, 1985). He has also published an English version of *Scheibe* in issue number 56 of the *Performing Arts Journal*.

filming in the theatre, but achieved outstanding and revolutionary results with his plays and his productions. It is time to acknowledge Fassbinder's achievements in the theatre and allow them to form a more rounded view of Fassbinder the creative artist whose works in three media of the performing arts were substantial and impressive. All we have left of the theatrical productions are reviews and the memories of those who performed in and attended them. The plays themselves are yet to be collected in full, but the majority are available in print. The lively and provocative texts have resonated with many a director, actor and theatre-goer over the years and there is little sign that this is set to end.

Bibliography

Note:

Some of the newspaper reviews were provided to me without dates. Despite attempts to establish their provenance, some remain undated. Theatre programmes and unpublished documents have not been recorded in the bibliography. Sources for all documents are given in the main text or in footnotes.

Primary materials

Barthes, Roland, 'Diderot, Eisenstein, Brecht', in *Image Music Text*, tr. Stephen Heath (London: Fontana, 1977), pp. 69–78.

Boal, Augusto, *The Theatre of the Oppressed*, tr. Charles A. and Maria-Odilia Leal McBride (London: Pluto, 1979).

Brecht, Bertolt, footnote to 'Anmerkungen zur Oper *Aufstieg und Fall der Stadt Mahagonny*', in Brecht, *Grosse kommentierte Berliner und Frankfurter Ausgabe*, vol. xxiv (Berlin and Frankfurt/Main: Suhrkamp, 1991).

Enzensberger, Hans Magnus, 'Gemeinplätze, die Neueste Literatur betreffend', *Kursbuch*, 15 (1968), pp. 187–97.

Fassbinder, Rainer Werner, *Die Anarchie der Phantasie. Gespräche und Interviews*, ed. Michael Töteberg (Frankfurt/Main: Suhrkamp, 1986).

   Antiteater (Frankfurt/Main: Suhrkamp, 1970).

   'Hanna Schygulla – kein Star, nur ein schwacher Mensch wie wir alle. (Unordentliche Gedanken über eine Frau, die interessiert)', in Hanna Schygulla, *Bilder aus Filmen von Rainer Werner Fassbinder. Mit einem autobiographischen Text von*

Hanna Schygulla und einem Beitrag von Rainer Werner Fassbinder (Munich: Schirmer/Mosel, 1981), pp. 169–87.

'Imitation of Life. Über die Filme von Douglas Sirk', in Fassbinder, *Filme befreien den Kopf. Essays und Arbeitsnotizen*, ed. Michael Töteberg (Frankfurt/Main: Fischer, 1984), pp. 11–24.

Katzelmacher (film script) in Fassbinder, *Die Kinofilme*, vol. I, ed. Michael Töteberg (Munich: Schirmer/Mosel, 1987), pp. 131–223.

Der Müll, die Stadt und der Tod. Nur eine Scheibe Brot (Frankfurt/Main: Verlag der Autoren, 1998).

Die Niklashauser Fart, in *Fassbinders Filme*, vol. II, ed. Michael Töteberg (Frankfurt/Main: Verlag der Autoren, 1990), pp. 125–55.

Plays, ed. and tr. Denis Calandra (New York: PAJ, 1985).

Sämtliche Stücke (Frankfurt/Main: Verlag der Autoren, 1991).

Stücke, vol. III (Frankfurt/Main: Suhrkamp, 1976).

'Volkstheater im weitesten Sinn', *Frankfurter Rundschau*, 28 November 1968.

'Vormerkungen zu *Querelle*', in Fassbinder, *Filme befreien den Kopf. Essays und Arbeitsnotizen*, ed. Michael Töteberg (Frankfurt/Main: Fischer, 1984), pp. 116–18.

'Wie stelle ich mir meine zukünftige Berufstätigkeit vor?', in *Filme befreien den Kopf*, ed. Michael Töteberg (Frankfurt/Main: Suhrkamp, 1984).

Fleisser, Marieluise, *Briefwechsel 1925–1974*, ed. Günther Rühle (Frankfurt/Main: Suhrkamp, 2001).

Gesammelte Werke. Erster Band. Dramen, ed. Günther Rühle (Frankfurt/Main: Suhrkamp, 1994).

Materialien zum Leben und Schreiben der Marieluise Fleisser, ed. Günther Rühle (Frankfurt/Main: Suhrkamp, 1973).

Goethe, Johann Wolfgang von, *Iphigenie auf Tauris* (Stuttgart: Klett, 1980).

et al., *Torquato Tasso. Regiebuch der Bremer Inszenierung*, ed. Volker Canaris (Frankfurt/Main: Suhrkamp, 1970).

Handke, Peter, 'Untitled [Notes to *Hilferufe*]', in *Stücke*, vol. 1 (Frankfurt/Main: Suhrkamp, 1972), p. 92.

Hebbel, Friedrich, *Maria Magdalene*, in *Gedichte und Dramen*, vol. 11 (Hamburg: Hoffmann und Campe, n.d.), pp. 211–63.

Hegel, Georg Wilhelm Friedrich, *Wissenschaft der Logik*, second part (Leipzig: Felix Meiner, 1934).

Marcuse, Herbert, *One-Dimensional Man. Studies in the Ideology of Advanced Industrial Society* (London: Ark, 1986).

Miller, Arthur, *Plays*, vol. 1 (London: Methuen, 1988).

Mulisch, Harry, *Das Theater, der Brief und die Wahrheit. Ein Widerspruch*, tr. Gregor Seferens (Munich and Vienna: Carl Hanser, 2000).

Runge, Erika, *Bottroper Protokolle. Vorwort von Martin Walser* (Frankfurt/Main: Suhrkamp, 1968).

Straub, Jean-Marie, *Der Bräutigam, die Komödiantin und der Zuhälter*, in *Filmkritik*, 12 (1968), no. 10, pp. 681–7.

Williams, Emlyn, *Beyond Belief: A Chronicle of Murder and its Detection* (London: Pan, 1968).

Zadek, Peter, *My Way. Eine Autobiographie 1926–1969* (Cologne: Kiepenheuer und Witsch, 1998).

Zwerenz, Gerhard, 'Nedine oder die fünfzehnte Rose', in *Nicht alles gefallen lassen. Schulbuchgeschichten* (Frankfurt/Main: Fischer, 1972), pp. 83–95.

Secondary materials

ab, 'Die kraftlosen Rituale von Geld und Liebe', *Süddeutsche Zeitung*, 17 October 1969.

Abendroth, Friedrich, 'Eine Julien-Parabel', *Stuttgarter Zeitung*, 2/3 November 1974.

Aly, Götz Haydar, 'Kuckuck klebt am Action-Theater', *Abendzeitung*, 8/9 June 1968.

Anon, 'Auf dem Weg von Ulm nach Frankfurt: Dietrich Hilsdorf. "Vor mir ist der Intendant genauso wenig sicher wie die Putzfrau"', *Theater heute*, 7 (1985), p. 43.

'[commentary on Peter Zadek's *Measure for Measure*]', in Burkhard Mauer and Barbara Krauss (eds.), *Spielräume – Arbeitsergebnisse. Theater Bremen 1962–73* (Bremen: Theater Bremen, 1973), p. 171.

'Empfindsames Kammerspiel', *Hanauer Anzeiger*, 16 October 1974.

'Geschehen auf drei Ebenen abgespielt', *Ruhr-Nachrichten*, 24 January 1979.

'Kanzler: Heilfroh über die Absetzung der Fassbinder-Affäre', *Offenburger Tageblatt*, 14 November 1985.

'Keine Krebs-Oper', *Frankfurter Allgemeine Zeitung*, 13 August 1979.

'Müll-Abfuhr', *Der Spiegel*, 9 July 1984.

'Notizen', *Theater heute*, 7 (1970), p. 57.

'Peter Zadek äussert sich zu Fassbinder-Interview', *Die Welt*, 19 August 1972.

'Prozess ohne die Angeklagten', *Süddeutsche Zeitung*, 15 October 1968.

'Rainer Werner Fassbinder am Theater am Turm?', *Frankfurter Rundschau*, 29 October 1973.

'Der Streit um Fassbinder', *Der Tagesspiegel*, 3 September 1998.

'Theater und Revolte', *Theater heute*, yearbook 1968, pp. 25–37.

'Tomaten für die Zuschauer', *Abendzeitung*, 30 September 1967.

untitled, *Frankfurter Allgemeine Zeitung*, 7 June 1972.

untitled, *Frankfurter Allgemeine Zeitung*, 24 August 1974.

'Was wird bei uns gespielt?', *Theater heute*, 10 (1970), pp. 52–3.

'Zadeks Engagements', *Süddeutsche Zeitung*, 4/5 December 1971.

Assenmacher, Karl-Heinz, 'Das engagierte Theater Rainer Werner Fassbinders', in Gerhard Charles Rump (ed.), *Sprachnetze. Studien zur literarischen Sprachverwendung* (Hildesheim and New York: Olms, 1976), pp. 1–86.

Aust, Stefan, *Der Baader Meinhof Komplex*, expanded and modernized edition (Munich: Goldmann, 1998).

Baer, Harry with Packer, Maurus, *Schlafen kann ich, wenn ich tot bin. Das atemlose Leben des Rainer Werner Fassbinder* (Cologne: Kiepenheuer und Witsch, 1982).

Barnett, David, 'Dramaturgies of *Sprachkritik*. Rainer Werner Fassbinder's *Blut am Hals der Katze* and Peter Handke's *Kaspar*', *Modern Language Review*, 95 (2000), no. 4, pp. 1053–63.

'The Simulation of a Reception. Or: Rainer Werner Fassbinder's *Der Müll, die Stadt und der Tod* in Germany, Holland, and Israel', *Contemporary Theatre Review*, 14 (2004), no. 2, pp. 29–40.

Baumgart, Reinhard, 'Erst bunter Seelenmüll, dann rote Idylle', *Süddeutsche Zeitung*, 18 September 1974.

Becker, Peter von, 'Fast verspielt', *Theater heute*, 12 (1985), pp. 3–9.

Bergmann, Werner, 'Sind die Deutschen antisemitisch? Meinungsumfragen von 1946–1987 in der Bundesrepublik Deutschland', in Werner Bergmann and Rainer Erb (eds.), *Antisemitismus in der politischen Kultur* (Opladen: Westdeutscher Verlag, 1990), pp. 108–30.

Berling, Peter, *Die 13 Jahre des Rainer Werner Fassbinder*, revised paperback edition (Bergisch Gladbach: Gustav Lübbe, 1995).

Bleisch, Ernst Günther, 'Neuer Lyrikerjob: Tango tanzen in der Witwe Bolte', *Münchner Merkur*, 8 September 1969.

Bock, Bertram, 'Orgie findet nicht statt', *Abendzeitung*, 3/4 August 1968.

Bock, Hans Bertram, 'Nacht der langen Messer', *Abendzeitung*, 16 June 1969.

Bohnen, Klaus, '"Raum-Höllen" der bürgerlichen Welt. "Gefühlsrealismus" in der Theater- und Filmproduktion Rainer Werner Fassbinders', in Gerhard Kluge (ed.), *Studien zur Dramatik in der Bundesrepublik Deutschland* (Amsterdam: Rodopi, 1983), pp. 141–62.

Borski, Arnim, 'Ich liebe dich, ich liebe dich, ham, ham, ham' and 'Wer schenkt uns ein Staatstheater?', *Berliner Zeitung*, no date supplied.

Brem, Rudolf Waldemar, '*action-theater*', *rupprechtonen* (sic), November 1967, n.p.

    'Büchner Theater', *rupprecht-tönchen* (sic), May 1968, n.p.

Brocher, Corinna, 'Gruppen sind ja vieles. Gespräche mit Rainer Werner Fassbinder über die Geschichte des antiteaters', unpublished manuscript, 1973.

Brustellin, Alf, '*Action-Theater* in München', *Theater heute*, 6 (1968), pp. 44–5.

    'Heisse Plattheiten', *Stuttgarter Zeitung*, 20 June 1969.

    'Jenseits des Kulturbetriebs', *Süddeutsche Zeitung*, 9 April 1968.

    'Kriegstänze um Sophokles', *Süddeutsche Zeitung*, 22 August 1967.

Buddecke, Wolfram and Fuhrmann, Helmut, *Das deutschsprachige Drama seit 1945. Schweiz. Bundesrepublik. Österreich. DDR. Kommentar einer Epoche* (Munich: Winkler, 1981).

Bügner, Torsten, *Annäherung an die Wirklichkeit. Gattung und Autoren des neuen Volksstücks* (Frankfurt/Main *et al.*: Peter Lang, 1986).

Burkhardt, Werner, 'Dreimal Broadway-Melodie . . . von 1936 bis 1941', *Süddeutsche Zeitung*, 7 October 1976.

Burns, Rob and van der Will, Wilfried, 'The Federal Republic 1968–1990: From the Industrial Society to the Culture Society', in Rob Burns (ed.), *German Cultural Studies. An Introduction* (Oxford: Oxford University Press, 1995), pp. 257–323.

Büscher, Barbara, 'Liebesmomente und Grausamkeiten: W. Schroeters und R. W. Fassbinders Filmessays über Theater – und andere Zustände um 1980', in Inga Lemke (ed.) with Sandra Nuy, *Theaterbühne – Fernsehbilder. Sprech-, Musik- und Tanztheater im und für das Fernsehen* (Anif/Salzburg: Müller-Speiser, 1998), pp. 119–35.

Canaris, Volker, 'Ist in Bochum wirklich alles ganz anders?', *Theater heute*, 1 (1973), pp. 16–20.

Carr, William, *A History of Germany. 1815–1985* (London: Edward Arnold, 1987).

Coberg, Klaus, 'Fassbinder bei der Modeschöpferin', *Münchner Merkur*, 7 June 1971.

Cornelsen, Dirk, 'Für Kohl sind die Bundesbürger "immun" gegen Antisemitismus', *Frankfurter Rundschau*, 27 February 1986.

Cz, *'Axel Cäsar Haarmaan'*, *Frankfurter Rundschau*, 23 May 1968.

Czaschke, Annemarie, *'antiteater* gegen Sophokles & Co', *Frankfurter Rundschau*, 13 December 1968.

      'Die Bettleroper als Subkultur', *Frankfurter Rundschau*, 6 February 1968.

      'Neue Impulse von Aussenseitern', *Frankfurter Rundschau*, 24 April 1968.

Daiber, Hans, *Deutsches Theater seit 1945. Bundesrepublik Deutschland. Deutsche Demokratische Republik. Österreich. Schweiz* (Stuttgart: Reclam, 1976).

Dannecke, Hermann, 'Umfunktioniertes Kaffeehaus', *Rheinischer Merkur*, 19 September 1969.

Deutscher Bühnenverein (ed.), *Vergleichende Theaterstatistik 49/50 bis 84/5* (Cologne: Deutscher Bühnenverein, 1987).

Donner, Wolf, 'Barocker Faltenwurf statt Agitation', *Die Zeit*, 13 November 1970.

Eckardt, Bernd, *Rainer Werner Fassbinder. In 17 Jahren 42 Filme – Stationen eines Lebens für den deutschen Film* (Munich: Wilhelm Heyme, 1982).

The Editors, 'Subkultur. Zur Klärung eines Schimpfwortes und einer verschrieenen Sache', *Song*, 4 (1969), no. 4, pp. 3–4.

Eichholz, Armin, 'Bei den H-Entfernungen in der Amalienstrasse', *Münchner Merkur*, 16 October 1969.

      'So früh schon soviel vom ganzen RWF', *Münchner Merkur*, 29 May 1985.

Elsaesser, Thomas, *Fassbinder's Germany. History Identity Subject* (Amsterdam: Amsterdam University Press, 1996).

Emigholz, Erich, 'Erst lauter Namen, dann ein Begriff', in Burkhard Mauer and Barbara Krauss (eds.), *Spielräume – Arbeitsergebnisse.*

Theater Bremen 1962–73 (Bremen: Theater Bremen, 1973), pp. 244–5.

'Gesellschaft mit Echo', *Bremer Nachrichten*, 5 April 1971.

Ettl, Hubert, *Kurt Raab. Hommage aus der Provinz* (Vietach: edition lichting, n.d.), pp. 49–50.

Everding, August, Schwiedrzik, Wolfgang, and Stein, Peter, 'Was ist demokratisches Theater?', *Theater heute*, 9 (1968), pp. 1–3.

Fest, Joachim, 'Linksfaschismus', *Frankfurter Allgemeine Zeitung*, 19 March 1976.

Finnan, Carmel, 'Volkstümlichkeit als Alltagsritual. Der Einfluss Marieluise Fleissers auf Rainer Werner Fassbinder am Beispiel von *Fegefeuer in Ingolstadt* und *Katzelmacher*', in Ursula Hassel and Herbert Herzmann (eds.), *Das zeitgenössische deutschsprachige Volksstück. Akten der internationalen Symposions. University College Dublin 28. Februar–2. März 1991* (Tübingen: Stauffenburg, 1992), pp. 131–7.

Firaza, Joanna, *Die Ästhetik des Dramenwerks von Rainer Werner Fassbinder. Die Struktur der Doppeltheit* (Frankfurt/Main *et al.*: Peter Lang, 2002).

'Flucht vor Mimesis: Rainer Werner Fassbinders *Anarchie in Bayern*', in Sascha Feuchert (ed.), *Flucht und Vertreibung in der deutschen Literatur. Beiträge* (Frankfurt/Main: Peter Lang, 2001), pp. 239–48.

Friedrich, Regina, '"Mündel will Vormund sein". Oder: die TAT-Story', in Katherina Bleibohm and Wolfgang Sprang (eds.), *Neue Szene Frankfurt. Ein Kultur-Lesebuch* (Frankfurt/Main: Waldemar Kramer, 1976), pp. 22–7.

Fröhlich, Hans, 'Ein bürgerliches Trauerspiel', *Stuttgarter Nachrichten*, 13 December 1971.

Funke, Hajo, 'Bitburg, Jews and Germans: A Case Study of Anti-Jewish Sentiment in Germany during May, 1985', *New German Critique*, 38 (1986), pp. 57–72.

Gniffke, Kai, *Volksbildung in Frankfurt am Main 1890–1990. Festschrift zum hundertjährigen Jubiläum* (Frankfurt/Main: Waldemar Kramer, 1990).

gr, 'Die Last des Anfangs', *Frankfurter Allgemeine Zeitung*, 17 September 1974.

'Das schöne Bild der Verbrecher', *Frankfurter Allgemeine Zeitung*, 23 November 1974.

'Das Theater als Melange', *Frankfurter Allgemeine Zeitung*, 9 November 1970.

Grack, Günther, 'Unheilige Nacht', *Der Tagesspiegel*, 28 December 1968.

Gurreck, Klaus, Johler, Jens, Sichtermann, Barbara and Stein, Stefan, 'Zerschlägt das bürgerliche Theater', *Theater heute*, 2 (1969), pp. 29–30.

Gutermuth, Walter, 'Sie wollten sogar Zigaretten rauchen', *Abendzeitung*, 15 October 1968.

Güthlein-Fritzsche, Karin, 'Zur totalen Langeweile umfunktioniert', *Nordwest-Zeitung*, 12 September 1969.

halef, 'Märchen vom antiteater', *Nürnberger Zeitung*, 22 March 1971.

Harmssen, Henning and Peters, Karsten, 'So geht es nicht', *Abendzeitung*, no date supplied.

Hartmann, Rainer, '*Aspekte* im TAT', *Frankfurter Neue Presse*, 17 January 1975.

'Kulturschutt in der endzeitlichen Szene', *Nürnberger Zeitung*, 29 May 1974.

'TAT-Ensemble fühlt sich genasführt', *Frankfurter Neue Presse*, 6 June 1975.

Hayman, Ronald, *Fassbinder: Film Maker* (London: Weidenfeld and Nicolson, 1984).

hd, 'Keine Lust zum Kindertheater?', *Frankfurter Allgemeine Zeitung*, 21 January 1975.

HD, 'Liliom als Ritual', *Hildesheimer Neue Presse*, 14 December 1972.

Heer, Hannes, 'Um des lieben Friedens willen', *die tageszeitung*, 6 November 1985.

Hemler, Stefan, 'Protest-Inszenierungen. Die 68er-Bewegung und das Theater in München', in Hans-Michael Körner and Jürgen Schläder (eds.), *Münchner Theatergeschichtliches Symposium 2000* (Munich: Herbert Utz, 2000), pp. 276–318.

Henrichs, Benjamin, 'Fassbinder, Rainer Werner. Oder: immer viel Trauer dabei', *Theater heute*, Sonderheft 1972, pp. 69–70.

'Warnung vor einer Theaternutte', *Süddeutsche Zeitung*, 24 January 1973.

'Wohl doch ein guter Mensch', *Süddeutsche Zeitung*, 23 March 1971.

'Zeit der Kunstlosen', *Die Zeit*, 20 September 1974.

Hensel, Georg, 'Monster-Modelle', *Theater heute*, 3 (1970), p. 14.

Herrmann, Wilhelm, 'Amoklauf der Dörfler', *Weser-Kurier*, 9 November 1970.

'Play Goldoni mit Dürers Adam und Eva', *Münchner Merkur*, 12 September 1969.

HH, 'Aus dem Lebenskuchen', *Abendzeitung*, 12 September 1969.

'Kleinbürgermief', no further details supplied.

HL, 'Fleisser-Montage im Büchner Theater', *Abendzeitung*, 20 February 1968.

Hofer, Hermann, 'Brutalität der Sprache', *Donau-Kurier*, 22 March 1971.

Holefleisch, Heiko, 'Frankenstein am Main', in *Programme for Rainer Werner Fassbinder's 'Der Müll, die Stadt und der Tod'*, Schauspiel Frankfurt, première 4 November 1985, n.p.

Horn, Effi, 'Büchner-Happening mit Bauchtanz', *Münchner Merkur*, 5 October 1967.

'Verhör mit Walzerbegleitung', *Münchner Merkur*, 20 December 1967.

HS, 'Am deutschen Wesen will das TAT genesen', *Frankfurter Rundschau*, 14 February 1975.

Iden, Peter, 'Der Eindruck-Macher. Rainer Werner Fassbinder und das Theater', in Peter W. Jansen and Wolfram Schütte (eds.), *Rainer Werner Fassbinder*, fifth expanded edition (Frankfurt/Main: Fischer, 1985), pp. 17–28.

'Es ist schade um die Menschen', *Frankfurter Rundschau*, 24 March 1971.

'Frechheit, gealtert', *Frankfurter Rundschau*, 30 October 1974.

'Freundlich und rührend', *Frankfurter Rundschau*, 17 September 1974.

'Ein mähliches Trauerspiel', *Frankfurter Rundschau*, 15 October 1974.

'Nur veraltete Fragen?', *Frankfurter Rundschau*, 23 November 1974.

'Revolution als Orgasmus', *Theater heute*, 12 (1970), pp. 33–5.

'Rituale und Spiele aus anderen Spielen', *Frankfurter Rundschau*, 6 November 1969.

'Der Sache nur geschadet', *Frankfurter Rundschau*, 24 March 1975.

Die Schaubühne am Halleschen Ufer. 1970–1979 (Munich and Vienna: Carl Hanser, 1979).

'Verweigerte Wirklichkeit und verweigertes Theater', *Frankfurter Rundschau*, 27 May 1974.

'Wer dem Wind ins Gesicht bläst', *Frankfurter Rundschau*, 19 August 1972.

Intendanz Frankfurt (ed.), *Der Fall Fassbinder. Dokumentation des Streits um 'Der Müll, die Stadt und der Tod' in Frankfurt* (Frankfurt/Main: Stadt Frankfurt, 1987).

Fassbinder ohne Ende. Eine Dokumentation anlässlich der Uraufführung von Rainer Werner Fassbinders 'Der Müll, die Stadt und der Tod' im Kammerspiel von Schauspiel Frankfurt am 31. Oktober 1985 (Frankfurt/Main: Stadt Frankfurt, 1985).

Jäger, Gerd, 'Erinnerung an das Weltgefühl des Herrn Quitt', *Theater heute*, 7 (1974), pp. 25–34.

'Fassbinders Anti-BO Theater', *Theater heute*, 3 (1973), pp. 22–3.

'Hin zu Hollywood', *Theater heute*, 11 (1976), pp. 26–9.

Jenny, Urs, 'Chaos macht Spass', *Süddeutsche Zeitung*, 16/17 June 1969.

'Enteignet Thoas', *Süddeutsche Zeitung*, 31 October 1968.

'Saubermann greift durch', *Süddeutsche Zeitung*, 5 August 1968.

Jeremias, Brigitte, 'Der Kölner Dom in grünen Wiesen', *Frankfurter Allgemeine Zeitung*, 13 November 1981.

JK, 'Ionesco mit Bier', *Süddeutsche Zeitung*, 10 March 1967.

JSch, 'Fassbinder inszeniert in Hamburg', *Stuttgarter Zeitung*, 18 August 1976.

JvM, 'Kriminelle Reflexionen', *Süddeutsche Zeitung*, 21 December 1967.

Karasek, Hellmuth, 'In den Folterkammern des Gutgemeinten', *Der Spiegel*, 11 November 1985.

    'Mörderin, Vorläuferin', *Theater heute*, 1 (1972), pp. 14–15.

Kardish, Laurence, in collaboration with Juliane Lorenz, *Rainer Werner Fassbinder* (New York: Museum of Modern Art, 1997).

Karsunke, Yaak, '*Der amerikanische Soldat* und *Ajax*', *Kulturspiegel*, Bayerischer Rundfunk, no transmission date supplied.

    'Das "antiteater" gastiert mit *Orgie Ubuh* im Theater 44', *Kulturspiegel*, Bayerischer Rundfunk, no transmission date supplied.

    '*Hands Up, Heiliger Johannes*', *Kulturspiegel*, Bayerischer Rundfunk, no transmission date supplied.

    '*Hilferufe* von Peter Handke im *antiteater*', *Kulturspiegel*, Bayerischer Rundfunk, 18 November 1968.

    '*Iphigenie auf Tauris von Johann Wolfgang von Goethe*', *Kulturspiegel*, Bayerischer Rundfunk, no transmission date supplied.

    '*Jakob oder der Gehorsam*', *Kulturspiegel*, Bayerischer Rundfunk, transmitted 22 March 1967.

    'Korrigieren ohne zu verfälschen', *Programme of Yaak Karsunke's 'Germinal'*, TAT, première 15 September 1974, pp. 63–6.

    '*Leonce und Lena*', *Kulturspiegel*, Bayerischer Rundfunk, no transmission date supplied.

    '*Publikumsbeschimpfung*', *Kulturspiegel*, Bayerischer Rundfunk, no transmission date supplied.

    'Zur Schliessung des Action-Theaters in der Müllerstrasse am 6. Juni', *Kulturspiegel*, no transmission date supplied.

Kässens, Wend and Töteberg, Michael, 'Fortschritt im Realismus? Zur Erneuerung des kritischen Volksstücks seit 1966', *Basis*, 6 (1976), pp. 30–47.

Kayser, Beate, 'Langweiligkeit als Stilprinzip', *Donau-Kurier*, 20 February 1968.

Keller, Nina, *Report über junge Künstler in München* (Iching and Munich: Kreisselmeier, 1968).

Ketelsen, Uwe K., *Ein Theater und seine Stadt. Die Geschichte des Bochumer Schauspielhauses* (Cologne: SH, 1999).

Kirn, Thomas, 'Lauter miese kleine Schweine', *Frankfurter Neue Presse*, 3 April 1971.

Knabe, Gerd, *Bubis contra Fassbinder. Ein Theaterkrach in Frankfurt* (Knüllwald: Winkelberg, 1995).

Koch, Thomas, *Rainer Werner Fassbinder als Theaterregisseur* (unpublished MA thesis: Ludwig-Maximilians-Universität, Munich, 1994).

Kotschreuther, Hellmuth, 'So strapaziert man das geduldigste Publikum', *Abendpost*, 29 December 1969.

Kramberg, K. H., 'Büchner im Action-Theater', *Süddeutsche Zeitung*, 9 October 1967.

Krämer-Badoni, Rudolf, 'Es war nichts mehr zu retten', *Die Welt*, 6 June 1975.

'Ist die Jagd jetzt wieder offen?', *Rheinischer Merkur*, 9 November 1985.

'Dem Lieblingskind auf die Beine helfen', *Die Welt*, 16 November 1973.

Krebs, Dieter, 'Kamikaze oder Die lange Angst des Rainer Werner Fassbinder', in Rainer Werner Fassbinder, *Katzelmacher Preparadise Sorry Now Bremer Freiheit Blut am Hals der Katze* (Berlin: Henschel, 1985), pp. 170–87.

kth, 'Brot und Wein', *Abendzeitung*, 18 August 1967.

'Hippie à la Büchner', *Abendzeitung*, 6 October 1967.

'Ein kleines Wunder', *Abendzeitung*, 22 March 1967.

'Krawall auf Tauris', *Abendzeitung*, 28 October 1968.

'Mit Bar und Bühne', *Abendzeitung*, no date supplied.

Lange, Mechthild, 'Die abwesenden Männer spielen die Hauptrolle', *Frankfurter Rundschau*, 22 September 1976.

Langhans, Rainer and Teufel, Fritz, *Klau mich* (Berlin: Rixdorfer Verlag, n.d.).

Laube, Horst, 'Die Kuller des Systems zerstören', in Laube (ed.) with Brigitte Landes, *Theaterbuch*, vol. 1 (Munich: Carl Hanser, 1978), pp. 324–6.

Lehmann, Hans-Thies, *Postdramatisches Theater* (Frankfurt/Main: Verlag der Autoren, 1999).

Lennartz, Knut, *Theater, Künstler und Politik. 150 Jahre Deutscher Bühnenverein* (Berlin: Henschel, 1996).

Lichtenstein, Heiner (ed.), *Die Fassbinder-Kontroverse oder das Ende der Schonzeit* (Königstein: Athenäum, 1986).

Lietzau, Hans and Wendt, Ernst, 'Wie autoritär ist das deutsche Theater?', *Theater heute*, 5 (1968), pp. 1–3.

Limmer, Wolfgang, *Rainer Werner Fassbinder, Filmemacher* (Reinbek: Rowohlt, 1981).

Link, Jonathan, 'Theater in der Kneipe', *Sonntagsbeilage der Heidelheimer Zeitung*, 16 July 1967.

Lorenz, Juliane (ed.), *Das ganz normale Chaos. Gespräche über Rainer Werner Fassbinder* (Berlin: Henschel, 1995).

Luft, Friedrich, 'Ibsen auf der Untertreppe', *Die Welt*, 24 December 1973.

Lütgenhorst, Manfred, 'Kunst wird durch Bier erst schön!', *Abendzeitung*, 8/9 April 1967.

Mack, Gerhard, 'Die Sechziger als Zeit kümmerlicher Klischees', *Stuttgarter Zeitung*, 15 August 1995.

Markovits, Andrei S., Benhabib, Seyla and Postone, Moishe, 'Rainer Werner Fassbinder's *Garbage, the City and Death*: Renewed Antagonisms in the Complex Relationship between Jews and Germans in the Federal Republic of Germany', *New German Critique*, 38 (1986), pp. 3–27.

Mauer, Burkhard, 'Oberhäuptling Fassbinder', *konkret*, 1 (1977), pp. 30–1.

Maus, Sibylle, 'Die Gesellschaft ändern – aber wie?', *Stuttgarter Nachrichten*, 30 January 1970.

Mengershausen, Joachim von, 'Bitterböse Moormörder', *Süddeutsche Zeitung*, 19 March 1969.

    'Für R. von Praunheim und F. von Schiller', *Süddeutsche Zeitung*, 23 July 1969.

'Grabgesänge für Helden', *Süddeutsche Zeitung*, 11 December 1968.

'Mecki, der gammelnde Marxist', *Süddeutsche Zeitung*, 3 February 1968.

'Ein sommerliches Wintermärchen', *Süddeutsche Zeitung*, 12 July 1968.

'Sprung auf die Strasse', *Süddeutsche Zeitung*, 21 May 1968.

Meter, Peer, *Geesche Gottfried. Ein langes Warten auf den Tod* (Langenbruch: Jürgen, 1995).

Meyer-Bretschneider, Constanze, 'Fassbinders Team sucht das Kollektiv', *Frankfurter Rundschau*, 16 August 1974.

Michaelis, Rolf, 'Bestien im Käfig', *Die Zeit*, 28 December 1973.

'Deutscher Müll', *Die Zeit*, 13 June 1984.

'Ein Theater, das nicht sterben kann?', *Theater heute*, 7 (1974), pp. 23-4.

'Von den Barrikaden in den Elfenbeinturm. Aufbruch, Leerlauf, Stillstand: Die undeutlichen Jahre Schauspiel in der Bundesrepublik Deutschland zwischen 1967 und 1982', in Manfred Linke (ed.), *Theater 1967–1982* (Berlin: Institut International du Théâtre, 1983), pp. 7-25.

Militz, Klaus Ulrich, *Media Interplay in Rainer Werner Fassbinder's Work for Theatre, Cinema and Television* (unpublished PhD thesis: University of Edinburgh, 2000).

msch, 'Fasbinder in Zürich', *Die Weltwoche*, 23 April 1971.

Müller, F. K., 'Der grosse Fassbinder und der kleine Goethe', *Abendpost*, 30 October 1974.

Nahoun, Philippe, untitled article, in *Programme of Ferdinand Bruckner's 'Die Verbrecher'*, p. 28.

Naumann, Uwe and Töteberg, Michael (eds.), 'In der Sache Heinar Kipphardt', *Marbacher Magazin*, 60 (1992).

Niehoff, Karena, 'Schaf im Wolfspelz', *Süddeutsche Zeitung*, 22 December 1969.

Nolte, Jost, 'Seltsam in den Schlag gespielt', *Die Welt*, 12 September 1969.

'Die Verhältnisse, sie sind nicht mehr so . . .', *Die Welt*, 8 February 1971.

Offenbach, Jürgen, 'Gemeinde-Abend', *Stuttgarter Nachrichten*, 2 March 1970.

Pankau, Johannes G., 'Figurationen des Bayerischen: Sperr, Fassbinder, Achtenbusch', in Helfried W. Seliger (ed.), *Der Begriff 'Heimat' in der deutschen Gegenwartsliteratur* (Munich: iudicium, 1987), pp. 133–47.

Patterson, Michael, *German Theatre Today. Post-War Theatre in West and East Germany, Austria and Northern Switzerland* (London: Pitman, 1976).

Pflaum, Hans Günther and Fassbinder, Rainer Werner, *Das bisschen Realität, das ich brauche. Wie Filme entstehen* (Munich: Hanser, 1976).

Ponzi, Mauro, *Pier Paulo Pasolini. Rainer Werner Fassbinder* (Hamburg: Europäische Verlagsanstalt, 1996).

Poschmann, Gerda, *Der nicht mehr dramatische Theatertext. Aktuelle Bühnentexte und ihre dramaturgische Analyse* (Tübingen: Niemeyer, 1997).

Prinzler, Hans Helmut, 'The Application', in Laurence Kardish (ed.), in collaboration with Juliane Lorenz, *Rainer Werner Fassbinder* (New York: Museum of Modern Art, 1997) pp. 77–84.

r, 'Iphigenie im Drahtkorb', *Münchner Merkur*, 29 October 1968.

Raab, Kurt and Peters, Karsten, *Die Sehnsucht des Rainer Werner Fassbinder* (Munich: Bertelsmann, 1982).

Ralinofsky, Dagmar, *Die Gestaltung zwischenmenschlicher Beziehungen im Drama der Moderne. Tradition und Mutation* (Frankfurt/Main: Peter Lang, 1976).

Ramseger, Georg, 'Antigone im Mini-Rock', *Münchner Merkur*, 22 August 1967.

Raue, Gernot, '"Was man kapiert, ist wichtig". Ein Gespräch mit Rainer Werner Fassbinder', *Die deutsche Bühne*, 6 (1970), pp. 112–13.

Reichel, Verena, 'Klamauk statt Unbehagen', *Abendzeitung*, 11 December 1968.

Ringelband, Wilhelm, 'Fehlbesetzter Tschechow am TAT', *Trierischer Volksfreund*, 22 December 1974.

'Strindbergs *Julie* wurde Courths-Mahler Schnulze', *Rhein Zeitung*, 19 October 1974.

Rischbieter, Henning, 'Arbeit auf dem Theater', *Theater heute*, 10 (1974), pp. 6–11.

'Missverstandenes Melodram', *Die Zeit*, 8 December 1973.

RM, 'Hauptmann-Stipendien', *Frankfurter Allgemeine Zeitung*, 11 December 1969.

Roberts, David, 'Introduction. From the 1960s to the 1970s: the Changing Contexts of German Literature', in Keith Bullivant (ed.), *After the 'Death of Literature'. West German Writing of the 1970s* (Oxford, New York and Munich: Berg, 1989), pp. xi–xxiii.

RSt, 'Faktographie eines Verbrechens', *Der Tagesspiegel*, 11 April 1969.

Rühle, Günther, *Anarchie in der Regie? Theater in unserer Zeit*, vol. II (Frankfurt/Main: Suhrkamp, 1982).

'Fassbinder erhält ein Theater', *Frankfurter Allgemeine Zeitung*, 28 November 1973.

'Die letzte Chance', *Frankfurter Allgemeine Zeitung*, 29 January 1975.

'Die schöne Tochter des Generals', *Frankfurter Allgemeine Zeitung*, 24 December 1973.

Theater in unserer Zeit (Frankfurt/Main: Suhrkamp, 1976).

'Un-TAT', *Frankfurter Allgemeine Zeitung*, 24 March 1975.

'Die *Unvernünftigen* verlaufen sich sehr schön im Sand', *Frankfurter Allgemeine Zeitung*, 27 May 1974.

'Der Wille, der Spass, die Phantasie und die Kunst', in Burkhard Mauer and Barbara Krauss (eds.), *Spielräume – Arbeitsergebnisse. Theater Bremen 1962–73* (Bremen: Theater Bremen, 1973), p. 235.

Sabelus, Annette, *'Mir persönlich brachten sie allerhand Verdruss . . .'. Die Bearbeitung von Marieluise Fleissers 'Pioniere in Ingolstadt' durch Rainer Werner Fassbinder* (unpublished MA thesis: University of Hamburg, 1996).

Schauer, Lucie, 'Der Mensch – des Menschen Wolf', *Die Welt*, 22 December 1969.

Schenk, Irmbert, 'Widerspruchsbehandlung bei Rainer Werner Fassbinder am Beispiel von *Katzelmacher, Bremer Freiheit* und *Nora Helmer*', *TheaterZeitSchrift*, 33/4 (1993), pp. 163–80.

Schmidt, Dietmar N., 'Fassbinder – Goethe, uns und sich selbst verspottend?', *Recklinghauser Zeitung*, 8 November 1974.

'Fassbinder verhandelt mit Peter Zadek', *Stuttgarter Nachrichten*, 3 April 1971.

'Fassbinders Stück fürs Dürer-Jahr', *Die Welt*, 22 March 1971.

'Gescheiterte Kommune', *Die Welt*, 27 June 1969.

'Ob das wohl gut geht?', *Stuttgarter Nachrichten*, 28 November 1973.

'Tschechow, wie wir ihn lieben?', *Main-Echo*, 11 December 1974.

Schmidt, Jürgen, 'Fassbinderei', *Stuttgarter Zeitung*, 6 November 1969.

'Kälter als der Tod', *Deutsche Zeitung/Christ und Welt*, 5 February 1971.

'Trauerspiel mit Luft', *Stuttgarter Zeitung*, 15 December 1971.

Schmitz, Helmut, 'Müllkutscher Fassbinder', *Frankfurter Rundschau*, 12 March 1976.

Schönfeld, Gertie M., 'Eine Art Herrenabend', *Deutsches Allgemeines Sonntagsblatt*, 26 September 1976.

Schreiber, Ulrich, 'Heintjes Stimme dröhnt durch Zadeks Haus', *Frankfurter Rundschau*, 24 January 1973.

'Kunst als Ware – wahre Kunst', *Handelsblatt*, 16 June 1970.

Schütte, Wolfram, 'Doppel-Dokument', *Frankfurter Rundschau*, 10 October 1981.

Schwab-Felisch, Hans, 'Verbrecher und Verhöre', *Frankfurter Allgemeine Zeitung*, 11 June 1970.

Schwendtner, Rolf, *Theorie der Subkultur* (Cologne and Berlin: Kiepenheuer und Witsch, 1971).

Schygulla, Hanna, *Bilder aus Filmen von Rainer Werner Fassbinder. Mit einem autobiographischen Text von Hanna Schygulla und einem Beitrag von Rainer Werner Fassbinder* (Munich: Schirmer/Mosel, 1981).

sd, 'Die schönen glitzenden Ziele', *Frankfurter Neue Presse*, 27 November 1974.

Senate of Berlin (ed.), *25 Jahre Theater in Berlin. Theaterpremieren 1945–70* (Berlin: Heinz Spitzing, 1972).

Seibel, Wolfgang, *Die Formenwelt der Fertigteile. Künstlerische Montagetechnik und ihre Anwendung im Drama* (Würzburg: Königshausen und Neumann, 1988).

Seibert, Peter, 'Rainer Werner Fassbinder: Film wie Theater – Theater wie Film', in Inga Lemke (ed.), with Sandra Nuy, *Theaterbühne – Fernsehbilder. Sprech-, Musik- und Tanztheater im und für das Fernsehen* (Anif/Salzburg: Müller-Speiser, 1998), pp. 103–17.

Seybold, Eberhard, 'Auf der Suche nach neuen Heilmitteln', *Frankfurter Neue Presse*, 10 December 1974.

Shattuc, Jane, *Television, Tabloids and Tears. Fassbinder and Popular Culture* (Minneapolis: University of Minneapolis Press, 1995).

Sichtermann, Barbara, and Johler, Jens, 'Über den autoritären Geist des deutschen Theaters', *Theater heute*, 4 (1968), pp. 2–4.

with Bremer, Claus, Klaussnitzer, Horst, Utzerath, Hansjörg, and Wiebel, Martin, 'Wie autoritär ist das deutsche Theater?', *Theater heute*, 6 (1968), pp. 1–3.

Sinter, Gidy, 'Wie soll ein Intendant beschaffen sein?', *Theater heute*, 2 (1968), pp. 2–3.

Skasa-Weiss, Ruprecht, 'Ein Salonstück in den Sand gesetzt', *Stuttgarter Zeitung*, 12 June 1974.

Sormani, Laura, *Semiotik und Hermeneutik im interkulturellen Rahmen. Interpretationen zu Werken von Peter Weiss, Rainer Werner Fassbinder, Thomas Bernhard und Botho Strauss* (Frankfurt/Main et al.: Peter Lang, 1998).

Spaich, Herbert, *Rainer Werner Fassbinder. Leben und Werk* (Weinheim: Beltz, 1992).

Steets, Bernd, 'Ionesco in der Müllerstrasse', *Münchner Merkur*, 8 March 1967.

Steinweg, Rainer (ed.), *Brechts Modell der Lehrstücke. Zeugnisse, Diskussion, Erfahrungen* (Frankfurt/Main: Suhrkamp, 1976).

    Das Lehrstück. Brechts Theorie einer politisch-ästhetischen Erziehung (Stuttgart: Metzler, 1972).

Stern, Frank, *Im Anfang war Auschwitz. Antisemitismus und Philosemitismus im deutschen Nachkrieg* (Gerlingen: Bleicher, 1991).

Stöckl, Ula, Geisler, Achim, and Carstensen, Margit, 'Diskussion: Fräulein Julie', in *Programme of Ferdinand Bruckner's 'Die Verbrecher'*, TAT, première late November 1974, pp. 19–23.

Straeten, Joachim, 'Zadek verhandelt mit Werner Fassbinder', *Westfälische Rundschau*, 26 March 1971.

Strauss, Botho, 'Über Rührung und Emphase', *Theater heute*, 7 (1971), pp. 46–7.

Stubbendorff, Dietrich, 'Fassbinders Kaffeehausgespräche', *Hannoversche Allgemeine*, 12 September 1969.

Taberner, Stuart, 'The Final Taboo? Martin Walser's Critique of Philosemitism in *Ohne Einander*', *German Life and Letters*, 37 (2001), no. 2, pp. 154–66.

Tank, Kurt Lothar, 'Sieg mit einer Broadway-Satire', *Der Tagesspiegel*, 3 October 1976.

Thieringer, Thomas, 'Fassbinder kam gar nicht vor', *Süddeutsche Zeitung*, 13 November 1981.

Thomas, R. Hinton and Bullivant, Keith, *Literature in Upheaval. West German Writers and the Challenge of the 1960s* (Manchester: Manchester University Press, 1974), p. 38.

Thomasius, Jutta W., 'Drei Stunden in der Hölle der vom Leben Geschundenen', *Abendpost*, 17 September 1974.

Thomsen, Christian Braad, 'Conversations with Rainer Werner Fassbinder', in Laurence Kardish (ed.), in collaboration with Juliane Lorenz, *Rainer Werner Fassbinder* (New York: Museum of Modern Art, 1997), pp. 85–9.

    Fassbinder. The Life and Work of a Provocative Genius, tr. Martin Chalmers (London: Faber and Faber, 1997).

Töteberg, Michael, 'Fassbinders Erstling', *Theater heute*, 5 (1994), p. 29.

'Fassbinders Theaterarbeit. Eine Recherche im Nachlass', in Rainer Werner Fassbinder, *Anarchie in Bayern und andere Stücke* (Frankfurt/Main: Verlag der Autoren, 1985), pp. 151–64.

'Nachwort', in Töteberg (ed.), *Fassbinders Filme*, vol. II (Frankfurt/Main: Verlag der Autoren, 1990), p. 247.

Rainer Werner Fassbinder (Reinbek: Rowohlt, 2002).

'Das Theater der Grausamkeit als Lehrstück. Zwischen Brecht und Artaud: Die experimentellen Theatertexte Fassbinders', *Text und Kritik*, 103 (1989), pp. 20–34.

Treusch-Dieter, Gerburg, 'Was hat Karsunke von Zola verstanden?', *Theater heute*, 10 (1974), pp. 12–16.

ur, 'Bei *Käthchen*s Ausstattung griff der Intendant zum Rotstift', *Ruhrnachrichten*, 18 August 1972.

us, 'Ein Hamlet der Geschäfte', *Wiesbadener Kurier*, 27 May 1974.

usc, 'Basler Schauspielpläne 1970/71', *Neue Zürcher Zeitung*, 26 June 1970.

Various authors, 'Materialien zur Kollektivarbeit im Theater', *Theater heute*, 3 (1969), pp. 22–5.

Wagner, Eberhard, 'Ist die Mitbestimmung eine teuflische Idee des Kapitalismus?', in Programme of Ferdinand Bruckner's *'Die Verbrecher'*, TAT, première late November 1974, pp. 24–5.

Wagner, Klaus, '*Die Frauen in New York*, wie Fassbinder sie sieht', *Frankfurter Allgemeine Zeitung*, 20 September 1976.

Watson, Wallace Steadman, *Understanding Rainer Werner Fassbinder. Film as Private and Public Art* (Columbia: University of South Carolina Press, 1996).

Wefelmeyer, Fritz, 'Die Ästhetik sich schliessender Systeme. Judendarstellung bei Rainer Werner Fassbinder', in Pol O'Dochartaigh (ed.), *Jews in German Literature since 1945: German-Jewish Literature?* (Amsterdam: Rodopi, 2000), pp. 549–65.

Weigel, Sigrid, 'Shylocks Wiederkehr. Die Verwandlung von Schuld in Schulden oder: Zum symbolischen Tausch der Wiedergutmachung', *Zeitschrift für deutsche Philologie*, 114: Sonderheft (1995), pp. 3–22.

Wendt, Ernst, 'Fassbinder sinkt in den Bodensee', *Die Zeit*, 26 March 1971.

White, Ann and John, 'Marlene's Pistol and Brady's Rule. Elements of Mystification and Indeterminacy in Rainer Werner Fassbinder's Film *Die bitteren Tränen der Petra von Kant*', *German Life and Letters*, 53 (2000), no. 3, pp. 409–25.

Wilms, Bernd, 'Die Stadt, das Stück und die Kontroverse', *Süddeutsche Zeitung*, 11 November 1998.

wp, 'Rühle beharrt auf "Probe"', *Frankfurter Rundschau*, 6 December 1985.

Zi, 'Bochumer Freiheit', *Die Welt*, 18 August 1972.

Zweig, Stefanie, 'Die Vernunft hat Sand im Getriebe', *Abendpost*, 27 May 1974.

Zwerenz, Gerhard, *Der langsame Tod des Rainer Werner Fassbinder. Ein Bericht* (Munich: Schneekluth, 1982).

Unpublished interviews

Harry Baer, 19 March 2002.

Karlheinz Braun, 30 October 2001.

Rudolf Waldemar Brem, 19 and 21 November 2001.

Margit Carstensen, 6 November 2001.

Irm Hermann, 22 June 2002.

Hans Hirschmüller, 1 October 2001.

Kurt Hübner, 3 December 2001.

Yaak Karsunke, 19 November 2002.

Gunter Krää, 6 December 2001.

Renate Leiffer, 14 November 2001.

Juliane Lorenz, 17 September 2001.

Joachim von Mengershausen, 10 November 2001.

Peer Raben, 22 November 2001.

Günther Rühle, 2 November 2001.

Jörg Schmitt, 27 November 2001.

Hanna Schygulla, 25 February 2002.

Heide Simon and Eberhard Wagner, 18 November 2002.

Volker Spengler, 17 September 2001.

Gerhard Zwerenz, 20 April 2002.

Index

Index

Index

Lightning Source UK Ltd.
Milton Keynes UK
UKOW02n2206301115

263825UK00001B/32/P